The Sacred Desert

For Alison, with love

The Sacred Desert

Religion, Literature, Art, and Culture

David Jasper

Blackwell
Publishing

350 Main Street, Malden, MA 02148-5020, USA
108 Cowley Road, Oxford OX4 1JF, UK
550 Swanston Street, Carlton, Victoria 3053, Australia

First published 2004 by Blackwell Publishing Ltd

Library of Congress Cataloging-in-Publication Data

Jasper, David.
The sacred desert: religion, literature, art, and culture / David Jasper.
p. cm.
Includes bibliographical references and index.
ISBN 1-4051-1974-8 (hardcover: alk. paper) –
ISBN 1-4051-1975-6 (pbk.: alk. paper)
1. Spiritual life – Christianity. 2. Deserts – Religious aspects –
Christianity. I. Title.
BV4501.3.J37 2004
248–dc22
2003019365

A catalogue record for this title is available from the British Library.

Set in 10/12.5pt Galliard
by Graphicraft Limited, Hong Kong
Printed and bound in the United Kingdom
by MPG Books Ltd, Bodmin, Cornwall

For further information on
Blackwell Publishing, visit our website:
http://www.blackwellpublishing.com

1* I had forgotten what real darkness was like. At first it was frightening. I have a flashlight, and I was afraid I might not be able to find the little path which would lead me back to my door. I could see, literally, nothing. I could see only blackness, illuminated now and then by flashes of lightning to the far south, so far away there was no accompanying sound of thunder. I thought how terrifying that light must be to people who have never experienced it muted by the lights of cities and towns. A primeval light. And the silence. I think of my remark to my friend before I set out last week that "there is nothing there." No sound of traffic (the nearest road with cars is over ten miles away), or airplanes or trains or music or voices. It is silent, and yet there is sound everywhere. I suppose I must call it natural sound, and it is frightening. I am frightened by the rustling of the wind in the leaves of the palm trees. That is a heavy sound, quite unlike the gentle rustling of the leaves in the trees back home. The endless whirring of the crickets in the bushes – that I know and can identify. But there are also the mysterious noises – I am sure I heard breathing in the bushes. It may have been my imagination, which is working overtime, or perhaps one of the deer I saw this afternoon. There are odd whistles, and howling of dogs miles and miles away – farm dogs, I suppose. Or could they be wild?

2 "Every person is by nature solitary." I think it was Thomas Merton who said that. Well, of course we are – in the end. All of us. And maybe it is important to be reminded of that now and then, and go back to our "nature" in silence, without communication or distraction. Because it is silent here, it means that it doesn't really matter *where* I am. Odd things are happening to my sense of time and place. I have traveled 5,000 miles to be in this strange place, but I don't feel remotely lonely or cut off. I am where I am, touching base. This is my home for the time being, and it does very nicely.

---

* Notes made by the author during a solitary retreat in the Texas desert during November 2002, and during a visit to the sacred Indian lands of South Dakota in May 2003

3   It hasn't been quite what I expected, but then things rarely are. I had a much more romantic image, absurdly constructed from myth, film, books. Of course, it is different. It has not been the grand desert of limitless sands and rocks and hills. But it has been something more than that – a place which is neither exterior nor interior, and remote. I should have expected as much, of course – to travel all this way and find a place which has been familiar all along but hitherto largely unfrequented by me. It is a place we all know, individually, but rarely, if ever visit. I don't think I could live here for *very* long.

4   Tuesday May 6, 2003. To the Lakota Indians this country is known as "mako sica" – land bad. I have come to the Badlands of South Dakota, and it has not been hard to move beyond the tourist routes, to move out into this desert. It is not a place to stay in easily, and not a place to travel through easily either. A place of extremes, dry, dusty and arid and yet after rain a sea of slippery mud that defies walking. And even then I can feel the dry atmosphere drying me out, and I need to drink, though the water is what I have carried with me; there is nothing to drink here. Nothing grows on these slimy mounds and sharp peaks and gulleys, but look down and far below, in valleys blessedly inaccessible to human intrusion, there are secret kingdoms where junipers grow and birds sing. Probably there are antelope down there too, unseen. Life is tenacious, but I feel how fragile my life is in this desolate, beautiful place. I feel how out of touch I have become with the secrets of true survival with an unreconciled mixture of emotions. There is the immediate wonder, excitement, followed by a growing respect and then a hint of fear as I clamber and slide up this pass, each step becoming more uncertain and uncontrolled. There is the desolation of the short prairie grass which stretches on forever like a sea of green that will become brown dust in a few months. There is nowhere to stop and recover, nowhere to shelter. The land is indifferent. I can sense why the Sioux tribes regarded the land as sacred, for it is everything and upon it and its produce they were utterly dependent. It is nurturing mother and angry father, and I sense that ultimately it will not take kindly to our binding it with paved roads and campsites. Not far from here is Wounded Knee, where the hearts of the Indian tribes were finally broken. The desert is, indeed, other, defying and defining our constructions of the world, for against such places as this we build our fortifications. But to go out here, as Antony went out into the desert of Egypt, is also to touch a chord in our nature that sounds at the deepest levels of our religious being. Without it how can we speak? As I stand facing the driving rain that tomorrow will be a wind that is dry enough to wither the human body, looking across the mud to the peaks that are vertical and yet also cut across with the horizontal lines of deposits from an ancient inland sea, I cannot speak, for it literally blows my breath away – and only here does true utterance begin.

Contents

Contents

Plates

Plates

Foreword

Who wanders in the desert? In his extraordinary book, David Jasper converses with the poets, prophets, mystics, madmen, nomads, explorers, outlaws, warriors, seekers, thinkers, theologians, visionaries, and artists of the desert – dreamers all. What are they doing in the desert? They are passing beyond the familiar world of stable meanings and predictable events into a domain of openness and insecurity. Why do they leave the shelter of all things familiar, the world of "ten thousand things"? They do so in order to approach and to appropriate the nothingness that is at the heart of things – the heart of our thinking and the heart of our hearts. To wander in the desert is a metaphor for the human situation, once our eyes are opened to the truth that all philosophical theology reveals. What is that truth?

Although the religions – all of them – purport to know who God is, what God wants and demands of humans, and what God has in store for human history, we humans by our own light of reason do not and cannot know the truth about God. Philosophical theology – whether of Plato, Spinoza,

Kant, Fichte, Hegel, Schleiermacher, Buber, Heidegger, Tillich, Derrida, or whoever – knows that the coherence of rational thinking and purposive acting logically presupposes an ultimate ground of thinking and being, so long as we assume the coherence of rational thinking and purposive acting. But the circularity of such presupposing is a wandering in the desert, a staring into an abyss, from which we can return – but never all the way, never fully the same. Sensing this abyss, feeling this nothingness, humans have religion – images, narratives, wisdom sayings, and rituals. Religion fills the abyss with meaning and allows even the desert wanderer some orientation in a disorientating journey. Religion allows us to think on, even when we have nothing on which to think.

In this sense, *The Sacred Desert* is a book of religious thought. It presents an extended interdisciplinary meditation on the religious and theological meanings of the image, idea, and language of the "desert." The "desert" refers to a complex locus of experience and reflection; it is simultaneously an interior space of the mind; an exterior place where pilgrims, adventurers, and travelers can visit and dwell; and an intertextual space produced by cross-references among cultural creations dealing with the desert as archetype or icon of the imagination. The book is fascinating and unique as a meditation on meanings opened up within the complex locus by tracing interweavings or interconnections among a wide variety of "texts" dealing with the "desert." These texts include texts of the desert mystics, contemporary novelists, the Bible, poets, journalists, modern artists, current filmmakers, and theologians. The book proceeds through a series of dialogues among works, through which the meditation advances. In this regard, it is a demonstration of creative, interdisciplinary scholarly writing in which reflection and imagination are both maximally in play. What is the meditation about?

The desert meditation is about what it means for each of us to be the unique human being that "I" am. Minimally, this meditation, which grows richer and more amazing with each step of the "wanderings," includes reflection on human finitude: our capacities are bounded and limited by a vast, empty space that we can understand with the image of the "desert." In the desert, we encounter and experience this finitude – the limitations of our being human. But in addition, the meditation includes reflection on the paradoxical identity of this concrete and personal human finitude with the being of God (which can also manifest itself as Satan), with divine being. The experience of the desert is an experience of the overturning of human finitude, the opening of human being to the mystical basis of its identity. This place is where the divine as "God" empties itself into finite human being and where finite human being discovers its own deep participation in transcendence. This is the place of desert encounter: the encounter of the self with itself, encounter of the self with the other self, and encounter of the self with the unknowable Transcendent Other that in the end is not other than self or other self. With each step of the way, this meditation deepens the reader's understanding of the "desert" as a primordial place in discourse and experience, where conventional distinctions are overturned so as to manifest their origin and final destination in the unspeakable, unnamable Word and Name of God. "Desert" is a locus of theological experience and reflection in this text. Ultimately, this text is a reflection on the depth dimension of meaning in human experience.

The steps that I am speaking of include the nine core chapters of the book – core chapters which are framed between an introduction and a conclusion, in which things are pulled together around a beginning and an ending (that is still another beginning). The first core chapter (actually numbered as chapter 2) moves the reader through biblical archetypes of the desert in Genesis and Exodus, along with current explorations of these spaces in Schoenberg's opera and Heidegger's reflections on *Gelassenheit* (the state of openness or "letting be"). Chapter 3 focuses on the miraculous lives of the Desert Fathers and the literary modes of thought in which these lives of extreme asceticism and bliss are told and retold. It is important at this point to realize that the book is not about the Bible and Desert Fathers. It reads these texts as literary productions that in many ways ground the reader's reception and interpretation of the idea of the "desert" as a religious icon. Chapter 4 deals with the relationship between the (literary and physical) experience of the desert and mysticism. Here the idea of the "negative way" is introduced alongside the negative modes of discourse that characterize desert mysticism – not merely in its historical context but in the imagination of those who receive it in the variety of cultural forms. Chapter 5 brings the reflection into the modern mystical writings of Thomas Merton and Don Cupitt, to show that the fascination with the desert as a mystical place is just as serious in the present time as it was in the time of the Desert Fathers. Chapters 6 and 7 move into the wonderful literature of the desert, written by travelers, poets, and novelists. With these chapters in particular, teachers who use the book in the classroom can supplement its reading with some of the novels, poems, or travel accounts discussed by David Jasper. By this time in the reader's experience, the image, idea, and language of the "desert" are becoming more profound and vivid, as the reader finds herself enacting in the imagination the kind of limit-experiences presented through this array of materials. Chapter 8 explores the visual art that belongs to desert experience and reflection – Georgia O'Keeffe, Bill Viola, and the New York School. Chapter 9 moves into cinematic presentation of the desert. Finally, chapter 10 brings the image into the theological reflection of Thomas Altizer and the great thinker of negativity, Hegel.

The work as a whole is a *tour de force*. The text is post-postmodern, because it does not reflect on postmodern theory or method. It does not describe deconstruction or analyze the decentered self. Rather, it *enacts* postmodern theory and method. It deconstructs its various sources and performs a decentered subjectivity. In this way, the text participates in a new form of religious reflection that is both intertextual and interdisciplinary.

The Sacred Desert will of course reward those scholars and students of culture, who can follow the references cited here. However, I know from personal experience that the book can be used with great success in the classroom as the organizing text for an interdisciplinary study of the "desert." I have been privileged to host David Jasper for a semester as an Ida Cordelia Beam Distinguished Visiting Professor at the University of Iowa, where he had the students read the primary texts with which he enters into his hermeneutical conversations. The students were extremely excited to follow the shifting sands of thought. They rightly understood this work as a form of contemporary religious thought that is both theological and literary. One of its strengths is to help students make connections among works of enormous diversity from many different fields of human cultural endeavor. In making these connections, the text enacts what it is about: an image, idea, and discourse of the "desert" appear in the space between these works. It is a space where humans go to encounter themselves, their demons, and their god. This desert is at once an oasis, a paradise, where humans renew themselves and are transformed. I think that teachers are looking for just this kind of book to use in the classroom to help their students think beyond the current impasses of postmodern thought.

David E. Klemm
University of Iowa

Preface

The origins of this book are complex and have deep roots in my personal history. As a result of this it is difficult to assess its nature. It is certainly interdisciplinary, grounded in teaching and my lifelong concern for the relationship between theology and the study of literature, together with more recent interests in film, the visual arts, and now music. But it is also about real deserts, the people who have lived and traveled in them, and how they have perceived them and, above all, written about them. It is about places on the map, but also texts, and how text relates to place, and embodies it. Librarians should probably place it in the theology section of their libraries, and most of the chapters have been honed in the classrooms of departments of theology and religious studies, but at the same time much of the material with which it is concerned is anything but "religious," being narratives of desert journeys, descriptions of military campaigns, novels, or films. Parts I can even trace back in my imagination to boyhood reading of the wild romances of writers like Rider Haggard or R. M. Ballantyne. Saints, artists, writers, and theologians jostle together in these pages in unlikely fellowship, some whose only experience of the desert is the all-too-real, painful waste-land of their own spirit. It is also, and deliberately, repetitious – although to say something a second time is not necessarily to repeat it, but rather to deepen it in further explorations and new discoveries. Part of my purpose is to explore how the *same* experiences and expressions are repeated in the millennia of desert literature of all kinds – and unconsciously thereby old truths are reborn: even in my own brief desert sojourns. This explains also why the endnotes refer continuously backwards and forwards to the same point made in other chapters. The reader who finds this cross-referencing irritating should feel perfectly at liberty to ignore it! It has a precedent, however, in books like Jean-François Lyotard's *The Differend*, where the 264 sections endlessly point, in notes, to each other, the final section footnoted "No. 1ff."! This, in turn, has precedents in St. Mark's Gospel and *Finnegans Wake* – a goodly company who realize that in our end is our beginning.

Although I did not intend this to be a specifically Christian study, and other religious traditions will be discussed, my own limitations have inevit-ably led to a concentration on Christianity and the desert. Nevertheless its concerns and religious expressions will never be constrained by the dimensions of one confession or tradition, for the desert speaks a univer-sal language. Yet, for me, the Desert Fathers and Mothers who followed St. Antony into the deserts of Egypt and Judea are the first of our desert wanderers. These were the pioneers, and, after the Bible itself, provide the blueprint for all my later studies. I have not, however, pursued an academic and theological study of these men and women. There are many such studies, not a few of them referred to in chapter 3, and my concern has been rather different from most of them. As I read the accounts of their lives, I became fascinated with the way in which those lives became legends in these texts. The desert, so to speak, became a "text," and there is a great textual commonality between this ancient literature of the fourth and fifth centuries of the Christian era and almost everything else I read about the desert in later narratives and images. In other words, these texts, like the *Historia Monachorum* and the *Lausiac History*, first caught my attention as a student of *literature* and theology, and I read them in this way.

But I did not begin with the Desert Fathers. To start with I had wanted to write a book about what I called "twentieth-century wasteland texts," and I narrowed these down in my mind to four: T. S. Eliot's poem *The Waste Land*, Arnold Schoenberg's opera *Moses und Aron*, Karl Barth's "commentary" on St. Paul, the *Romerbrief*, and Martin Heidegger's great work of philosophy *Sein und Zeit*. The point was to embrace poetry, music, theology, and philosophy, concentrating on the years between the two world wars and the incredibly fertile wasteland of the spirit which they provided. Well, to start with, it was just too ambitious. A passion for interdisciplinarity had got the better of me and it quickly became clear that, even if this was a feasible project, I was not academically equipped to do it! Some of that unwritten book has survived into the present text, though not much, and yet it did give rise to much else that has borne fruit. Basically, I began to conclude that what I was really interested in was the desert as a *place*, one which indeed haunts the human spirit, but is also there on the map. And so I began to move from Eliot's *Waste Land* to the deserts of his later poetry, and especially the *Four Quartets*: from the unreal city to the midwinter spring of Little Gidding, a real enough place though also "nowhere," the utopia of the desert(ed) place that is nowhere yet more real than the unreality of the London where "death had undone so many."

By now the journey was becoming more than the academic work I was paid to do by my university. Yet at the same time it was very much to do with the nature, even the possibility, of doing theology now, and both where it is to be found and how pursued. On the whole I have chosen to avoid the technical language of theology mapped, as it too often is, against the current cultural, sociopolitical, and philosophical jargon. Rather, I have allowed the study of texts to develop its own poetics, and its own dialectic, and this will become apparent especially in chapters 4 and 5, and later in chapters 10 and 11. Its closest affinity is with the language of the mystical tradition in the West, but also the theology of Thomas Altizer. At the same time I have not just been sitting at my desk! The curious sacrality and beauty of desert landscapes was first borne in upon me many years ago when I lived for a time in North India. Since then I have been able to travel on more than one occasion to the Negev Desert south of Beer-Sheva, where the empty landscape is filled with the ghosts of peoples who have crossed the hills since biblical times and earlier. Most recently, I spent a while living as a solitary in the wide open spaces of South Texas – and some pages from my journal of that time have found their way into the opening of this book.

It was in writing that journal that it struck me that the desert gives rise to a universal community of unlikely dimensions. Quite simply, I found myself unconsciously recording impressions and thoughts in phrases and in a manner that I was to come across in other books that I had not at that time read. I was also beginning to behave in a way that is recognizable not so much through "normal" description, but in the legends of the Fathers, in the writings of people like T. E. Lawrence, and in the best fiction of writers like Cormac McCarthy (who knows what Texas and New Mexico are like because he lives there) and Jim Crace (who is, I assume, working entirely within his imagination). This, in itself, is not so very surprising, but it does lead to the question of what it is that holds this community together across the ages of literature. I was becoming interested not only in the desert as "text," but also the redescription of the world that takes place when one goes out and sees it from the "other," from the empty space where no one, or very few people, lives.

On the other hand, the desert does not come to us, very firmly non-desert dwellers, from nowhere. It has its own legend and a romance born of mystery and harsh beauty, but it is also construed for many of us through the Bible as the place where the Israelites wandered for forty years, where Jesus went out to be tempted by Satan, where Elijah is fed during the time of drought, and where, even in the Vale of Misery, a well can be found. The Bible is the first, and still, perhaps, the greatest of our desert texts, and when the first travelers from the West went into the deserts of the Middle East with cameras in the nineteenth century, they construed to take pictures of the desert so that it looked like the image that they had brought with them from their Bible reading. The desert is insistently *there*, and yet it is also inside us and our imaginations, a no place, a utopia, the land to which we are led back, as their God led the erring Israelites back into the desert as a "door of hope" in Hosea.

A place of wandering, a place to be crossed, a place to *enter into*, the desert is also a place of meeting, a meeting point; and so it has become for me. Its considerations and its literature had been leading me back to the theologian who, perhaps above all others, has fascinated and inspired me over the years: Tom Altizer. Still best known as *the* "death of God" theologian, profoundly mystical and yet deeply systematic, Altizer's sense of the total presence of God in language that is realized and absorbed in absolute self-giving, or kenosis, alone takes me back to where I began and to where I am going, the absolute desert, the "unimaginable zero summer."

Many people, wittingly and unwittingly, have contributed to the development of this book. Jim Harold has shared with me his own fascination for the desert, seen through the eyes of an artist and photographer. Ken Mitchell of the Glasgow School of Art, Andrew Hass of the University of Stirling, Lori Branch of the University of Iowa, Mel Schlachter and Gerda Elata-Alster, who introduced me to the Negev Desert, have all given me generous hospitality and ideas, and listened patiently to my obsessions. I am grateful to Bill Hall who introduced me to Bill Viola, a short meeting from which much has grown. Robert Detweiler and Tom Altizer have, for years, been unstinting in their readiness to correspond and share a common pilgrimage. To my gracious hosts in Texas, who quite properly wish to remain hidden, I give my thanks. The University of Glasgow granted me research leave to write the book, and my colleagues in the Department of Theology and Religious Studies at Glasgow have put up with me, granting me the honorary title of "desert father," an idea that pleases me more than many academic honors! Above all I thank Professor David E. Klemm, who invited me to stay in the University of Iowa for a semester as Ida Cordelia Beam Distinguished Visiting Professor, without which not half of this work could have been achieved. Not only were David and his wife Catherine extraordinarily generous and gracious hosts, but they also gave me the opportunity to interact with staff and students who took to my project with great readiness, and carried me through the later stages with hearty good will and penetrating insight.

But, inevitably, the brunt of the whole thing has been carried by my family, Alison, Hannah, Ruth and May, who have put up with my absences from home and abstractions when *at* home with a patience and understanding beyond any call of human duty or affection. My thanks can but be small return for all this.

The second part of chapter 8 is based on an earlier article entitled "Theology and American Abstract Expressionism" in *Arts: The Arts in Religious and Theological Studies*, 7: 3 (1998), pp. 17–24. Chapter 10 is partly based on an earlier essay on Thomas J. J. Altizer, to be published as part of a Festschrift volume in his honor. Chapter 11 is partly based on the essay "Literature and the Possibility of Theology" in the Festschrift in honor of Robert Carroll, *Sense and Sensitivity*, edited by Davies and Hunter (Crossroads, 2002). Unless otherwise stated, biblical quotations are from the New Revised Standard Version.

"The Second Coming" by W. B. Yeats is reprinted from *The Collected Works of W. B. Yeats, Volume I: The Poems, Revised*, edited by Richard J. Finneran. © 1924 by The Macmillan Company; copyright renewed 1952 by Bertha Georgie Yeats. Reprinted by permission of A. P. Watt Ltd on behalf of Michael B. Yeats and Scribner, an imprint of Simon and Schuster Adult Publishing Group.

David Jasper

1

Introduction

Meeting Points

Near the beginning of Book 5 of *The Prelude*, which is entitled "Books," William Wordsworth describes a dream of the desert.

> Sleep seiz'd him, and he pass'd into a dream.
> He saw before him an Arabian Waste,
> A Desart; and he fancied that himself
> Was sitting there in the wide wilderness,
> Alone, upon the sands. Distress of mind
> Was growing in him, when, behold! at once
> To his great joy a Man was at his side,
> Upon a dromedary, mounted high.
> He seem'd an Arab of the Bedouin Tribes,
> A lance he bore, and underneath one arm
> A Stone; and, in the opposite hand, a Shell
> Of a surpassing brightness. Much rejoic'd
> The dreaming Man that he should have a Guide

> To lead him through the Desart . . .
> My friend continued . . .
> . . . On he pass'd
> Not heeding me; I follow'd, and took note
> That he look'd often backward with wild look,
> Grasping his twofold treasure to his side.
> – Upon a Dromedary, Lance in rest,
> He rode, I keeping pace with him, and now
> I fancied he was the very Knight
> Whose Tale Cervantes tells, yet not the Knight,
> But was an Arab of the Desart too;
> Of these was neither, and was both at once.[1]

I start with this passage, which was used also by W. H. Auden to begin his brief book *The Enchafèd Flood* (1951), though with a very different purpose. Auden's concern was with the psychology of poetic symbols, with the desert as symbol and with the stone of abstract geometry and the shell of imagination which the desert rider carries. My concern, however, is in the first instance with the desert as a real place, experienced not in a dream but as a harsh actuality to be entered into and which gives rise to literature, art, and a deep sense of the sacred. Almost all of the texts and art with which this book will be concerned begin, in some sense, in a physical encounter with the desert. Yet to begin with Wordsworth and Auden is not irrelevant, since the desert encounter gives rise to poetic symbols and associations which meet in the imagination of the poet or novelist, as also in the spirit of the Desert Fathers[2] or later mystics, and in this dialectic they thereby become profoundly significant for us. We will become familiar with the themes of Wordsworth's dream – the desert as a place of solitariness and meeting; a place of fear and shifting identity. It is also, as Auden points out,[3] a place where the water of life is lacking, as in Ezekiel's vision of the Valley of Dry Bones (Ezekiel 37: 1–14). It is "a place where nobody desires by nature to be," a place of criminality or scapegoating, yet also a place where people escape from the evil city in order to become good. It is a place of purgation and temptation, "the place or displace where nothing occurs or almost occurs,"[4] not to be lived in but to be entered into and crossed and traveled through. It is place where meetings occur, and identities are lost and discovered in a silence that speaks. As the poet Edmond Jabès says:

> You do not go into the desert to find identity but to lose it, to lose your personality, to become anonymous. You make yourself void. You *become* silence. It is very hard to live with silence. The real silence is death and this is terrible. It is very hard in the desert. You must become more silent than the silence around you. And then something extraordinary happens: you hear silence speak.[5]

Wordsworth and Auden *begin* with the words and language of the poetic image and the dream, while we shall largely, though not entirely, be concerned with the men and women who have actually traversed the desert in both body and spirit, and endured its silences, from the Bible to the present day. Yet "from the desert to the book"[6] has never been a long journey. As the poet and philosopher Edmond Jabès remarks in one of his poems, through the lips of Reb Sullam, "What is a book but a bit of fine sand taken from the desert one day and returned a few steps further on?"[7] The desert sands of Arabia are saturated with poetry, and with good reason. For if in English, to "desert" means to leave or abandon a place, the Arabic word *ashara* means to enter the desert, for there, if one knows where to look, there are springs and wells of water and places of life. Furthermore, the Arabic language is intrinsically attuned to the life of the desert and shares its nature.

> It is impossible to find a word in the dictionary without knowing its etymology. Hence, an Arabic word can disappear because of its fixed roots and can fall into disuse, but can always be revived through its root . . .
>
> I will not dwell on the plasticity of the sign in the Arabic language, or on the intimate correlation between the sign and signification . . . It is like the grain of sand, eternally containing the memory of a language, an alphabet of sand.[8]

Although we shall be considering the visual arts and film in this book, it has been argued that the experience of the desert is primarily auditory rather than visual. For in a landscape where the eye is often blinded or confused by shifting sands and the distortions of heat, it is the ear that is most acutely attuned to the voice of the wind – Elijah's "still, small voice" – which is, perhaps, the voice of God. Perhaps it was no accident, therefore, that the Israelites, emerging from the desert where God spoke to Moses on Mount Sinai, became the people of the book.[9]

Language and the desert sands, wherein dried but living roots are buried waiting for the rain, share a common life, and it is that which we shall be exploring through a wide and varied literature, from the Hebrew Bible, to the lives and sayings of the Christian Desert Fathers, the words of poets and of travelers and soldiers, the narratives of modern novelists as they meditate upon the desert from the Judean wilderness of the New Testament to the desert of the Gulf War, from musical libretti into film and to the images, and beyond, of contemporary art. My purpose is not systematic, and by its very nature the task cannot be completed. There will always be more texts and texts I have omitted, for they are as many as the grains of sand. Rather, my intention is to draw together a deliberately heterogeneous collection of writings and pictures in order to discern the thread that runs through them, ultimately a theological thread, though contained by no single tradition or confession. The desert, then, provides a focus for something which we are in danger of losing sight of. At the deepest level, this book is in often silent dialogue with the work of other theologians and scholars of religion who express concern and anxiety for the place of religion and the voice of theology in Western culture after postmodernity. These are people for whom it is not enough that theology speaks merely to itself in the dusty sanctuaries of those churches which Nietzsche's madman in *The Gay Science* proclaimed "the tombs and sepulchers of God." Like Graham Ward in his book *True Religion* (2003), I see "religion" as a defining characteristic of postmodernity, yet risking liquidation through its commodification. Unlike Ward, however, I see its future in the paradoxical turn which it has ever taken since Jesus or St. Antony took refuge in the desert. For some, as we shall see, that journey is a mystical one, but no less a turn to the wilderness for that, and only on that path and its crossings can theology and its language find new life.

People sometimes go out into the desert to find new beginnings and a new place from which theological articulation can be found and recovered. In chapter 2 this may take us with Arnold Schoenberg in a musical, verbal, and dramatic quest for his "inconceivable God" in his great "desert" opera *Moses und Aron*, or with Heidegger in his reflections on the origin of the work of art, both wanderers in the intermediary space between presence and absence that alone bears the key to that pure presence that the theologian Tom Altizer names the "self-embodiment of God." This will be the theme of chapter 10. But at the heart of the argument is a much simpler claim – simple, but never easy. It was well described many years ago by David Jenkins in a paragraph that continues to energize and provoke me, both because it seems so obvious and yet is still not often taken wholly seriously:

> The dreadful thing about so much theology is that, in relation to the reality of the human situation, it is so superficial. Theological categories (really mere theological formulae) are "aimed" without sufficient depth of understanding at life insensitively misunderstood. Theologians need therefore to stand *under* the judgments of the insights of literature before they can speak with true theological force of, and to, the world this literature reflects and illuminates.[10]

Without the acknowledgment of this judgment, theology becomes isolated from the life of the spirit and is eventually rendered voiceless. Even more, as we shall see in chapters 4 and 5, at the heart of this life of the spirit is a mysticism which, once its utterance ceases to be heard or given our attention, becomes estranged from theology and that is the first step in the death of the spirit. Only in the purity and the silence of the desert can this still small voice be heard and that is what the desert wanderer seeks to recover. There, as a place outside the law where nothing superficial can be tolerated, we stand under judgment, and theology stands under the judgments of its literature and art. This modern isolation of theology is the theme of Mark A. McIntosh's book *Mystical Theology* (1998) (to which we shall return in due course), while the dangers of this estrangement have been described by the Dutch Carmelite Kees Waaijman:

> It [modernity] had to eliminate mysticism – precisely to the degree that mysticism lays bare man's inner powerlessness – as an unproductive element, often falsely labeled as quietistic, irrational and occult. In reaction, mysticism – a living indictment against every form of self-interest, self-will, and technicalism – developed a language and a logic of its own which in turn rendered it unintelligible to cultural rationality.[11]

Theologians have paid little heed to this language,[12] and its recovery is what is traced in the texts explored in this book. Many of them are far from being theological, or even dismissed as the voices of fools and madmen, and that, in a way, is precisely the point, for only in the *space* of literature (to use Maurice Blanchot's term)[13] can be entertained a genuinely theological humanism precisely when literature is not "doing theology" – and *it must not do so*, or it will cease to be what it is within the broader reaches of culture. Only such literature has the potential to reconfigure theological discourse after that discourse has been rendered almost impossible in anything like its own terms.

In the space of the desert, where life itself becomes almost impossible and unbearable, language is transfigured and the impossible necessity of theology may be rediscovered. The truth of this is acknowledged in one of the texts we shall be considering in chapter 3, the *Historia Monachorum in Aegypto* (*The Lives of the Desert Fathers*) of the late fourth century CE, where the Prologue speaks thus of the Fathers:

> Indeed, it is clear to all who dwell there that through them *the world is kept in being*, and that through them too human life is preserved and honored by God.[14]

In a pattern of retreat remarkably similar to the Fathers, though in quite different cultural circumstances, Henry David Thoreau gave a lecture before the Concord Lyceum on April 23, 1851, which contained the words:

Let me live where I will . . . on this side is the city, on that the wilderness, and ever I am leaving the city more and more, and withdrawing into the wilderness. . . *in Wilderness is the preservation of the World.*[15]

The Fathers, while dwelling on earth, "live as true citizens of heaven": Thoreau speaks for the "absolute freedom" of Nature. In both, the opposition to the "city" represents the very preservation of the world, a claim both explored and sustained in the texts and art that emerge from the desert. Their difference exemplifies another theme of this book. The desert entertains and nurtures religion and its languages beyond the limits of any specific confession. As Theodore Roszak, with the eclectic fervor of the late 1960s, put it in his book *Where the Wasteland Ends*:

> The religion I refer to is not that of the churches; not the religion of Belief and Doctrine, which is, I think, the last fitful flicker of the divine fire before it sinks into darkness. Rather, I mean religion in its perennial sense. The Old Gnosis. Vision born of transcendent knowledge. Mysticism if you will.[16]

But we need to go beyond Roszak's broad and rather dated rhetoric. For, although the religious experiences we shall be examining may or may not be specifically Christian, what can often emerge from the desert is a deepening of a particular faith through a spirituality that is also universal, and profoundly so. There is in the sands a true ecumenism, human experience drawn into a unity through the universal encounter with the basic demands of life felt at the edge. That is why art and literature can offer an authentic response to the desert, since they too are universal, beyond all confessional limitation. There may, for some of us, be an ancient and deep interaction between art and Christianity, the former both provoking and illuminating the latter, but there is no such thing as "Christian art": there is only art which is universal though some, perhaps, is by Christians.

Among the great triumphs of modern art, the Rothko Chapel in Houston, Texas, which will be discussed further in chapter 8, functions as a "spiritual sanctuary, open to all religious faiths and nonbelievers alike."[17] What the dense monochrome paintings of the chapel offer is an internal desert, taking us, as this book will do continually, from external to internal, from physical to spiritual. For in the desert the categories of human experience, as of time and space, are disintegrated and extremes meet. At the very edge of physical possibility, the mind turns inward and the oppositions which we create between physical and spiritual, body and soul, collapse into a *coincidentia oppositorum* that is a Total Presence. Yet this is not the solipsistic experience which is so often wrongly ascribed to mystical souls, but a universal and potentially shared moment of utter sociability, a true meeting of the one and the many. The Rothko Chapel provokes an experience of seeing which is also a physical action, a moment of the reductive sublime, which is finally one with the ascetic world of the Desert Fathers. Being becomes seeing and seeing becomes being. Mark Rothko and the New York School of artists where nothing if not physical.

> That first experience of the Chapel paintings was – in the light of what I had known before – staggering . . . Before monochromatic painting can function outside itself, as it does in the greater scheme of the Chapel, it must hold its shape – i.e., work in itself – by stimulating and conducting eye movement up, down, across the surface, so that the painting is not merely seen but continuously and vividly experienced . . . The extraordinary variegated and breathing surfaces of Rothko's monochromes . . . accomplished this and more.[18]

Not simply the chapel, but the paintings themselves are a "place" of extraordinary experience. Neither inside nor outside, but both at once, the desert is a place of terror and hauntings, a place of miracles and visions, a hell and a utopia. There the Fathers lived as "true citizens of heaven" in a utopia which was truly "no place" on earth. From their solitariness and eremitical isolation emerged, quite naturally, the greatest of affirmations of community in the great monasteries that lived under the rule of St. Benedict, and the "ideal" life envisioned by St. Francis, whose Rule required that "the brothers shall possess nothing, neither a house, nor a place, nor anything. But as pilgrims and strangers in this world, serving God in poverty and humility . . . Let this be 'your portion,' which leads you to 'the land of the living' (Ps. 142:5)."[19] This link between the desert and the traditions of utopia will be explored further in chapter 5. For now, we may do well to reflect on the irony of that modern wilderness of the spirit that has been constructed in the desert of southern Nevada, the dangerous illusion that is Las Vegas, where at the hotel called the Mirage, the chairman has promised, with a grim echo of Christ's words from the Cross, that "Our guests will be in paradise."[20] We shall also have occasion to return to the theme of the desert mirage.

Theology, it has recently been affirmed (by a literary critic), has never not dealt in the desert experience, the aporetic and the *via negativa*.[21] Much has been said and written in recent years about Jacques Derrida, postmodernism, the aporetic and the negative way. Graham Ward, as we have seen, claims "religion" as a defining characteristic of postmodernity "testifying to the implosion of both secularism and liberalism and the re-enchantment of the world."[22] I hope this may be so, although I am not entirely clear what it means. Although we are children of the Enlightenment in the West, we have indeed begun to lose faith in the reason which sets the self at the center of all things or to believe in the truth of Descartes' dictum, *cogito ergo sum*. Indubitably, we have been formed by, and yet now begin to doubt, Kant's exhortation in his essay "What is Enlightenment?" (1784) "*Sapere aude!*" – "Dare to know," or perhaps "Think for yourself."[23] Kant claims this as the "motto of the Enlightenment," which he goes on to describe as

> the exodus of human beings from their self-induced minority. Minority is the inability to make use of one's reason without calling on the leadership of another.[24]

The image is significant, if not ironic, in the context of the present book. For the biblical Exodus, though a flight from bondage in Egypt, was also a journey into the desert, a school in which the Israelites learned by hard knocks the lessons of leadership under God. Kant's exodus into the freedom of reason has also become for us a journey across what Paul Ricoeur has described as the "desert of criticism" beyond which we hear another calling.[25]

I am deliberately mixing my images here. We are indeed (or most of us, at least) heirs to the Enlightenment and have been called to cross its deserts in which we have both grown and fallen far short of our ambitions. Yet, and most particularly in recent years, these deserts have only led us deeper into other wildernesses, more ancient deserts that are even more harsh and demanding, though they have a mysterious fertility that we had almost forgotten. Daphne Hampson begins her book *After Christianity* – which is the story of her own odyssey both out of and into the desert – with a reminder of Dietrich Bonhoeffer, the young German pastor imprisoned in Nazi Germany in 1945. He, too, in his way, was a "desert father," and we shall return to him in due course. In his *Letters and Papers from Prison*, Bonhoeffer returns us to Kant's words *sapere aude*, and reflects upon the consequences of a human daring that assumes a power which the desert reminds us is claimed illegitimately and must finally be relinquished in the self-forgetting and "kenosis" of a more ancient and humbler understanding.[26] That understanding acknowledges not the courage of *knowing*, but in Paul Tillich's phrase the courage *to be* – the courage of being. This is our true majority, the opposite of our self-induced minority, for which men and women have dared to lose themselves in the desert.

It may be that all such journeys are profoundly "postmodern." That term itself, representing an inevitable and proper critique of modernism, without which it could not exist, has now, like a river at its estuary mouth, become so broad as to be indefinable. It has certainly changed its temper considerably since we wielded it with such abandon in the 1970s and 1980s. And yet it retains some value and Graham Ward has a legitimate point about the "re-enchantment of the world" (although I am uneasy about his specific claims for "religion"). For postmodernity, it may be, is not to be temporally restricted to the late twentieth century, but it has always been there, a hidden move in human affairs, when someone, perhaps for no definable reason, recklessly walks into the desert armed only with the courage "to be" and a vision barely articulated. It is the moment when, along with Buber and Levinas, the over-riding claims of the "other" are acknowledged as supreme.

Yet, somehow, we have remained, positively or negatively, dazzled by the glamor, the complexities, and the intellectual acrobatics of "the post-modern," and very few have been prepared to take up seriously the third term, the desert – and even fewer theologians (there is not very much of any substance in print in English by or even on Charles de Foucauld, the French monk and hermit who died in the French North African desert in 1916, and to whom we shall return in chapter 5). The desert has largely remained a resource for biblical archeologists and not what it most truly is, a place of profound religious experience. Its surface has been scratched in the pop-ular imagination from Lawrence of Arabia to *The English Patient*, inhabited at one remove in the cushioned comfort of the cinema, but even these scratches, as we shall see, may have their value as tiny fissures allowing us to glimpse something of the vast interiority of St. Antony's mountain.

Travelers from the West, since the nineteenth century, have visited and romanticized the desert, while novels and films have realized the desert in our imaginations, and in their grainy photographs and sweaty journals, they have tended to see the desert with the eyes of Wordsworth's dreamer. But what has been missed is that, once the veneer of romanticism has been rubbed off by the abrasions of sand and rock and burned off by the sun (physical-ities unknown to *The Prelude*), these texts and pictures bear remarkable sim-ilarities to the literature of all those men and women, pious, mad, or mystic, who have "gone out" into the desert and found something there which we have missed in our cities and civilizations. It has been described by Edward Said in an essay on T. E. Lawrence (to whom we shall return later), as found in "a special but extreme form of life: the decentered one."[27] Art, too, saw something of that in its mysterious turn to abstraction, a turn which led Wassily Kandinsky to write about the "spiritual" in art, and the coming together of all arts in the figure which, perhaps above all, symbolizes for us the desert – the pyramid, yet a spiritual pyramid that is the very antithesis of the vaunting human ambition and reckless daring of the Tower of Babel.

> And so the arts are encroaching one upon another, and from a proper use of this encroachment will rise the art that is truly monumental. Every man who

steeps himself in the spiritual possibilities of his art is a valuable helper in the building of the *spiritual pyramid* which will some day reach to heaven.[28]

This spiritual pyramid is realized in Moses' ascent of Mount Sinai, when he is summoned into the clouds to meet the Lord who *descends* to the top of the mountain (Exodus 19:20). It is realized again in the climbing of Antony's "interior mountain," and the "ascent" of Mount Carmel by St. John of the Cross. And yet again in Thomas Merton's climb from his monastery in Kentucky to his simple hermitage. All of these journeys we shall follow in due course.

The spirituality of these journeys, their decenteredness, which is a losing of the self (for good or ill), will finally take us back to the theology of the last two chapters of this book, from meeting points to a meeting point arrived at when all "centeredness" has been shed and scorched away and the soul, as John Cassian once described it, has found its fertile places. T. E. Lawrence, as a "decentered" person, is an unlikely and finally tragic companion for the religious souls who preceded him into the sands of Egypt and Arabia, or the deserts of mystical spirituality. Nevertheless, it is perhaps not *finally* an accident, that two literary monuments to the "desert" experience in the twentieth century – by men different in almost every respect imaginable – bear closely similar titles: Lawrence's *The Seven Pillars of Wisdom* (1935), and Thomas Merton's *The Seven Storey Mountain* (1952).[29] This unlikely, and certainly accidental, resonance oddly contributes to the harmony of this book.

The word "harmony" is deliberately chosen here, for some people may find this an odd and dissonant book to read. It does not progress through an obvious and consecutive narrative based on either chronology or thematic development. Neither is it one of those books that is a series of separate essays sewn together to form some kind of a whole. As is made clear in the notes, it is not intended to form an introduction to college courses on the Desert Fathers and their theology or spirituality, and the standard textbooks are referred to if that is what you want. Rather, the chapters are in the form of a series of meditations on the place (rather than the literary idea) of the desert, as an environment in which theological reflection is uniquely possible, its echoes and resonances perceptible not merely in the work of theologians or "religiously" inclined people, but in the whole variety of people who have gone out into the desert and written about their experience, or painted pictures or made films.

It is important for the harmony that the chapters are read in order, forming as they do a link from the Bible to the present day. Each, in a sense, revisits the same space and builds upon the reflections of the chapters that have gone before, while at the same time each circles around and is a whole unto itself. Why the Bible, Schoenberg, and Heidegger? It is because Schoenberg, in his unfinished opera *Moses und Aron*, takes us again on the biblical wilderness wanderings – reenacting that which is first enacted in the Book of Exodus, while at the same time the composer shares with the philosopher Martin Heidegger the desert vision of Total Presence, a vision that will haunt each chapter until the final two chapters form a meditation – a space – upon that which has been present all along in writing and image. This early chapter, then, beginning with the Bible, binds all together. In the last of the *Four Quartets*, "Little Gidding," the poet T. S. Eliot reminds us that visiting the place Little Gidding (and reading the poem) is an action pursued not simply to verify, to instruct, to inform curiosity, or to carry report. It is to enact what he calls "prayer" in the physical act of kneeling. I do not wish to claim that this book should have the same effect. That is not my purpose, and I hope that the reading of it will be instructive and informative. But its primary concern is to make something possible – possible only in that most impossible and remotest of places, the desert, through literature and art and the lives of certain extraordinary men and women, so that a genuine theological reflection becomes the essence of the reader's response. This might come as a surprise, for its manner will be neither "churchy" nor even particularly pious, but profoundly real and ultimately, I believe, inescapable if we are to remain human in the profundity of our being.

It has often been noted that the desert is a place of purity and cleanness. Looking at a map of the Sahara we might be tempted to say "there is nothing there." It is a place of absorption and scouring, where bones are bleached white until they are absorbed into the very sand itself by the action of the wind. In *The Lausiac History* written by Bishop Palladius, a pupil of the great Evagrius of Pontus and a colleague of St. John Chrysostom, in about 417 CE, we read of the story of a mad scullery maid in a convent who is the recipient of scorn and abuse from the whole community of sisters. She eats only the scourings and scraps which are left over, never even chewing her food, and drinking only dishwater. She is dressed in rags and sleeps on the kitchen floor. She is, in a word, disgusting. When finally, under God's direction, the saintly Piteroum recognizes her as a holy person and actually the spiritual center of the convent, she vanishes into the desert and is never heard of again. Though regarded by all as an idiot, her self-effacement makes actual idiots of all her sisters in the convent, for they have failed to see her true worth. She becomes as nothing. It is only then, in her final absence, that the community recognizes that she has been, in fact, the true and necessary heart of the convent who has made the community possible – the sponge and the empty desert who has absorbed its dross and excess. Her very "being" is "to be nothing" and she is the quiet, unrecognized wisdom who is perceived only as a negation.[30]

Let us begin our travels with her.

Notes

1 William Wordsworth, *The Prelude* (1805) Book 5: "Books," lines 70–83, 110, 117–26.
2 I will use the term Desert Fathers throughout as a shorthand for the early Christian wanderers, men and women, who followed St. Antony into the deserts of Egypt and Judea in the fourth and fifth centuries.
3 W. H. Auden, *The Enchafèd Flood, or the Romantic Iconography of the Sea* (London: Faber, 1951), pp. 22–3.
4 Mark C. Taylor, *Disfiguring: Art, Architecture, Religion* (Chicago: University of Chicago Press, 1992), p. 270.
5 Ibid.
6 *From the Desert to the Book* (1980) is the title of a collection of dialogues with Edmond Jabès, and will be discussed in chapter 6.
7 Edmond Jabès, *The Book of Resemblances 2. Intimations: The Desert*, translated by Rosemarie Waldrop (1991), quoted in Jim Harold (ed.), *Desert* (Southampton: John Hansard Gallery, 1996), p. 47.
8 Mounira Khemir, "The Infinite Image of the Desert and its Representations," in *The Desert*. Fondation Cartier pour l'art contemporain (London: Thames and Hudson, 2000), pp. 58–9.
9 I am particularly indebted to David E. Klemm for this observation.
10 David Jenkins, "Literature and the Theologian," in John Coulson (ed.), *Theology and the University: An Ecumenical Investigation* (London: Darton, Longman and Todd, 1964), p. 219.
11 Kees Waaijman, "Towards a Phenomenological Definition of Spirituality," *Studies in Spirituality*, 3, 1993: 5–57, p. 35.
12 See, for example, William Johnston, *The Inner Eye of Love: Mysticism and Religion* (London: Collins, 1978).
13 Maurice Blanchot, *The Space of Literature*, translated by Ann Smock (Lincoln: University of Nebraska Press, 1982).
14 *The Lives of the Desert Fathers*, translated by Borman Russell, with an introduction by Benedicta Ward SLG (Oxford: A. R. Mowbray, 1981), Prologue, 9, p. 50 (emphasis added).
15 Henry David Thoreau, "Walking," in *Excursions: The Writings of Henry David Thoreau*, Riverside edn., 11 vols. (Boston, 1893), vol. 9, pp. 267, 275 (emphasis added). See also Roderick Nash, *Wilderness and the American Mind*, 3rd edn. (New Haven, CT: Yale University Press, 1982), ch. 5, pp. 84–95.
16 Theodore Roszak, *Where the Wasteland Ends: Politics and Transcendence in Post-industrial Society* (London: Faber, 1974), p. xx.

17 Walter Hopps, "The Rothko Chapel," in *The Menil Collection* (New York: Harry N. Abrams, 1997), p. 314.

18 Harris Rosenstein, in Hopps, *The Menil Collection*.

19 "The Rule of St. Francis," in Gregory Claeys and Lyman Tower Sargent (eds.), *The Utopia Reader* (New York: New York University Press, 1999), p. 70.

20 Quoted in Taylor, *Disfiguring*, p. 187.

21 Valentine Cunningham, *In the Reading Gaol: Postmodernity, Texts and History* (Oxford: Blackwell, 1994), p. 402.

22 Graham Ward, *True Religion* (Oxford: Blackwell, 2003), p. viii.

23 See also Daphne Hampson, *After Christianity*, 2nd edn. (London: SCM, 2002), p. 1.

24 Quoted in Hampson, *After Christianity*, p. 1. I have followed Hampson's own translation.

25 Paul Ricoeur, *The Symbolism of Evil*, translated by Emerson Buchanan (Boston, MA: Beacon Press, 1969), p. 349.

26 See Hampson, *After Christianity*, p. 1. The word "kenosis" will recur throughout this book. It is used by St. Paul in Philippians 2:7 to describe the "emptying" of God, by himself, so that he takes on the form of humanity in Christ.

27 Edward W. Said, *Reflections on Exile and Other Literary and Cultural Essays* (London: Granta Books, 2001), p. 32.

28 Wassily Kandinsky, *Concerning the Spiritual in Art* (1914), translated by M. T. H. Sadler (New York: Dover Publications, 1977), p. 20.

29 The point is all the more odd when we remember that Lawrence gave this title to his history of the Arab Revolt only because he transferred it from an earlier book which he wrote but never published, and he used its title "as a memento." It refers to the verse in Proverbs 9:1: "Wisdom hath builded a house: she hath hewn out her seven pillars." Merton's title is born of an equally literary passion – his love of Dante's *Divine Comedy*.

30 Palladius, *The Lausiac History*, translated by Robert T. Meyer (New York: Newman Press, 1964), p. 110. See also Michael de Certeau, *The Mystic Fable, Vol. 1: The Sixteenth and Seventeenth Centuries*, translated by Michael B. Smith (Chicago: University of Chicago Press, 1992), pp. 32–4.

2

The Bible, Schoenberg, and Heidegger

Veronica Smiles was crossing the Sahara desert, minding her own business, when she ran into God . . .

"I think there'll be a sandstorm," He said, and passed on His way. No salute, no salaam, no goodbye, no form of leave-taking in any culture, and He should have been aware of them all, since enough of them had bid adieu to Him in their time.

Veronica looked after Him and thought He was very rude indeed. She got quickly back into her jeep, thought about offering Him a lift, but decided against it. If He was arranging a sandstorm, He could jolly well weather it. In any case she couldn't afford to waste time with God.[1]

Veronica Smiles, in Bernice Rubens' novel *Our Father* (1988), enters the desert alone and leaves it alone and unchanged, her time still her own. In the Sahara she encounters God, though to her he could equally well have been the Devil, and throughout the novel he continues to haunt her, like a guilty conscience, at moments either opportune or inopportune. To the difference he himself is indifferent – the indifferent God of the desert. At the beginning of his ministry, Jesus, too, violently driven by the Spirit,[2] enters the desert alone and experiences a traumatic encounter. But when he leaves after forty days, he does so transformed and resolved immediately to start his work and engage with the community. For him,' unlike Veronica, the desert is a place of preparation, and from its solitariness the church, a "city" of people, is begun to be built. Whether their encounters were with the same person – God or Satan – is hard to discern. Perhaps they were simply the hauntings of their own innermost being – the demons of uncaring or the demons of temptation.

At the beginning of his ministry Jesus walks alone into the desert. At its end he walks alone again, along the *Via Dolorosa* to the cross, to another desert outside the walls of the city, and towards another community through the Passion and crucifixion. Before Jesus, the wildman John the Baptist had "appeared" in the desert (the Greek word for desert in Mark 1:4 is *eremos*, from which we derive the term "hermit") to preach and baptize, and people went out from the cities to hear him. For this wilderness of John "was the place from where many Jews expected the final eschatological deliverance to appear."[3] "All great religions were born between the desert and the steppe," said Carlo Carretto.[4] For the character in the modern novel, it is and remains a place of loneliness and isolation; for Jesus and John, it becomes a place of community, though for each of them it is also a place of self-discovery through pain, solitariness, and suffering.

In the monasticism of the Western church, which grew out of the Egyptian and Judean deserts through people like John Cassian, the practice of *lectio divina* was the slow and meditative reading of the Bible in order imaginatively and actually to enter into its life and experience, and above all the life and sufferings of Jesus. The Franciscan Bonaventure (1217–74) urges us actually to live our own lives within these narratives, experienced above all in the liturgical practice of the church. This is a solitary way that is also deeply social, so that "thus using the rod of the cross . . . he [the reader] may pass over [*transeat*] the Red Sea, going from Egypt into the desert, where it is given for him to taste the hidden manna, [and] he may rest with Christ in the tomb, as one dead to the world."[5] The reader lives within the text as desert itself. For Bonaventure, the mystical knowledge which this journey engenders is anything but the lonely encounter of Veronica Smiles or even the isolated experience of the eremitic mystic. It is not, as Mark McIntosh expresses it, "an apprehension of bare deity, but precisely the awareness of the eternal *ekstasis* of deity by which the divine draws all creation into loving union in Christ."[6] The desert journey, through the *lectio divina*, is a going out to meet God, who meets the traveler half way, like the father of the prodigal son in Luke's parable. For other travelers, where this journey is experienced as an erotic participation in the bodily suffering of Christ, the imagery of communion maintains its association with the physical extremes of the wilderness that is at once both heaven and hell. The Flemish woman poet and visionary Hadewijch (mid-twelfth century) describes this participation as of those who "wander in the storms of Love, / Body and soul, heart and thought – / Lovers lost in this hell."[7]

In the Bible, these often hellish wanderings exist between a lost garden and an envisioned city, folded between the pages of the sacred text: from the Eden of Genesis 1–2 to the Heavenly City described in Revelation 21. The journey traverses the entire book.[8] Abram journeys towards the Negev, the great desert to the south of Canaan (Genesis 12:9), from where he "looked forward to the city which has foundations, whose builder and maker is God"(Hebrews 11:10). In the wilderness, at Mount Horeb, Moses first meets with God in the Burning Bush (Exodus 3:2–4:17), and a revelation takes place in the desert place. From this encounter unfolds the forty years of desert "wanderings" of the Israelites. These wanderings, however, are not vague and indeterminate, but rather under the purposes of God, who leads them in the desert of Sinai in order to avoid the more obvious coastal route from Egypt where (anachronistically in the Book of Exodus) the Philistines block the way "although that was nearer", with the danger that "the people [might] repent when they see war, and return to Egypt" (Exodus 13:17). Rabbinic argument is unresolved about the translation of the word "although" (in Hebrew, *ki*). It can also be translated as "because": "*because* that was nearer." God, it might be said, took the Israelites into the desert precisely *because* the other way was easier. For the desert is a harsh place of testing, of judgment and also learning when, on Mount Sinai, the Law is delivered to Moses. In Exodus (19–31) and Numbers (15), statutes are given with a view to the time "when you come into the land" (Numbers 15:2), though the desert still remains a place of repeated rebellion and the necessary renewal of the covenant bond between Yahweh and his people. In Exodus 32, thinking that Moses has deserted them, the Israelites turn to his brother Aaron and together they construct and worship the Golden Calf, thus breaking the first commandment.

The desert tests the people up to and beyond their limits. In the desert, God speaks to Moses "face to face," yet mysteriously remains unseen – an intimately present absence, so that Moses is to remain hidden in a cleft of the rock "while my glory passes by" (Exodus 33:22). And so these forty years are paradoxically a time of closeness to God and a time of rebellion against him; a time of suffering, but also a time in which God's care is yet profound and tender. In the words of Moses' song in Deuteronomy 32,

> He sustained him [Israel] in a desert land,
> > In a howling wilderness waste;
> he shielded him, cared for him,
> > guarded him as the apple of his eye.
> As an eagle that stirs up its nest,
> > and hovers over its young;
> as it spreads its wings, takes them up,
> > and bears them aloft on its pinions.
> > > (Deuteronomy 32:10–11)

In the prophetic literature of the post-exilic period, the blossoming of the desert becomes the symbol of God's enduring love for his people, when "The wilderness and the dry land shall be glad, / the desert shall rejoice and blossom; / like the crocus it shall blossom abundantly, / and rejoice with joy and singing" (Isaiah 35:1–2). It is the dream of all desert peoples. Yet at the same time, the return to the desert and the wilderness is never far away, for it is there, and only there, that God's covenant and love for Israel are renewed. Hosea makes this quite explicit, as God entices his people back into the wilderness, despite punishing them ("her") for their waywardness and the worship of other gods. Yet he will come to her as a lover.

> Therefore, I will now allure her,
> > and bring her into the wilderness, and speak tenderly to her.
> From there I will give her her vineyards,
> > and make the Valley of Achor a door of hope.
> And there she shall respond as in the days of her youth,
> > as at the time when she came out of the land of Egypt.
> > > (Hosea 2:14–15)

Paradoxically, the forty years of the desert wanderings have now become not a time of misery, but a halcyon period in Israel's history, the time when God's love for his people was in its first prime and bloom. And so, too, Jesus begins his ministry in the desert, in a time of conflict and temptation, but one that will bear much fruit. For if the desert is for Jesus a time of testing, it is also a place of refreshment where he goes to be alone and to pray (Mark 1:35). Yet from there he is dragged back to the town by his disciples to fulfill his ministry. But the desert remains, for him, the necessary "other."

It is in the time of the Exodus, of Israel's desert wanderings, that the German composer Arnold Schoenberg set his opera *Moses und Aron*, begun in 1930 and never completed. In 1933 Schoenberg was dismissed from his post at the Prussian Academy of Arts in Berlin because he was a Jew and shortly afterwards he left Germany to wander himself as an exile in the United States. The opera is one of the greatest examples of the twelve-tone method with which Schoenberg had experimented as early as 1908 in the *Three Pieces for Piano*, Opus 11. This method abandons the Western tradition of harmonic progression and cadence by giving an equality to each of the twelve tones of the scale.[9] No harmonic preferences are given and hierarchy is abandoned. This advent of "atonal" music in the twentieth century established a profound subversion of the relationship between time and space such as exists in most tonal music.[10] It is, we might say, in musical terms, a leaving of the ordered life of the city for the disorientation of the desert, where the experience of time and space is also radically deconstructed. (This is a theme to which I shall return in more detail in chapter 4.) In the words of Jeremy Begbie:

> The twelve-tone method proposed by Arnold Schoenberg (1874–1951) was in part an attempt to solve the difficulties posed by the abandonment of tonality. Pitch relationships were organized according to non-hierarchical and non-functional harmonic principles. Even here, however, the musical phrase, related to meter, was not abandoned, though it became more supple and asymmetrical.[11]

By his method, Schoenberg is actually exploring in musical terms the experience of the desert, and thereby inviting us as listeners into the very environment of the biblical narratives, such that we, too, must learn to listen to a new sound and find our way in an unfamiliar, perplexing, and often threatening place. It is a place both strange and yet also known and familiar, a "place" of sometimes harsh musical atonality, but also sometimes of extraordinary lyrical beauty. Apart from its musical form, *Moses und Aron*, for which Schoenberg also wrote the libretto, is also a search for a perfect and ultimately impossible language. Drawing from the Bible story in Exodus and Numbers (though deliberately excising the influences of Luther's great but too familiar German version), and exercised by its contradictions, Schoenberg gives Moses voice in *Sprechgesang*, an utterance harshly and even painfully midway between speaking and singing, which he had used in earlier works to suggest a lack of harmony with the surrounding reality; a lack of being at home in the world. At the end of Act 2, which is musically the end of the opera, Moses finally sinks to the ground in despair with the great cry: "O word, thou word, that I lack!" (*O Wort, du Wort, das mir fehlt!*).[12] By contrast, Aron, an eloquent tenor, will only die at the end of Act 3, for which no music was ever written, with Moses uttering the very last words which have never been uttered or heard on any stage:

> But in the wasteland you shall be
> invincible and shall achieve the goal:
> unity with God.
> (*Aber in der Wuste seid ihr unuberwindlich*
> *und werder das Ziel erreichen:*
> *Vereinigt mit Gott.*)

This unity is the persistent theme of the early Christian literature of the desert, a recovery of the unity inherent in creation but which was lost in the departure from Eden, a unity with God that is the final ground of human "being."

Paradoxically, Schoenberg's music is a quest for language, Gabriel asserting in the last of his *Modern Psalms*, "in the beginning was the spirit, the spirit of creation. And what it produced by perpetuating itself could only be less than it was itself. That is how infinite space and time came about – the infinite yielded what is without end."[13] That is the insurmountable problem faced by Moses as he searches for words in the desert where God is revealed to him yet hides his face, and language is defeated by the very infinity which it has revealed. Language reaches out to express the unutterable. In *Moses und Aron*, above all, as George Steiner has suggested, "music has celebrated the mystery of intuitions of transcendence . . . Music is plainly uncircumscribed by the world."[14]

Even to witness the opera is, in a real way, a liturgical experience. It is more than simply an experience of watching and listening to an opera being performed on the stage. To move from the figure of Moses to Aron is a move from the urbane city to the wilderness, and at the heart of this journey is the great staging of the "Golden Calf and the Altar" in Act 2, scene 3, drawn from Exodus 32. In the biblical narrative it is the very inversion of proper liturgy, a turning away from Yahweh and true worship in which, in the wilderness of despair, "the people sat down to eat and drink, and rose up to play" (Exodus 32:6). In the opera, the scene begins with Aron reversing the otherness and transcendence of the desert God of Moses by investing everything in the utter immanence and immutability of the golden image which has been made. Aron sings:

> This gold image attests
> that in all things that are, a god lives.
> Unchangeable, even as a law,
> is the stuff, the gold
> that you have given.
> (*Dieses bild bezeugt,*
> *dass in allem, was ist, ein Gott lebt.*

Unwandelbar, wie ein Prinzip,
ist der Stoff, das Gold,
das ihr geschenkt habt.)

What follows is unmatched in operatic performance for its violence, sexuality, gluttony, and din. Crucially, Schoenberg insisted that there should be
no synchrony between what is heard and what is seen, between ear and eye.
(It is impossible to appreciate the impact of the scene simply by *listening*
to a recording of the opera. It has to be witnessed, even participated in, on
the stage.) As the music descends into a primitive anarchy of sound which
beats upon the ear, so the eye is distracted by a puppet-like performance of
dancing butchers, beggars, old and young, in an orgy of drunkenness and
dancing (*Orgie der Trunkenheit und des Tanzes*). It is a scene of absolute
dislocation and chaos, in utter contrast to the purity of Moses' demands,
though even this is, he finally realizes, a purity which is itself, inevitably,
tainted, as he acknowledges that even the Tables of the Law themselves are
images and nothing can attain to the purity of the demands of the desert
and its God. This purity is a word beyond all human speaking. Thus we
witness the tragedy of Moses' last speech in Act 2, which opens us to
the very edge of language and to the God who is revealed only in utter
mystery. It is Schoenberg's finest expression of his own reaching out in
speech and music to that which is beyond all utterance, acknowledged by
Moses as he sinks onto the sands of the desert in despair. Yet it is also his
realization of truth, his victory beyond which there can only be silence.

Inconceivable God!
Inexpressible, many-sided idea,
will you let it be so explained?
Shall Aron, my mouth, fashion this image?
Then I have fashioned an image too, false,
as an image must be.
Thus I am defeated!
Thus, all was but madness that
I believed before,
and can and must not be given voice.
O word, thou word, that I lack!
(*Unvorstellbarer Gott!*
Unaussprechlicher, vieldeutiger Gedanke!
Lässt du diese Auslegung zu?
Darf Aron, mein Mund, dieses Bild machen?
So habe ich mir ein Bild gemacht, falsch,
wie ein Bild nur sein kann!

So bin ich geschlagen!
So war alles Wahnsinn, was ich
gedacht habe,
und kann und darf nicht gesagt werden!
O Wort, du Wort, das mir fehlt!)

The opera cannot be finished, for beyond this there is only infinity. Yet there is more to come. There is always more to come, although the third act has never been and can never be heard. For the paradox is that Moses' despair and defeat are his triumph – and thus it must be in the wilderness, as it was in the Passion, and as it was for the solitary monk, Charles de Foucauld. This is an odd company – but there are more.

The final turn of this chapter from the Bible and Schoenberg to Heidegger might seem indeed to be an encounter with what Kierkegaard describes in *The Concept of Irony* (1841) as "the prodigious daemon dwelling in the empty wastelands of irony."[15] The desert is always the dwelling place of demons, as we shall see. And yet Schoenberg and Heidegger share a vision of Total Presence[16] that is only encountered in the spaces of the desert, whether of the body or of the spirit, and finally only of both as such distinctions are dissolved. Once a candidate for the Catholic priesthood, Heidegger wrote towards the end of his life, in a letter to Ingeborg Böttger:

> Behind the technological world there is a mystery. This world is not just a creation of human beings. No one knows whether and when humans will ever experience this emptiness as the "sacred empty." It suffices that this relation remains open.[17]

This emptiness may be a space or it may be an experience – or both at once. Paradoxically, Heidegger seeks for this emptiness in words, as Schoenberg sought for it in music. In his great early work, *Sein und Zeit* (1927), Heidegger deliberately uses a non-technical language to explore Being, because, as George Steiner puts it, "the simple word, the antique vulgate will serve precisely because it contains . . . the greatest charge of initial and valid human perception."[18] The greatest riches lie within the old and plainest of words and yet they are the most difficult of all. For in this apparently simple and stripped down language, "we are to be slowed down, bewildered and barred in our reading so that we may be driven deep." To read Heidegger's work is an experience in reading which is akin to the asceticism of the desert, and ultimately just as mysterious. It takes us to the very basis of thinking, until that which is simple becomes that which is most apart, separate and therefore, in a sense, "sacred." Thus, Steiner concludes, "a Heideggerian text is often strange and impenetrable beyond that of even the most difficult of preceding metaphysicians and mystics."[19] In his early monograph on Duns Scotus, for which he obtained his *Habilitation* in 1916, Heidegger took his first steps back into medieval mysticism in what becomes a process of retrieval or recovery of its roots by a breaking down of the conceptual surface of traditional metaphysics.[20] At the limits of philosophy or theology we cease to "do" and begin to "become." In the abyss of this space, theology or philosophy becomes a threat to Being in its pure detachment, and yet without this detachment there can be no thought and no theology. As with the Desert Fathers as they wandered deep into the wilderness, Heidegger's thinking is absolutely not a flight from the world but actually a rediscovery of our roots and place in the world.

In his book *The Mystical Element in Heidegger's Thought* (1986), John Caputo makes a comparison between the mystical reflections *On Detachment* of the medieval mystical writer Meister Eckhart (whom Heidegger read carefully) and Heidegger's inaugural lecture in Freiburg, *What is Metaphysics?* (1929), which he later defended in a "Postscript" of 1943 against the charge of "nihilism" and "irrationalism." For Heidegger, "nothing" is precisely something which we experience or encounter, just as Moses experienced God in the desert yet without seeing him, such that "pure Being and pure Nothing are then the same." This experience of Nothing is an absolute otherness, since "that which never and nowhere is a being reveals itself as that which differentiates itself from all beings, which we call Being."[21] At this extreme point of anxiety is encountered an utter "serenity and the gentleness of a creative longing" that is yet not incompatible with the active life.

Meister Eckhart and Heidegger agree that in this encounter (whether it be with God or Being) we are not called to deal with it, but to allow ourselves to be dealt with in a letting be. In its serenity or composure (Heidegger uses Eckhart's term *Gelassenheit*), anxiety becomes a sense of wonder or awe akin to the "awefulness" which Rudolf Otto famously described as that which is experienced in the face of the numinous.[22] And in this "letting be" we should respond as to a graceful gift, in a thanking which is to engage actively with "thinking." Caputo describes it in words of a liturgical nature, for thus to "think" is none other than to "be," both liturgically and biblically:

> In giving thanks one attains to the "nobility of poverty" and "the treasures of the sacrifice." This is the essential paradox known to every religious man and every mystic: that in giving up all one attains all. It was the lesson which Jesus tried to teach the rich young man. Meister Eckhart himself described the detached heart as living a life of perfect poverty . . . Dasein is poor in spirit

because by its essential thinking it knows nothing useful or productive; it has acquired no scientific knowledge. Indeed, it knows "nothing" at all, just as Eckhart's detached heart possesses "nothing" at all.[23]

It is then in Eckhart's thinking that we take our leave of God for God's sake.[24] The problem of Heidegger's mystical thought has been much discussed.[25] My purpose here is not to conflate Eckhart's mysticism with Heidegger's thinking. That would be a foolish venture, for their concerns and cultures are far different in many ways. Nevertheless, it is intrinsic to the purpose of the present book to trace likenesses in difference through many works, separated by time and circumstance, religious and otherwise, in order to recover or retrieve (Heidegger's term is *Wiederholung*) a commonality which is both and at the same time on the edge and at the heart of what it is to be human and "to be." It is a commonality found most deeply in the deserts of human experience and wanderings.

Here Eckhart and Heidegger stand beside Schoenberg with Moses, and they are not alone. In the next chapter we shall turn to that odd assortment of men and women who followed Antony into the Egyptian desert in the fourth century CE who, in their solitariness and their communities, take their place among those who have lived on the edge of things worldly and comprehensible, "wasting" their time with God and thereby transforming both time and space. The paradox, we shall discover, is that it is these strange people by whom the world is truly kept in being.

Notes

1 Bernice Rubens, *Our Father* (London: Abacus, 1988), pp. 1–3.
2 In Mark's Gospel the Greek verb is *ekballo*, which means literally to "throw out."
3 C. M. Tuckett, "Mark," in John Barton and John Muddiman (eds.), *The Oxford Bible Commentary* (Oxford: Oxford University Press, 2001), p. 888.
4 Quoted in Andrew Louth, *The Wilderness of God* (Nashville, TN: Abingdon Press, 1991), p. 37.
5 Bonaventure, *The Journey of the Mind to God*, translated by Philotheus Boehner, OFM (Cambridge: Hackett Publishing, 1993), VII, 37–8.
6 Mark A. McIntosh, *Mystical Theology* (Oxford: Blackwell, 1998), p. 77.
7 Hadewijch, *Poems in Couplets*, 16, in *Hadewijch: The Complete Works*, translated by Mother Columba Hart, OSB. Classics of Western Spirituality (New York: Paulist Press, 1993), p. 358.
8 See chapter 4, pp. 43–4.
9 See Albert L. Blackwell, *The Sacred in Music* (Louisville, KY: Westminster John Knox Press, 1999), pp. 70–1.

10 Jeremy Begbie, *Theology, Music and Time* (Cambridge: Cambridge University Press, 2000), p. 141.

11 Begbie, *Theology, Music and Time*, p. 142. See also Richard Norton, *Tonality in Western Culture: A Critical and Historical Perspective* (University Park: Pennsylvania State University Press, 1984), pp. 231ff.

12 The English translation is by Allen Forte, in the book accompanying the 1984 recording by Sir Georg Solti with the Chicago Symphony Orchestra and Chorus (London: Decca Record Company, 1985).

13 Quoted in Alexander L. Ringer, *Arnold Schoenberg: The Composer as Jew* (Oxford: Clarendon Press, 1990), p. 39.

14 George Steiner, *Real Presences* (London: Faber and Faber, 1989), p. 218.

15 Søren Kierkegaard, *The Concept of Irony, Schelling Lecture Notes*, translated by Howard V. Hong and Edna H. Hong (Princeton, NJ: Princeton University Press, 1989), p. 125.

16 Capital letters are used throughout the book for this term, which will become ever more central as we move towards chapter 10 and a consideration of the theology of Thomas Altizer.

17 Quoted in Timothy Clark, *Martin Heidegger* (London: Routledge, 2002), p. 97.

18 George Steiner, *Heidegger* (London: Fontana, 1978), pp. 14–15.

19 Ibid, p. 16.

20 See John D. Caputo, *Demythologizing Heidegger* (Bloomington: Indiana University Press, 1993), pp. 170–1.

21 Martin Heidegger, *What is Metaphysics?*, quoted in John D. Caputo, *The Mystical Element in Heidegger's Thought* (New York: Fordham University Press, 1986), p. 21.

22 Rudolf Otto, *The Idea of the Holy*, translated by John W. Harvey (Oxford: Oxford University Press, 1923).

23 Caputo, *The Mystical Element in Heidegger's Thought*, p. 28.

24 Don Cupitt's *Taking Leave of God* (1980), a phrase drawn from Meister Eckhart's sermon *Qui audit me*, will be discussed further in chapter 5.

25 Works on this question by Paul Huhnerfield, Karl Lowith, and Laszlo Versenyi are discussed by Caputo, *The Mystical Element in Heidegger's Thought*, pp. 31–45.

3

The Desert Fathers
Wanderings and Miracles

And so for nearly twenty years he [Antony] continued training himself in solitude, never going forth, and but seldom seen by any. After this, when many were eager and wishful to imitate his discipline, and his acquaintances came and began to cast down and wrench off the door by force, Antony, as from a shrine, came forth initiated in the mysteries and filled with the Spirit of God. Then for the first time he was seen outside the fort by those who came to see him. And, when they saw him, they wondered at the sight, for he had the same habit of body as before, and was neither fat, like a man without exercise, nor lean from fasting and striving with the demons, but he was just the same as they had known him before his retirement.[1]

Whether St. Athanasius (ca. 296–373) actually wrote the *Life of St. Antony* remains disputed. What is clear, however, is that it was a widely known and influential document in the early history of the Egyptian Desert Fathers. Even in its elaborate stylization, the *Life* touches perhaps more closely than any other work the primal imperative and spirit of the first desert monks in Egypt.

It was almost immediately translated into Latin by Evagrius, who was Bishop of Antioch (in Italy, 364–73); it is mentioned by Jerome (ca. 345–420); and in an oration delivered only a few years after the death of Athanasius, Gregory of Nazianzus (ca. 329–89) states: "Athanasius compiled the biography of the divine Antony." The life of this obscure hermit was of immense importance for the church throughout the world.

The son of a well-to-do landowner in the Fayum in northern Egypt, the young Antony fought the "demon of fornication,"[2] gave away his money, and "began to abide in places outside the village."[3] It was about the year 270. Followed by disciples, as Simon and those who were with him pursued Jesus when he went into the wilderness to pray and be alone (Mark 1:35), Antony wandered ever deeper into the desert, living among the tombs that were set between the empty desert and inhabited country – the cities of the dead – until finally at the end of his travels coming to rest after a journey of three days and three nights in the eastern desert close to the Red Sea at "a very lofty mountain, and at the foot of the mountain ran a very clear stream, whose waters were sweet and very cold; outside there was a plain and a few uncared-for palm trees."[4] Here he remained in the "inner mountain," living the life of a solitary, but still visited by many people. At first, the narrative runs, he was supplied with basic necessities by Arabs who "saw his earnestness," and later by his own followers. However, realizing the trouble which this caused to others, he took up simple husbandry and provided for himself and those who came to him in order that they "might have some slight solace after the labor of that hard journey." And when the wild beasts damaged his crops, he spoke to them and they desisted. Yet, even here, Antony did not live apart from the great theological controversies in the wider church, being closely associated with Athanasius in his support of the Nicene party in its debate with the Arian heresy, a theological imperative for which we shall, later in this chapter, see the reason.[5]

It is the passage quoted at the beginning of this chapter, with its description of a miraculous asceticism, that encapsulates the spirit of the current discussion. For almost twenty years, the *Life* tells us, Antony lived alone in the desert, almost like one who had died. It is that landscape which forms and defines his spirituality and being, a place outside human habitation though not entirely cut off from it, for many came eager to imitate him. In Egypt, the desert was never far away, yet it was the place of mystery and harshness, a place outside life. It was where a few lived as wanderers, but none could settle in its vastness and extreme conditions. Even (perhaps even more) in Antony's time the desert was a place of legend, well described by Peter Brown:

The myth of the desert was one of the most abiding creations of late antiquity. It was, above all, a myth of liberating precision. It delimited the towering presence of the "the world," from which the Christian must be set free, by emphasizing a clear ecological frontier. It identified the process of disengagement from the world with a move from one ecological zone to another, from the settled land of Egypt to the desert. It was a brutally clear boundary, already heavy with immemorial associations.[6]

Beyond this boundary and in the desert Antony lived in a fort "so long deserted that it was full of creeping things, on the other side of the river."[7] And yet, like Lazarus from his tomb, he emerges in perfect health of both body and soul. The journey into the desert is, literally, a descent into the place on earth most feared, where the demons, both inside and outside, are most powerfully encountered, and where Antony, the pioneer, faces that which is most fearful and discovers what he most deeply seeks, so that he is able, finally, to say, "I no longer fear God: I love Him."[8] This perfection lies at the heart of the asceticism of the desert. "Asceticism" is derived from the Greek word *askesis*, meaning exercise or training, such as an athlete must pursue if the body is to be subdued and fit to win the race or competition. It explains Antony's perfect health and it is the image taken by St. Paul to encourage the Corinthian church to strive for the "imperishable wreath" which will be their prize as Christians, for they must run not merely to compete in the race, but to win it (1 Corinthians 9:24). Antony does not go into the desert to destroy his body, but to perfect it, and so he emerges from his "tomb" full of life and vigor.

It is clear that the *Life of St. Antony* is a deliberate reworking of an image, already by then a legend, and a fictionalizing of his life, composed probably under the influence of the impact of the writings of Origen on the desert spirituality of the fourth century.[9] This is a characteristic of the writings of the early Desert Fathers to which we shall return later in this chapter, and it has an important bearing on the relationship between these ancient texts and more recent, and very different, desert literature considered in the later chapters of this book. Nevertheless, there remain striking similarities between the *Life* and the seven Epistles of Antony, which are almost certainly genuine, though the original Coptic version has been lost.[10] In the Epistles the emphasis is on *gnosis*, or "knowledge," which is above all a knowledge of the self, whereby we are saved and thus return to God. According to Antony, since through our "intellectual participation" we may participate in God, then knowledge of God is possible. This is achieved by the subjection of all bodily passion that attacks us both physically and mentally. By the ascetic cleansing of the body, the soul too is cleansed and we return to our natural, virtuous condition. As Thomas Merton, who was in many ways a true spiritual descendent of Antony, was to express it, people first went into the desert "to recover the lost innocence and purity of heart that belonged to Adam and Eve in Eden."[11] Nor, for Antony, was nature subject to the punishment of the Fall. (As we shall see later, the demands of Christian theological "orthodoxy" and its later insistences is a matter of indifference to Antony and the desert monks. Although, in their way, deeply theological, they were led by other and even more powerful visions.) As the critic Samuel Rubenson sums up Antony's teaching:

> Nature is not fallen and should not be rejected. God thus calls human beings primarily through the natural law laid down in their hearts. The written (scriptural) law, and the teaching of the Holy Spirit, those other ways in which God calls human beings, do not contain anything new. The coming of Jesus, his presence, reveals what is already laid down in creation – it reestablishes the unity that once existed.[12]

Thus, in the purity of the desert, Antony and the monks of the great settlements of Nitria and Scetis in the northern Egyptian desert, near Alexandria, sought the paradise which is our true home, and in the words of the *Historia Monachorum* (a text discussed in more detail below), "while dwelling on earth . . . they live as true citizens of heaven." The theme of utopian paradise is a frequent one in early monastic texts and in all desert literature, and the order sought in the desert is a reconfiguration of the disorder of the fallen world of the cities. It is a theme which will be pursued further in chapter 5.[13]

And yet, paradoxically, these strange figures, both men and women, emerge from the early literature of the desert as perfectly "earthy" folk, through their intuitive grasp of their own inner selves, the fruit of which, as Thomas Merton perceived, was *quies*, or "rest." Merton describes this not as anything ecstatic or extravagant, but as "simply the sanity and poise of a being that no longer had to look at itself because it is carried away by the perfection and freedom that is in it."[14] This is, quite literally, a coming into the self and is a freedom from that restless and dislocated self-consciousness experienced by Adam and Eve when they first saw that they were naked and were afraid, so that they hid themselves from God (Genesis 3:7–11). Nor is it so very far from the Buddhist doctrine of *anatta* or "selflessness" that is the realization of the totality of *dharma*, which perhaps goes far to explain Merton's persistence in, and even identification with, Zen Buddhism. Such *quies* is the reason for the unselfconscious humanity of the Fathers, their humor and the natural wit of their sayings. Their emphasis on the natural goodness of human nature lies at the heart of their utopian vision of a life lived in earth's harshest places, which grants, at the same time, a vision of heaven that is given in the stripping away of all material things. For, as Antony says in the sermon attributed to him in the *Life*,

> when the soul hath its spiritual faculty in a natural state virtue is formed. And it is in a natural state when it remains as it came into existence. And when it came into existence it was fair and exceeding honest.[15]

And so, as we turn now to the literature of the Desert Fathers, what we find is often highly romanticized and fictionalized. It is a literature that follows the pattern of legend and hagiography in its attentiveness to concrete experience, its insistence on narrative, and a narrative articulation in which events are disclosed and take on the character of what Edith Wyschogrod calls an "ontological matrix."[16] It is a point made also by Maurice Blanchot:

> If we regard the tale [le récit] as the true telling of an exceptional event which has taken place and which someone is trying to report, then we have not come close to sensing the true nature of the tale. The tale is not the narration of an event, but the event itself, the approach to that event, the place where that event is made to happen – an event which is yet to come and through whose power of attraction the tale can hope to come into being too.
> . . . The tale is a movement towards a point . . . unknown, obscure, foreign [and] such that apart from this movement it does not seem to have any prior existence, and yet it is so imperious that the tale derives its power of attraction only from this point, and cannot even "begin" before reaching it.[17]

In such tales, such places, the real is precisely that which is inexpressible, an acknowledgment of difference that confounds the totalizing of the discourse and reorders time in what Wyschogrod calls the "understanding of past and future as modalities of the present."[18] As the travelers of the *Historia Monachorum* enter the desert, they leave, at the same time, cultural and historical definitions of space and time, entering, quite literally, a text in which the voice is that of the radical Other that speaks with an imperative force, a hagiography that only makes sense as "a *practice* through which the addressee is gathered into the narrative so as to extend and elaborate it with his or her own life."[19] Yet at the same time we should be profoundly aware of the *impossibility* of finally following the saint into the deep desert. As Geoffrey Galt Harpham has written: "We must imitate the model; we must not think that the model is or ought to be imitable."[20]

In other words, we read not *through* the text, somehow consuming it in a search for its meaning, but read only by extending in ourselves the very existence of the text. In the oxymoronic text the saintly body becomes a total presence only in its absolute self-forgetfulness, in pure kenosis, and thus the impossible *imitatio Christi*, an impossibility which we therefore entertain in our reading. For in this act of reading, the letters that we *see* are only possible against the greater reality of the pure, blank spaces that allow them to become visual. The desert, we may say, is the blank page upon which the lives of the Fathers are mere markings across which the eye travels for a moment in brief encounters that, like Antony in his mountain, provide necessary refreshment for travelers otherwise lost in time and space. Yet they are markings which both define and are defined by the purity of the deserted page, which is also what Rufinus, the friend of Jerome, in the Latin version of the *Lives of the Desert Fathers*, calls the *quies magna* (the "huge silence") of the desert. Here, in these texts, the three travelers – the desert father (subject), the speaker, perhaps Rufinus (narrator), and you the reader (addressee) – become companions in a journey towards the "other" that demands much of the self. For this is a desert literature that is haunted by demons that are the demons of the self (as Jesus was haunted and tempted in his forty days in the desert), a self obsessed with sexual temptation, and a literature replete with miracles and visions of gardens and fair fruit. Such things are to be expected in the lonely privations of the wilderness, and they prompt extremes of often highly eccentric practices, of which perhaps the most spectacular are those of the "pillar ascetics" like Simeon Stylites (ca. 390–459), whose singular manner of life perched on top of a pillar did not prevent him from exercising considerable theological and pastoral influence.[21] Furthermore, Simeon's extreme asceticism, outside the law, was not uncontroversial among his fellow monks, who accused him of trying to "undo the rule of the monastery."[22] Simeon moves beyond rule and order to a deeper place in which he battles not with any human failure to keep the law, but with the human condition itself, as it finds itself confronting the absolute perfection of God. To go into the deep desert is to go far beyond the claims of law and order – and yet it is also a guarantee of justice, for in the act of reading the lives of such saints "the divine shrinks somehow, the infinite becomes calculable in exchange."[23]

Yet this is also a literature of profound humanity and humor. Here is an example from the *Verba Seniorum*, the *Sayings of the Fathers*, which found their way into the West in a Latin translation made at the request of St. Martin of Dumes, as early as the later part of the sixth century.[24] It concerns the issues of self and possession.

> There were two elders living together in a cell, and they had never so much as one quarrel with each other. One therefore said to the other: Come on, let

us have at least one quarrel, like other men. The first said: I will take this brick and place it here between us. Then I will say: It is mine. After that you will say: It is mine. This is what leads to a dispute and a fight. So then they placed the brick between them, one said: It is mine, and the other replied to the first: I do believe that it is mine. The first one said again: It is not yours, it is mine. So the other answered: Well then, if it is yours, take it! Thus they did not manage after all to get into a quarrel.[25]

Our concern here will not be with the history of early desert monasticism (which is popularly available through the work of Derwas Chitty, Peter Brown, and others, or through the massive volumes of Père Migne's *Patrologiae* (1844–66)). Rather, our more modest purpose is to take some of the early texts written directly from the experience of the deserts of Egypt and Judea, often by "tourists" who visited the men and women living the ascetic life, sometimes alone, sometimes in great communities after the manner of pioneers like Pachomius (d. 346), and gave them life in texts that are often highly imaginative, but bear remarkable resemblances to later desert texts, written for very different purposes and within different cultures. Later, in chapter 6, we shall consider the work of the modern travel writer William Dalrymple, whose book *From the Holy Mountain* (1997) follows in the footsteps of the Byzantine monk John Moschos, who died in Rome in 619. Believing that the early purity of the desert life was being eroded, John Moschos traveled with his pupil Sophronius to the monasteries of the Judean desert and later into Egypt, where together they spent ten years on Mount Sinai. The result was the text of the *Pratum Spirituale* (*The Spiritual Meadow*), which translates the theme of paradise and utopia, a meadow found in the sands of the wilderness, into the form of a text. At the outset, Moschos writes:

> I have called this work *meadow* on account of the delight, the fragrance and the benefits which it will afford those who come across it. For the virtuous life and habitual piety do not merely consist in studying divinity: not only of thinking on an elevated plain about things as they are here and now. It must also include the description in writing of the way of life of others.[26]

Here the image of the meadow is internalized, as the sands of the desert lead the monks to paradise itself, and contemplating their lives, deeds, and words in Moschos' text becomes a meadow in the mind of the reader. For Moschos, the vocation of the writer is crucial. At the heart of the religious life is the text that translates the desert for the reader and also situates the desert in the texts of scripture and later theological debate. In this account, the monks, whose lives and deeds are indeed nothing short of parables, live utterly *within* biblical experience as they are visited by John the Baptist himself, who encourages them, as they in their turn baptize.[27] Or they still live close beside their forebear Elijah the Tishbite in the Wadi Cherith, to which he was sent by the word of the Lord during a drought (1 Kings 17:1–7).[28] At the same time in Moschos' narrative, the desert burns with the fire of heretics like Nestorius, Severus, or Arius.[29] Church politics themselves give rise to the humor of the Fathers, such as the story of the elder who sees a dead brother up to his neck in the fire of hell:

> The elder said, "Was it not because of this retribution that I called on you to look after your own soul, my child?" The brother answered and said to the elder: "I thank God, my father, that there is relief for my head. Thanks to your prayers I am standing on the head of a bishop.[30]

In the loneliness of the desert the monks are visited by angels and devils, and in this place they are always strangers.[31] They practice extraordinary and often bizarre forms of asceticism, yet at the same time live a common life of humble, practical service to others, like the elder who would "sit down and repair the footwear of men and women,"[32] or the bishop who left his diocese to become a builder's laborer.[33] They are called to a life that is both active and passive, and they experience a harmony with nature that was lost after the exit from Eden, but is envisaged in Isaiah 11:69, like the elder who fed lions in his own cave[34] or the brother who never lit a lamp as a "light shone from heaven to allow him to read the scriptures."[35] In them, indeed, is realized the text of scripture: "They will not hurt or destroy on all my holy mountain."

The Spiritual Meadow is a strange mixture of the fantastic and serious theology, at the heart of which is a spirituality centered on the eucharist – a mixture recorded in the lives of the present-day desert monks by Dalrymple with the same combination of humor and seriousness, as for example in his photograph of Fr. Dioscorus discussing with his brothers the latest sighting of St. Antony in the Monastery of St. Antony in Egypt.[36] Exactly the same mixture of tone and, indeed, reverence for the slightly absurd is to be found in Bishop Palladius' *Lausiac History* (ca. 417), which also begins with a journey into the desert, but a journey which "leads to the kingdom of heaven."[37] Helen Waddell has written rather disparagingly that Palladius speaks of the Fathers "with bated breath,"[38] and he frequently writes from hearsay and hagiographic legend. But the elements of the desert life remain consistent and perhaps all the more so: immense practicality ("since the place was a desert")[39] is mixed with the miraculous and an extreme asceticism bordering on the mystical. (Palladius was a pupil of Evagrius of Pontus, who is often referred to as the father of monastic mysticism.) The men (and especially in the one notable case of Silvania, the women) of the desert abandoned the world but not learning. Yet it is a scholarship which, like their control of the physical body, was pursued only as a liberation "from knowledge, so called,"[40] after the demand of 1 Timothy 6:20 to "avoid the godless chatter and contradictions of what is falsely called knowledge." Thus Silvania, it is claimed, read 3 million lines of the works of Origen, and 2.5 million lines of Gregory, Stephen, Pierius, and Basil. These ascetics are dead to the world, indifferent to its judgment, and so, asks Palladius, "what does it matter that they say you are insane and demon-ridden?",[41] for they are all wanderers on a journey where they are beset by the demons of lust and willfulness, and yet like Christ himself, and Elijah before him, they survive because they are fed by angels on their walk to God.

Palladius, we might say, could only convey the truth of his *History* through "fictions" and legends, for his characters were simply larger than life, living in every sense on the edge of the world in ambiguities and with a vision that only a text of this nature can convey. He was, in a way, writing in direct literary descent from the biblical evangelists and even the writers of the many "apocryphal" gospels, whose imaginations and narratives were stretched by the extreme and extraordinary subject they were addressing. Neither folk tales nor fairy stories, they were writing of actual experiences, yet such as could only be constituted textually in a "proto-novelistic discourse"[42] that properly inhabits the realm of our imaginations. This is why, in the end, so many of the works of modern scholars and editors of these writings, and even Chitty's classic study of early Christian monasticism, *The Desert a City* (1966), have a certain aridity that misses the essence of such texts and the experiences which they convey. Perhaps the greatest of them are the *Historia Monachorum in Aegypto* (*The Lives of the Desert Fathers*), and the various collections of the *Apophthegmata Patrum* (or in the Latin the *Verba Seniorum*) that were collected and circulated among the monks themselves and "have a kind of authenticity which is unique."[43] But it is upon the former that we shall concentrate for a few moments, since this *History* is clearly a conscious work of literature, a reflection upon a journey, and almost certainly a real journey, made into the desert from which the pilgrims then stand back and reflect upon what they have seen and heard in a text that is written for public readership and edification. The text itself is a "place" of spirituality and vision, like the work of John Moschos, a veritable spiritual meadow into which we enter and participate in the reading. The origins of the text are complex and debatable. The Greek text is the earliest, and describes the journey of a party of pilgrims, some of whom could not face the final journey into "the terrible desert" of the interior. The later Latin version is probably the work of Rufinus of Aquileia (though Jerome, wrongly, regards him as the original author), who nevertheless was able to draw upon his own experience of a visit to the monks in Nitria in 375. This debate about origins is not specifically our concern here. What we do have is an echo of a real and powerful vision in these harsh places. In one of his letters to his friend Rufinus, Jerome wrote:

> I hear that you are penetrating the hidden places of Egypt, visiting the bands of monks and going the round of heaven's family on earth . . . at last the full weight of truth has burst upon me: Rufinus is in Nitrias and has reached the blessed Macarius.[44]

While at Scetis, Rufinus records:

> This is the utter desert where each monk remains alone in his cell . . . There is a huge silence and a great quiet here.[45]

Throughout the *Lives* there is a sense of a task of description that lies beyond the powers of the writer. In the encounters with this place and with these men and women, the pilgrims enter an experience that is quite simply outside the reach of common language and concept, and what emerges can only be described as a kind of poetics, a visionary narrative that is realizable only in the imagination – in the encounters with demons and in descriptions of a way of life beyond anything known – yet rooted in real lives. In the Prologue the pilgrims admit that "their powers are not equal to the task of explaining the truth in a fitting manner, particularly when they presume to commit themselves to writing and give an inadequate expression to difficult matters."[46] Their problem is a literary one, and they address it by referring back to the Bible as the only proper source of description – and thus the *Lives* take on a tone that is at once fabulous and yet also familiar and authentic. Indeed, the very rhythms of the Prologue reflect the language of the New Testament, and in particular the Epistle to the Hebrews, the epistle of the high priesthood of Christ. The faith of the monks is like that of the prophets and heroes of Israel. We read in the Epistle to the Hebrews:

> By faith the people passed through the Red Sea as if it were dry land . . . who through faith conquered kingdoms, administered justice, obtained promises, shut the mouths of lions . . . of whom the world was not worthy. They wandered in deserts and mountains, and in caves and holes in the ground.[47]

Similarly in the Prologue to the *Historia Monachorum*:

> Why should we speak at length about their faith in Christ, seeing that it can
> even move mountains? For many of them have stopped the flow of rivers and
> crossed the Nile dry-shod. They have slain wild beasts. They have performed
> cures, miracles and acts of power like those which the holy prophets and apostles
> worked. The Savior performs miracles through them and in the same way.
> Indeed, it is clear to all who dwell there that through them the world is kept
> in being, and through them too human life is preserved and honored by God.[48]

Following the Bible and the life of Christ as they themselves emerged from
the desert, the desert monks live and travel toward heaven. Of course, from
them, miracles that are equal to those in the Bible itself are to be expected.

From the beginning, the *Lives* set out to tell stories, each a kind of
parable upon which a particular life is stamped, and yet which takes on a
universal and exemplary quality in the telling. In them the miraculous
becomes almost matter of fact, transfigurative of a world that has been
left behind. In them also we find embedded in the very structure of the
language itself, in its generous exchanges and its refusal to impose rules of
conclusion, that "infinite hospitality" that is part and parcel of the culture
of the desert – the obligation to feast upon the text. As Jacques Derrida
says in a "conversation":

> "One must eat well" does not mean above all taking in and grasping in itself,
> but learning and giving to eat, learning-to-give-the-other-to-eat. One never
> eats entirely on one's own: this constitutes the rule underlying the statement,
> "One must eat well." It is a rule offering infinite hospitality.[49]

There is a clear shift from this world to the more codified texts of John
Cassian (ca. 360–430), who, with his companion Germanus, set out into
the Egyptian desert during the last decade of the fourth century to visit the
hermits and groups of monks. It was some twenty years later, when he was
settled in Marseilles, where he founded two monasteries, that he wrote his
twenty-four *Conferences* recounting his recollections of conversations in the
desert, together with his *Institutes*, in which he distilled the rules for the
monastic life that were later to blossom in the great Rule of Benedict and
the monasticism of the West.[50]

It is not so much that Cassian moves from the physical desert to the interior life, for on the "inner mountain" of St. Antony the distinction between
the inner and the outer life is already utterly blurred, but we see now a shift
towards an intellectual and spiritual reflection upon the experience of the
desert. Cassian's writings remain exterior to the events upon which they reflect.

Thus, in Cassian's work, the lives of the Fathers are made into a new and different text that provides the basis for the theology and discipline of medieval Western monasticism. There is continuity, but a profound change from the restless wanderings of the Fathers to the ideal of "stability" within the walls of the monastery, and a life formed upon static contemplation and focused on the church and sanctuary rather than the boundless horizons of the desert. The idea of *quies*, "rest," had taken on a new meaning and the dimensions of time and space were reconfigured back into the history of the church and society. In a sense, with the writings of John Cassian we are returned to earth and to a more familiar world, although one upon which the desert has left an indelible mark. As Owen Chadwick puts it:

> Thus the Egyptian ideal as interpreted by Cassian received a frame by which it was modified and in which it was bequeathed to the Middle Ages. A recognition of Benedict's stature should not obscure a recognition of the thought on which he depended. It should not be overlooked that in one sense the powerful influence of the Rule upon monastic thought consisted in its transmission of an ideal descended at last from Egypt.[51]

The shift is not only physical and spiritual, it is also textual, from a literature that is one with the sands of the desert to a theology that establishes itself in the heart of Western society. The Desert Fathers had moved beyond a boundary from the world of the city and the cultivated plain into a "counterworld" where alone the City of God could be built.[52] Paradoxically, in this impossible place, whose immensity could be embraced only by the imagination and of which, seemingly, there was no end, the world is defined anew. It was no longer the "world" of farms, villages, and towns ordered under human government and shaped by human hand. Rather, it stood over against the fragility of all human endeavor, and yet in the sterile sands the ascetic realized what it is to be most truly human, for, in Peter Brown's arresting phrase, "he could not sink like an animal into its alluring density,"[53] for to remain human required the utmost tenacity, discipline, and *askesis*. It also required a certain indifference to hardship, which was conducive to serenity, and a silence at one with the desert itself. Quite deliberately, monks' cells were constructed after the manner of tombs.[54] What is learnt is a new harmony with the natural world, and a new respect, so that in the training of his body the monk learns also to lie down with the lion and the wild beasts, indifferent to either life or death. In this giving up of selfish desires and the demands of the body, the monk of the desert achieves, paradoxically, the opposite of the ideal of later monasticism – not a centering upon the self in a giving to God, but a radical decentering of the self in a perpetual wandering, though often remaining physically in one place, and a sociability that is lost in the social and competitive world of the city. Paradoxically, the desert combines the place of stillness and wandering: it is the still turning point. At the end of his life, the greater miracle of Antony was not his bodily perfection, but his charm and social openness. In the desert, there is always a rule of refreshment and shelter and words of wisdom offered – a rule found everywhere in the writings of modern desert travelers like T. E. Lawrence, Gertrude Bell, and Wilfred Thesiger, as we shall see later. In the *Life of St. Antony* we read that

> by frequent conversation he increased the eagerness of those already monks, stirred up in most of the rest the love of the discipline, and speedily by the attraction of his words, cells multiplied, and he directed them all as father.[55]

Although, as we have seen, the desert was not a place remote from learning and the theological debates of the church, its literature derives from a different base and enacts for the reader a different function from the later texts of John Cassian and those who followed him in Marseilles and elsewhere at a distance from the desert. Indeed, we might say that the passionate resistance of Antony and the monks to a "heresy" such as Arianism, which denied the consubtantiality of Christ the Son with the Father, was precisely because their very *lives*, and not simply their intellects, spoke out in opposition to its claims for such a distinction. They literally embodied a theology. We shall see in chapter 10[56] that their passion had little to do with the politics of Trinitarian debate in the church, which led eventually to the "resolution" of the Council of Chalcedon in 461. Indifferent to the demands of any orthodoxy, the Desert Fathers inscribed a theology with their lives and mode of being that only emerges again from time to time, in spite of the church, in the vision of deeply religious poets like William Blake, or the unconscious insights of desert artists and travelers.

The point here is the same as that made in chapter 1, where we considered Wordsworth's purely literary description of the desert in *The Prelude*.[57] Although learned, Antony was said to have replied to a "certain Philosopher" who asked him how he could be so happy when deprived of the consolation of books: "My book, O philosopher, is the nature of created things, and any time I want to read the words of God, the book is before me."[58] Perhaps even more significant is the Abbot Serapion of whom we read in the *Verba Seniorum*. Serapion sold his only book, a copy of the gospels, and gave the money to the poor, thereby selling "the very words which told him to sell all and give to the poor."[59] He had, quite simply, *become* the book. Peter Brown puts this another way when he suggests that "the monk's own heart was the new book."[60] This movement from the culture of the book to the *cultura Dei*, the term used to translate the Greek word *askesis* in the earliest Latin translation of the *Life of Antony*, inscribed within the monks a new "alphabet of the heart"[61] that was later to provide the seeds for a literature of the desert in the texts we have been considering.

In the first instance, this literature of the Fathers grows from a primacy given to experience with which the texts become, in a sense, coterminous: texts as sands, and the sands as texts. This quality they share with the other later literature and texts explored in this book, as they celebrate a shift from the culture of the book to the desert and then back to a new culture of the book, a new poetics.

Unlike the mystical writings of Plotinus and others who followed him (as we shall see in the next two chapters), the Desert Fathers did not abandon the body, but took it with the utmost seriousness. The body was a text to be read and preserved with care, just as for later medieval mystics like Richard Rolle, the body of Christ itself was a text to be read and learnt from.[62] Their scholarship, their spirituality, and their way of life were inseparable, and thus they corrected the imbalance of fallen nature in all its aspects. Living in the body, the monk lives a life of incorporeal purity – a pure poetics of the body – and yet, as John Climacus (ca. 570–649), an Abbot of Sinai and author of *The Ladder of Divine Ascent*, wrote, "Violence and unending pain are the lot of those who aim to ascend to Heaven with the body."[63] At the same time, the monk "finds himself in an earthly and defiled body, but pushes himself into the rank and status of the incorporeal angels."[64]

In the next two chapters we shall consider the emergence of mysticism from the desert in this complex interplay between body and text. It is a journey that takes us to the present day, and the recovery of a sense of the mystical not as a subjective, bodiless experience of the Divine, but as a physical encounter with the "other" and a narrative which is recovered for us in text and word; but they are words that, like the lives of the Fathers, embody and embrace an immediacy with things of most practical concern, so that they become ours in the reading, at once painful and liberating.

Notes

1   *The Life of St. Antony* (ca. 356–62). A Select Library of Nicene and Post-Nicene Fathers of the Christian Church, 2nd series, vol. 4, St. Athanasius: *Select Works* (Edinburgh: T. & T. Clark, 1991), 14, p. 200.

2   See Peter Brown, *The Body and Society: Men, Women and Sexual Renunciation in Early Christianity* (New York: Columbia University Press, 1988),

p. 214. The lurid account of Antony's sexual and philosophical temptations in Gustave Flaubert's dramatic poem in prose, *La Tentation Sainte-Antoine* (1874), will be discussed briefly in chapter 7.

3   *Life*, 3, p. 196.

4   Ibid, 49, p. 209.

5   See below, p. 37.

6   Brown, *The Body and Society*, p. 216. See also A. Guillaumont, "La Conception du désert chez les moines d'Égypte," *Revue de l'histoire des religions* (1975), 188:3–21.

7   *Life*, 12, p. 199.

8   See Derwas Chitty, *The Desert a City* (New York: St. Vladimir's Seminary Press, 1999), p. 16.

9   See Samuel Rubenson, "Christian Asceticism and the Emergence of the Monastic Tradition," in Vincent L. Wimbush and Richard Valantasis (eds.), *Asceticism* (Oxford: Oxford University Press, 1998), pp. 53–5.

10 The Epistles are probably the first original writings in Coptic. See Samuel Rubenson, "St. Antony, The First Real Coptic Author?" in *Actes du IVe congres copte* (Louvain, 1992), pp. 16–27.

11 Thomas Merton, *Zen and the Birds of Appetite* (New York: New Directions, 1968), p. 117.

12 Rubenson, "Christian Asceticism," p. 54.

13 See also Philip Sheldrake, *Spaces for the Sacred* (London: SCM, 2001), p. 42 and ch. 4, "The Practice of Place: Monasteries and Utopias."

14 See Thomas Merton, *The Wisdom of the Desert: Sayings from the Desert Fathers of the Fourth Century* (London: Sheldon Press, 1961), p. 8.

15 *Life*, 20, p. 201.

16 Edith Wyschogrod, *Saints and Postmodernism: Revisioning Moral Philosophy* (Chicago: University of Chicago Press, 1990), p. 7.

17 Maurice Blanchot, *The Gaze of Orpheus and Other Literary Essays*, translated by Lydia Davis (Barrytown, NY: Station Hill Press), p. 109. See also Wyschogrod, *Saints and Postmodernism*, p. 7.

18 Ibid, p. xvi.

19 Ibid, p. xxiii.

20 Geoffrey Galt Harpham, *The Ascetic Imperative in Culture and Criticism* (Chicago: University of Chicago Press, 1987), p. 88.

21 See *The Syriac Life of Symeon Stylites*, translated by F. Lent. *Journal of the American Oriental Society* (1915), 35, pp. 103–18. See also *The Lives of Simeon Stylites*, translated and edited by Robert Duran (Kalamazoo, MI: Cistercian Publications, 1992).

22 Ibid, p. 89. For this part of my discussion I am indebted to Lori Branch, and especially her article "The Desert in the Desert: Faith and the Aporias of Law and Knowledge in the Sayings of the Desert Fathers," *Journal of the American Academy of Religion*, forthcoming.

23 Branch, "The Desert in the Desert."

24 See Helen Waddell, *The Desert Fathers: Translations from the Latin* (London: Constable, 1936), pp. 211–13.
25 Merton, *The Wisdom of the Desert*, p. 67.
26 John Moschos, *The Spiritual Meadow*, translated by John Wortley. Cistercian Studies Series: 139 (Kalamazoo, MI: Cistercian Publications, 1992), p. 3.
27 Ibid, p. 5.
28 See chapter 4, pp. 46–7.
29 Ibid, p. 18.
30 Ibid, p. 35.
31 "Do not consort with heretics; keep a watch over the tongue and the belly, and wherever you stay, keep on saying [to yourself], 'I am a stranger.'" Ibid, p. 10.
32 Ibid, p. 16.
33 Ibid, p. 27.
34 Ibid, p. 5.
35 Ibid, p. 42.
36 William Dalrymple, *From the Holy Mountain* (London: Flamingo, 1998). The photograph is opposite p. 305.
37 Palladius, *The Lausiac History*, translated by Robert T. Meyer (New York: Newman Press, 1964), p. 17. One of the most widely read of the texts relating the lives of the Desert Fathers, *The Lausiac History* existed in Syriac, Coptic, Ethiopic, Arabic, Old Sogdian, and Greek versions.
38 Waddell, *The Desert Fathers*, p. 239.
39 Palladius, *Lausiac History*, p. 49.
40 Ibid, p. 136.
41 Ibid, p. 105.
42 Wyschogrod, *Saints and Postmodernism*, p. 11.
43 Benedicta Ward SLG, introduction to *The Lives of the Desert Fathers*, translated by Norman Russell (Oxford: A. R. Mowbray, 1981), p. 3. The best introduction to the *Sayings*, in my view, is in the short work by Thomas Merton. See above, note 14. I have used Merton's collection in preference to much more "scholarly" works by Owen Chadwick or Sister Benedicta Ward or the great collection of the *Verba Seniorum* in Migne's *Latin Patrology* (Volume 73), as Merton himself lived and wrote in direct descent from the desert monks of Egypt, and we will consider his writings at more length in chapter 5.
44 *Letters of Jerome*, translated by T. C. Lawler (London: ACW, 1963), Letter 3, p. 31.
45 Rufinus, *Historia Monachorum in Aegypto*. Quoted in Ward, introduction to *The Lives of the Desert Fathers*, p. 3.
46 Ward, *The Lives of the Desert Fathers*, p. 49.
47 Hebrews 11:29–38.
48 Ward, *The Lives of the Desert Fathers*, p. 50.

49 Jacques Derrida, "Eating Well, Or, The Calculation of the Subject: An Interview with Jacques Derrida," in Eduardo Cadava, Peter Connor, and Jean-Luc Nancy (eds.), *Who Comes After the Subject?* (London: Routledge, 1991), p. 115. Again, I must thank Lori Branch for drawing my attention to this reference.

50 See Owen Chadwick, *John Cassian*, 2nd edn. (Cambridge: Cambridge University Press, 1968), pp. 13–15.

51 Ibid, pp. 155–6.

52 See Peter Brown, *The Body and Society*, p. 217.

53 Ibid, p. 218.

54 Ibid, p. 219. Brown refers also to H. Torp, "Le Monastère copte de Baouit: Quelques notes d'introduction," *Miscellanes Coptica Acta Instituti Norvegiae Romani* (1981) 9:1–8.

55 *The Life of St. Antony*, 15, p. 200.

56 Chapter 10, pp. 146–7.

57 Chapter 1, p. 2.

58 Merton, *The Wisdom of the Desert*, p. 62.

59 Ibid, p. 19.

60 Brown, *The Body and Society*, p. 229.

61 Ibid. See also Benedicta Ward, *The Wisdom of the Desert Fathers: Systematic Sayings from the Apophthegmata Patrum* (Oxford: SLG Press, 1986), p. 31. "An old man said, 'The prophets wrote books, then came our Fathers who put them into practice. Those who came after them learnt them by heart.'"

62 See Gabrieli Finaldi, *The Image of Christ* (London: National Gallery, 2000), p. 148.

63 John Climacus, *The Ladder of Divine Ascent*, translated by C. Luibheid and N. Russell (New York: Paulist Press, 1982), p. 75.

64 Ibid, p. 74.

4

Time and Memory, Wind and Space

The Desert and Mysticism

You are alone now in spite of these stars,
The center is near you and far from you,
You have walked, you can walk, nothing changes anymore,
Always the same night that never ends,
And behold you are already separated from yourself
Even that same cry, but you do not hear it;
Are you he who is dying, you who have no more anguish,
Are you even lost, you who do not seek?[1]

Michel de Certeau concludes his book *The Mystic Fable* (1992) with these lines from the French poet Yves Bonnefoy to illustrate his claim that conversion, "which presupposes the Western paradigm of one sole truth . . . ceases being a putting into social circulation of places of meaning in order to become the ethical gesture of defiance, crossing a desert of meaning."[2] The poem, as it were, always goes ahead and precedes our progress.

This chapter will begin to explore the pattern of Western Christian mysticism as it finds its origins in the desert, moving between the landscapes of the wilderness and the texts of mysticism that take us on journeys of the spirit across deserts of meaning. The larger part of the chapter will place de Certeau's text as a kind of map upon the geography of the desert itself, thereby exploring the complex and subtle interaction between the interior deserts of the mind and spirit and the rocks and sands of Palestine, Sinai, and Egypt. In no respect, in this interplay, do I wish to fall into the trap of John Ruskin's pathetic fallacy, the Romantic departure from the harsh and necessary indifference of landscape through the betrayal of the "true appearance of things" under "the influence of emotion."[3] To do that would be a double betrayal – both of the desert itself and of the texts of mysticism. These are no constructs of a dreamy Orientalism. We are in real places of both body and spirit.

Yet we must begin with a reassembling of our sense of time and space. The early ascetics went into the desert seeking a lost paradise. What they bequeathed to the mystical tradition in the West was a haunting by two biblical images that impelled and grounded their search. The first was that of the lost Eden (Genesis 3:23). The second was that of the New Jerusalem of Revelation 21, for they literally sought a new earth and the old had passed away.

> Then I saw a new heaven and a new earth; for the first heaven and the first earth had passed away, and the sea was no more. And I saw the holy city, the new Jerusalem, coming down out of heaven from God.[4]

Just as God comes down to meet Moses on Mount Sinai, so the heavenly city comes down from heaven and meets humanity halfway. These ascetics were people embraced by scripture from its beginning to its end, by two images which were also, in a way, one, both mythical and eschatological. At one and the same time they were traveling towards the paradise garden and the heavenly city, of which they lived as true citizens, and thus past and future become one and time moves from the sequential narratives of history. Memory, as a nostalgia for a time that never was, is liturgically gathered up into the total presence of the eternal present which is also perpetually anticipated.

In his book *Spaces for the Sacred* (2001), Philip Sheldrake makes a vital connection between three things: place, memory, and human identity. Repeatedly, he explores the theme of life as a perpetual departure and a preparation for a journey that has already begun, expressed in R. S. Thomas' poem "Journeys" as

The deception of platforms
Where arrivals and departures
Coincide.[5]

Seen thus, life is a sort of endless pilgrimage that parallels the mystical journey to an imagined end that is known also as a beginning – as home. The natural world may be seen as a theater for such a journey, inviting us to realize in its landscapes the interior geography of our spiritual imaginations. To put this in another way, Simon Schama has suggested "landscapes are culture before they are nature; constructs of the imagination projected onto wood and water and rock."[6] The desert, as a kind of theater of memory,[7] is both "out there" and "in here," and necessarily so, and on the journey into the interior, understood in two senses, we seek for the home that is our origin and end, familiar yet wholly other in its "counter-domesticity."[8] It is precisely this idea and place that lies at the heart of Wim Wenders' film *Paris, Texas* (1984), which we examine in more detail in chapter 9. Early in the film, Travis emerges from the desert into which he disappeared years before. He is met by his brother, who had assumed that he had died, and he is carrying an old photograph of an empty space of land in Texas. It is nowhere, and there is nothing there, but it is his land, and it is in Paris, Texas – a real place, not far from Dallas, but in his imagination, and in the mind of his dead father, it is also the Paris of dreams, the fabled and beautiful city in another continent that he shall never visit. In this empty, nondescript place, Travis believes, he was conceived. There his parents brought him into being through an act of love – and it is therefore his true home. Truly there is nowhere else on earth like this place of dust and sand.

The particularity of this place links Travis, curiously, with the theology of the thirteenth-century Scottish Franciscan Duns Scotus, with its emphasis on the particularity and individuality of the Incarnation. Scotus, you will recall, was the subject of Heidegger's *Habilitation*.[9] The connection is not without significance. Christ's incarnation, Scotus affirms, "was immediately foreseen from all eternity by God as a good proximate to the end";[10] that is, the final purpose of all things. Furthermore, all things realize themselves in the particularity of Christ's incarnation by the realization of themselves specifically in their own being. The being and place of the self become then not merely a symbol of the Incarnation, but indispensably one with the life of the incarnate Lord in its self-realization, and that self-realization is at the same time an absolute loss and surrendering of the self. (At the end of *Paris, Texas*, Travis, having brought his family to reconciliation, must disappear again. Where, we are never told.) Nowhere has this self-realization been better explored than in the poetry of the nineteenth-century follower of Scotus, the Jesuit Gerard Manley Hopkins.

> Each mortal thing does one thing and the same:
> Deals out that being indoors each one dwells;
> Selves – goes itself; *myself* it speaks and spells,
> Crying *What I do is me: for that I came.*[11]

The Desert Fathers would have understood this sense of purpose, as would their close brethren the Cappadocian Fathers, themselves no strangers to rocky landscapes, in their deeply Christocentric lives. And yet their profound and deeply specific Christianity is, at the same time, universal. Each person and being seeks its individuality – what Scotus calls its *haecceitas* or "thisness" – and in its realization loses itself in the universal being of Christ. As in the poetry of Hopkins, this begins with a concrete realization of individuality that is the (perhaps) painful beginning of the redemption of place in order that it may become a space for the realization of God – whether that place be the innermost desert or the dungeon of St. John of the Cross.

In this space the forgotten dream is remembered and realized and then this unitive process becomes a kind of feasting in the desert. Perhaps this is why the feast, beyond all imaginative excess, is so important in the culture of the desert, as we find in *The Seven Pillars of Wisdom*, in Wilfred Thesiger, and in all literature of desert travelers. The desert law of hospitality is paramount. Out of nothing comes an excess of plenty and hospitality:

> Ho, everyone who thirsts,
> Come to the waters,
> And you that have no money,
> Come, buy and eat!
> Come, buy wine and milk
> Without money and without price.[12]

And so, through these prophetic words of Isaiah, we return to the two ancient scriptural archetypes of desert wanderers – to Moses and to Elijah. Moses is the central figure in Pseudo-Dionysius' brief but seminal work *The Mystical Theology*. Its influence on the Western mystical tradition is incalculable. A Syrian monk of the sixth century, Pseudo-Dionysius, or Dionysius the Areopagite as he is otherwise known, appropriately hidden behind his pseudonyms, focuses attention on the moment of Moses' ascent of Mount Sinai to meet the Lord and receive the Tables of the Law. It is a moment in memory that is the abandonment of everything "perceived and understood, perceptible and understandable."[13] In Moses' abandonment of self, says Pseudo-Dionysius, is all that is not and all that is. It is neither for the uninformed nor for the intellectual, for it is the negation of and prior to all such affirmations. On Mount Sinai, Moses is literally plunged into darkness and into the interiority of "the truly mysterious darkness of unknowing" and the "completely unknowing inactivity of all knowledge." At the moment when the Lord descends and Moses ascends the mountain (Exodus 19:20), in that moment of meeting and encounter between the human and the divine, Moses, according to *The Mystical Theology*, knows beyond the mind by knowing nothing.

At the same time and in this stillness – it was the third day after the Israelites' arrival at the mountain – according to Exodus, there was thunder and lightning on the mountain. And so it was for Elijah on Mount Horeb in 1 Kings 19:11–13, when he stood on the mountain before the Lord in the midst of wind and storm.

> Now there was a great wind, so strong that it was splitting mountains and breaking rocks in pieces before the Lord, but the Lord was not in the wind; and after the wind an earthquake, but the Lord was not in the earthquake; and after the earthquake a fire, but the Lord was not in the fire; and after the fire *a sound of sheer silence*.[14]

That last phrase is almost untranslatable from the Hebrew: *qol demamah daqqah*. *Qol* is voice, sound, or noise. *Demamah* is calmness or stillness or silence, even a whisper. It is the word used in Psalm 107:29: "He made the storm be *still*, and the waves of the sea were hushed." *Daqqah* is that which has been reduced and made fine, soft, or gentle.[15] What Elijah "hears" in this theophany is a paradox – a perceptible silence or stillness: a silence so profound that it can be heard like the gentlest of winds.

It is the still small voice – the pure, soundless wind of the desert that has no taste or sound and comes from nowhere and is going nowhere. It is the wind described by T. E. Lawrence in the opening pages of *The Seven Pillars of Wisdom*.[16] It is a movement and yet carries with it a silence that is profound beyond all earthly silence, neither perceptible nor conceptual. "It is not soul or mind, nor does it possess imagination, conviction, speech or understanding."[17] It is the very heart of all speech itself, and in the words of Stephen Prickett, "the whole effect of Elijah's mysterious experience seems to be to be to deny, *and* simultaneously affirm, certain connections."[18] The Yahweh of Elijah's theophany both *is* and *is not*, a natural phenomenon of the wilderness, and utterly "other."

Already by the time of this encounter, Elijah has earned his place as the "founder" of desert monasticism. He had been driven by the Lord to the east of the Jordan to the Wadi Cherith and there he had been fed by the ravens (1 Kings 17:2–7). Later, to the south of Beer-Sheva, in the Negev Desert, alone in the wilderness, he experienced the depths of despair and asked that the Lord might "take away my life, for I am no better than my ancestors" (1 Kings 19:4). Yet the Lord provides bread and water in this desolate place, so that, strengthened for forty days and nights, he is able to travel to Mount Horeb. Like Jesus after him, Elijah endures his period of quarantine. And finally, Elijah becomes the first of the succession of riders in the chariot.[19] Like the desert monks, who in their purity became flames to those who saw them, Elijah in his death, an absolute separation from Elisha – a moment of the conjoining and the separation of heaven and earth – becomes one with the wind and the fire: the everyday becomes the moment of change and transfiguration.

> As they continued walking and talking, a chariot of fire and horses of fire separated the two of them, and Elijah ascended in a whirlwind into heaven. Elisha kept watching and crying out, "Father, father! The chariots of Israel and its horsemen!" But when he could no longer see him, he grasped his own clothes and tore them in two pieces.[20]

Time and memory: wind and space. The desert deconstructs and cleanses our categories of history and place and leads us physically to a space that is beyond the physical to the frustration of our quotidian earthly experience. In his excellent book *The Darkness of God: Negativity in Christian Mysticism* (1995), Denys Turner has clearly shown how the development of an experientialist focus in Western culture has given rise to the supplanting of mystical theology by a rather vague notion of "mysticism" understood in terms of a solipsistic and unutterable experience of the divine.[21] From the theological language of Pseudo-Dionysius' description of the "negation of experience," this sense of mysticism shifts to a profoundly *untheological* discussion of "having negative experiences." Such language is quite alien to the monks of the desert, the great mystical writers of later times like Meister Eckhart and St. John of the Cross, and the more recent literature of the desert that we shall consider in later chapters. To the contrary, this deeply apophatic language of negation is precisely a move beyond consciousness in a manner unrecognized by the understanding of mysticism pursued by Bernard McGinn in his multi-volume work *The Presence of God* (a title which is, it seems to me, misleading). McGinn writes:

> This experience [of the presence of God] is presented as subjectively different [from ordinary religious consciousness] in so far as it is affirmed as taking place

on a level of the personality deeper and more fundamental than that objecti-
fiable through the usual conscious activities of sensing, knowing and loving.
There is also an objective difference to the extent that this mode of the divine
presence is said to be given in a direct or immediate way, without the usual
internal and external mediations found in other types of consciousness.[22]

Yet it is clear that this experience remains at some level in the category of
a type of consciousness. Furthermore, what we see in the mysticism of the
desert is not a presence but an absence as we enter into the cloud or mirage
of unknowing. This is not even what McGinn calls an "experience of
absence," but an absolute unknowing that is precisely an absence of experience. It is an attentiveness born of indifference, the condition minutely explored
by T. S. Eliot in "Little Gidding":

> There are three conditions which often look alike
> Yet differ completely, flourish in the same hedgerow:
> Attachment to self and to things and to persons, detachment
> From self and from things and from persons; and, growing
>   between them, indifference
> Which resembles the others as death resembles life.[23]

This indifference is found first in the very being of God, in God's aseity,
which is a divine indifference that, in the desert, draws us even as it repels
and negates. Nor is this simply a theological or even religious condition, for
in our own times the irascible Edward Abbey admits that what draws him
to the wilderness is precisely this indifference. He writes:

> The finest quality of this stone, these plants and animals, this desert landscape
> is the indifference manifest to our presence, our absence, our coming, our stay-
> ing or our going. Whether we live or die is a matter of absolutely no concern
> whatsoever to the desert.[24]

And that is exactly why Abbey is drawn to it and loves it, for it is, in turn,
only through an indifference to the overwhelming harshness of the desert
that the desert dweller can learn to survive in it and indeed, come to love
it. Such necessary indifference lies at the heart of the apophatic tradition that
seeks not to experience but to abandon experience and become indifferent
to it. As Denys Turner puts it:

> If a "present" God were "just another *thing*" of which we had "a sense" (or
> "consciousness") then the absence of God would be nothing more than
> the absence of *just that thing*, and the sense of the absence of God but the

consciousness of the absence of just that thing. I have argued that not even in *The Cloud of Unknowing* (which McGinn also cites in support of his position) is the apophatic "unknowing" to be described as the *experience of negation* (McGinn's "experience of absence"); rather it is to be understood as the *negativity of experience* (the absence of "experience"). The apophatic is not to be described as the "consciousness of the absence of God," not, at any rate, if such a consciousness were an awareness of *what* is absent. For if we do not know what God is, and if we cannot be conscious of God's presence, then we do not know, and cannot be conscious of, what it is that is absent: *eadem est scientia oppositorum.*[25]

It is for this very reason that travelers into the desert of interiority like St. John of the Cross discourage all "mystical" indulgence in extravagant and solipsistic experiences, preferring the spare wastelands where everything must be let go – the desert journey must be one in which we travel light. In the same way, the early desert monks were people of few words, though when they spoke it was always to the point. They were not people who eschewed language, and they often engaged in theological debate. And although often deeply solitary, they recognized their journey and the interior condition as profoundly liturgical, in other words as a "communion," and their life as sacramentally one with others and with all things. Paradoxically, therefore, the desert leads us into a mystical theology, not a "mysticism," that is both instantiated in the lives of those who have journeyed deep into the cloud of unknowing and in a textuality that is profoundly poetic and tautly disciplined. The apophatic way is therefore only completed in a cataphatic awareness and a life fulfilled in being for the other in a "compassion whose shape is justice,"[26] a journey which we will see repeated in the wholehearted compassion of Tom Altizer's theology of Total Presence. At the heart of the solitariness there is a deep community of spirit.

It is this textuality of the mystical theology of the desert that we shall explore in the second part of this chapter and in chapter 5, first by briefly placing a text – Michel de Certeau's study of the mystic way of the sixteenth and seventeenth centuries, *The Mystic Fable* (1982) – as a kind of textual map over the landscapes that we have been traversing, a double journey of interiority and exteriority that is yet one and the same.

Writing of the late Renaissance, de Certeau speaks of a time when "a utopian space, opening up in the margins of a no longer decipherable historical reality, supplied a non-place for a new kind of reason to use its capacity to produce a world as text and make texts themselves generate worlds."[27] This textual utopian space was a repetition, a true *anamnesis* and remembering of the desert space opened up by Antony as he moved beyond the margins of a culture whose "text" he could no longer decipher. De Certeau describes his own "journey" as paradoxically one written "during travels through a country from which I am away" (p. 1). This journey is an endless restlessness that becomes its place of origin and ultimate destination, its still, moving point. Like Kafka's petitioner waiting endlessly for the doorkeeper to grant him entrance in the great parable in *The Trial*, de Certeau (let us call him the mystic) experiences time as a waiting period, but for the mystic, unlike Kafka's anxious figure (who is, of course, K. himself), time ceases to be an interim but becomes a condition, a waiting period to be lived in indifferently. Yet the story remains to be told, and this desert lives in the very fables and narratives that it consumes. It is a utopia that the act of utterance alone makes possible (p. 163), and yet at the same time all speech is lying (as K. sadly concludes, "lying is a universal condition"), but a nevertheless necessary lie, a necessary fiction to lead us to the silence that is the vanishing point into truth (p. 177). Thus, as we saw in chapter 2, Moses in Schoenberg's opera acknowledges that even the Tables of the Law themselves are images and that nothing in him can attain to the purity of the demands of the desert and its God – the word that he lacks is precisely that perfect speech which can never be spoken, except in utter silence.[28]

De Certeau's textual world is a utopian retreat into nothingness. *The Mystic Fable* begins in texts – from *The Trial*, to the *Lausiac History*, to Hieronymus Bosch's visual text of the *Garden of Earthly Delights*. The mystic, like the desert traveler, is drawn to venture into a new land that is at the same time a memory of one that has been lost, a new yet somehow familiar world realized only in words, just as Adam realized the newly created world in his act of naming (Genesis 2:20). Yet this is not to deny its utter reality. For the mystic world is rooted in sites that become both semi-real and semi-mythical, above all Mount Carmel, where Elijah met with the prophets of Baal and Asherah, and Mount Sinai, where Moses received the Tables of the Law. In his extended commentary on the *Garden of Earthly Delights*, a vision which is a (non-) space that is at once visual and demanding of language, de Certeau shows us an enclosed space in which "no language comes from without to fill [the] lack of meaning" (p. 49). It is a surface on which our gaze wanders, a space organizing not meaning but rather the loss of meaning, and in the process a gain in wisdom. In Bosch's world we lose our way, and yet in it stories are endlessly told in the deferral of the ultimate loss of meaning, exactly like the 1,001 stories of the *Arabian Nights*. And yet they lead us ever deeper into the mystery and the interior of the maze that is all surface – the signifier progressively losing touch with the signified until there is nothing other than the signifier, a pure tautology that, like Kafka's texts, is nothing but glistening surface.[29]

Here, as the monks and all travelers know in their wilderness, the deconstruction and suspension of all categories and terms of referral ushers us into a place of miracle and the most dangerous of all places, where the encounter may be with the Devil or with God, and they are indistinguishable. Thus, as de Certeau points out, Bosch's *Garden* may as well be the precursor to the nocturnal theater of the Marquis de Sade in his *120 Days of Sodom* or *Juliette*, that are also pure abandonments of identity and social structure, journeys into the wastelands of sexual (rather than spiritual) anonymity. De Sade, the desert mystics: both pure perversions, pure negations, pure *texts*.[30] And yet there is an absolute difference, and it is why Bosch's *Garden*, with all its grotesques, is finally the Garden of Delights (though that is a matter of faith). For de Sade offers us pure oblivion in sexual excess, a loss of identity that is also a loss of memory, while Bosch offers us the very opposite – a map which is an "art of memory" (p. 63), of space that is "nomadized," yet in our wanderings there we begin to find a home, a memory, as in the sacrament of the eucharist that was the Christological heart of the wisdom of the desert. Here is not hostility and atomy, but communion.

This art of memory has its counterpoint in the ancient cultures of Greece and Rome, in the Renaissance Memory Theater and its esoteric mnemonics, but finds its clearest echo in the curious work of the Venetian Cosmos Rossellius, the *Thesaurus artificiosae memoriae* (1579). Rossellius offers us diagrams of Hell and Paradise, the latter indeed a city after the manner of Revelation 21, with its company of the heavenly host – a place of dream and true imagination where "we are to imagine the Throne of Christ so that it may most move the sense and excite the memory."[31] This was the textual artifice that was inhabited by Teresa of Avila and constructed in the Paneremos or the Deep Desert of the inner mountain by Antony in his stillness.

Thus, de Certeau reminds us that Christianity was founded upon loss: the loss of a body and the empty tomb, a body that is sought in the negations of the desert and text, and in the Word made flesh. And because what is sought is a hidden body (the tomb must remain empty, as at the true end of Mark's Gospel in 16:8, with the women fleeing in terror, or perhaps in recognition of the extraordinary truth), it cannot be the edifice of the church as the "social" body of Christ, but the hidden body, the *Corpus mysticum* (p. 80), that is both and absolutely interior and exterior, of which there is no signified, for there is nothing outside the signifier that is the Word, and the flesh made word. Antony in his Interior Mountain is the true *coincidentia oppositorum* of John 1:14, "And the Word became flesh": the impossible *imitatio Christi*. This speculative utopia that begins with the experiment of Antony and is realized in Pseudo-Dionysius' *Mystical Theology* is "a myth comparable to what would later be the Hegelian discourse during a century and a half of sociopolitical conflicts" (p. 90), another true kenosis, to which we shall return in chapter 10.

The journey into the desert is a self-imposed exile from the solidity of things (p. 65), yet into a harsh landscape that demands not less than everything. It demands a detachment and a silence that realizes and is realized by a purely oxymoronic language, a language that feeds on otherness which, in its abysses and pitiless horizons, becomes a theater of memory painfully assembling the fragments of lost unity that is the speech of God (p. 114). Gustave Flaubert's extravagant setting of Antony in a theater in the desert, assailed by masques of demons and specters, may not, perhaps, in the end, be so far off the mark. It is precisely what Antony was engaged in – a theater of memory in which language moves into semantic exile; it is a deictic – "it shows what it does not say" (p. 143) – and by saying creates a space for the unsayable. Language itself is wounded in its own trope of oxymoron, and like Jacob limping away from his wrestling with the stranger at Peniel (Genesis 32:22–32), like Travis in *Paris, Texas*, finds that it is no sin to limp,[32] for it is the wounds that God's stubborn, indifferent silence makes in language that alone make for memory and healing, as is found absolutely (and as Karl Barth realized afresh in the *Romerbrief*, overshadowed by the horrors of the Great War) in Christ's final cry of dereliction and forsakenness (Matthew 27:46; Mark 15:34).

This place of dereliction is a necessity imposed by the actual disorder of the assumed order of cultural and political structures. De Certeau points out (p. 156) that mystical theology finally faded in the West as monarchs in the seventeenth and eighteenth centuries imposed order upon society from claims for their own being, their divine right which claimed to set upon temporal affairs the seal of atemporal authority. But it was precisely such political claims in church and state that once drove men and women out into the desert and that impelled the visions and texts of Meister Eckhart, St. John of the Cross, and Teresa of Avila.[33] Politicians, as Desmond Tutu once wisely remarked, should fear the power of apophatic prayer, but rarely even hear it, for they are not concerned with silence. In the eighteenth century, the mystic fable was replaced by another story, the bourgeois myth of *Robinson Crusoe* (1719), whose wanderings in a place of the imagination exchanged abandonment and negation for appropriation and production (p. 200). Defoe's Crusoe was a true herald of the modern world in which the old fables were (almost) forgotten. Of Robinson Crusoe, Jean-Jacques Rousseau observed:

> The practice of simple manual arts, to the exercise of which the abilities of the individual are equal, leads to the invention of the arts of industry, the

exercise of which requires the concurrence of many. *The former may be practiced by hermits and savages*, but the latter can be exercised only in a state of society, and render that state necessary.[34]

Among the former, I am reminded of the hermit Abbot Agatho in the *Verba Seniorum*, whose work was to weave baskets and sieves, taking whatever price people would offer him without argument, however far it diverged from their actual value. "For he said: What is the use of me arguing with them, and leading them perhaps into sin by perjuring themselves."[35]

Truly a foolish man, but one whose speech never drew him out of the place where he was, alone in his cell. His word and the text of the *Sayings* confine him and provide that space for a new kind of reason (p. 161) where the power of discourse is not in its reference or its "denominative function" (163), but lies in its performance in the narrativizing of the speaker as "I" in perpetual and generous dialogue with the "other," enabling the self to forget the self utterly in the realization of a fiction of the soul that is the pure and real theater of Antony's Interior Mountain and Teresa's Interior Castle. That is why Abbot Agatho may give himself without limit to the "other" in the form of a social gesture that is a symbol of his utter openness to the absolute Other – the indifferent God who is absolute negation.

In this chapter we have been, as it were, laying two maps on each other, so that in the one we find the pure trace of the other. The true desert traveler is tough and realistic, for otherwise he or she would simply be consumed by the desert's excess of heat, cold, dryness, and storm. The true mystic, also, is not one given to solipsistic and rhapsodic indulgence in the presence of God, but quite the opposite. Mystical theology, since Pseudo-Dionysius, has given textual form to the very loss of all such experience in the cloud of unknowing. Desert as text: text as desert; and in each the stories are told that point beyond the very possibility of language. These are the mystic fables, from Elijah to Jim Crace. In chapter 5 we shall examine the recovery of this fable, not in the modern literature of desert travel, novel, film, and poetry (they will follow), but in the work of contemporary theologians and mystical travelers – unlikely traveling companions though they may seem.

Notes

1 Yves Bonnefoy, *Hier régnant desert* (Paris: Mercure de France, 1964), p. 14. Translated in Michael de Certeau, *The Mystic Fable*, translated by Michael B. Smith (Chicago: University of Chicago Press, 1992), p. 293.
2 De Certeau, *The Mystic Fable*, p. 293.

3   See Deborah Tall, *From Where We Stand: Recovering a Sense of Place* (New York: Alfred A. Knopf, 1993), p. 215.

4   Revelation 21:1–2.

5   R. S. Thomas, "Journeys," in *Mass for Hard Times* (Newcastle-upon-Tyne: Bloodaxe Books, 1992), p. 28.

6   Simon Schama, *Landscape and Memory* (London: HarperCollins, 1995), p. 61.

7   The classic study of the Renaissance theater of memory is Francis A. Yates' *The Art of Memory* (Chicago: University of Chicago Press, 1966), which is discussed further below, p. 51.

8   Philip Sheldrake, *Spaces for the Sacred* (London: SCM, 2001), p. 10. Gaston Bachelard has written on the idea of "home" in *The Poetics of Space* (Boston, MA: Beacon Press, 1994), remarking that it is more than simply our native place: "For our house is our corner of the world. As has often been said, it is our first universe, a real cosmos in every sense of the word" (pp. 4–5).

9   See above, p. 22.

10 Quoted in Sheldrake, *Spaces for the Sacred*, p. 23. See also D. McElrath (ed.), *Franciscan Christology* (New York: Franciscan Institute, 1980), pp. 141, 153.

11 Gerard Manley Hopkins, "As kingfishers catch fire," in W. H. Gardner and N. H. MacKenzie (eds.), *The Poems of Gerard Manley Hopkins* (Oxford: Oxford University Press, 1989), p. 90.

12 Isaiah 55:1.

13 Pseudo-Dionysius, *The Mystical Theology*, in *The Complete Works*, translated by Colm Luibheid, with Paul Rorem. The Classics of Western Spirituality (New York: Paulist Press, 1987), p. 135.

14 1 Kings 19:11–12 (emphasis added).

15 Gene Rice, *Nations Under God: A Commentary on the Book of I Kings* (Grand Rapids, MI: Eerdmans, 1990), p. 160.

16 See below, chapter 7, p. 101.

17 Pseudo-Dionysius, *The Mystical Theology*, ch. 4.

18 Stephen Prickett, "Towards a Rediscovery of the Bible: The Problem of the Still Small Voice," in Michael Wadsworth (ed.), *Ways of Reading the Bible* (Brighton: Harvester Press, 1981), p. 113.

19 For a modern Australian treatment of this theme, see Patrick White's novel *Riders in the Chariot*. See also Bernard McGinn, *The Presence of God: A History of Western Christian Mysticism, Vol. 1: The Foundations of Mysticism* (London: SCM, 1991), p. 16.

20 2 Kings 2:11–12.

21 Denys Turner, *The Darkness of God: Negativity in Christian Mysticism* (Cambridge: Cambridge University Press, 1995), pp. 148ff. Another useful discussion of his theme is in Mark A. McIntosh, *Mystical Theology* (Oxford: Blackwell, 1998).

22 Bernard McGinn, *The Presence of God*, vol. 1, p. xix. I am following the editing of Turner, *The Darkness of God*, p. 263.

23 T. S. Eliot, *The Complete Poems and Plays, 1909–1950* (New York: Harcourt, Brace, and World, 1952), p. 142.

24 Edward Abbey, *Desert Solitaire: A Season in the Wilderness* (New York: McGraw-Hill, 1968), p. 267.

25 Denys Turner, *The Darkness of God*, p. 264.

26 Belden C. Lane, *The Solace of Fierce Landscapes* (New York: Oxford University Press, 1998), p. 75.

27 Michel de Certeau, *The Mystic Fable*, p. 161. Henceforth, page references to *The Mystic Fable* will be in the text. On the organization of space as text, as the non-place of utopia, see Louis Marin, *Utopiques: jeux d'espaces* (Paris: Minuit, 1973).

28 See above, p. 20.

29 See pp. 156, 163–4 for more on Blanchot's *The Space of the Text*, and Kafka.

30 See Camille Paglia, *Sexual Personae: Art and Decadence from Nefertiti to Emily Dickinson* (New Haven, CT: Yale University Press, 1990), p. 241. "Sade's multisexed hybrid is like Scylla or Hydra or other chthonian horrors of Greek myth. Such grotesques in Spenser or Blake are always negative. But not in Sade, who substitutes sexual for social relations. His libertines swarm together in mutually exploitative units, then break apart into hostile atomies."

31 Yates, *The Art of Memory*, p. 122.

32 Valentine Cunningham, "It Is No Sin To Limp," *Literature and Theology*, vol. 6, no. 4, December 1992, pp. 303–9.

33 See above, p. 27, and Peter Brown, *The Body and Society: Men, Women and Sexual Renunciation in Early Christianity* (New York: Columbia University Press, 1988), pp. 216–17.

34 Jean-Jacques Rousseau, *A Treatise on Natural Education* (1762), quoted in the Norton Critical Edition of *Robinson Crusoe*, edited by Michael Shinagel (New York: W. W. Norton, 1975), p. 282 (emphasis added).

35 Thomas Merton, *The Wisdom of the Desert: Sayings from the Desert Fathers of the Fourth Century* (London: Sheldon Press, 1961), p. 61.

5

Mysticism and Modernity

Thomas Merton Meets Don Cupitt

Art Spiegelman, contemporary artist and son of a Holocaust survivor, admits that nothing can be said to explain the horrors of history, including events like those of Nazi Europe. Some silences seem endless. "Every word is like an unnecessary stain on silence and nothingness," Samuel Beckett once insisted. But after pondering Beckett's truth for a long time, Spiegelman adds with a spark of humor, if not hope, "On the other hand, he SAID it."[1]

So I will disappear.[2]

Father S—, who had to go to the doctor in Louisville, came back with a clipping about a man out in the Kentucky mountains, an old coal miner who, for thirteen years, has lived as a hermit with his dog in a pitiful little shack without even a chimney. He used an old car seat for his bed. When he was asked why he chose to live such a life he replied: "Because of all these wars." A real desert father, perhaps. And probably not too sure how he got there.[3]

This chapter, which forms a kind of pair with chapter 4, is called "Mysticism and Modernity" because, as will become clear, these two things have almost nothing in common with one another. Modernity has failed to understand anything about the desert except as a place to be wearily traversed by one or two brave souls in the service of Empire, and has absorbed the mystic path into its positivisms, though, miraculously, the desert wind is again blowing in the unlikely wastes of postmodernity. Maybe not so unlikely. Both mysticism and the postmodern, in all its many and varied forms, ultimately acknowledge a crisis in language and yet also, paradoxically, trust in language, its power to tell stories and make places, and its capacity to turn back on itself in apparent defiance of meaning and yet miraculously remain in being. Beckett speaks of silence – but yet he speaks. Thomas Merton tells the story of the old man in the mountains, and reaches back to the *Historia Monachorum*: his words construct the loony old saint of the Kentucky mountains. Actually Merton is doing that of himself in most of his writings about silence, mysticism, and solitude: all the time he is writing autobiographically; like all autobiographers, constructing a fictional self which he can inhabit and where he can both lose himself and also be himself most fully.[4] Merton was, above all, a writer, and from that condition springs the man and his vocation.

Saints – and I suppose that Merton is getting on for that state – become present to us in the hagiographical narratives that embrace their lives. Like mysticism, hagiography has got itself a bad name and become largely a pejorative term. That is a pity and uncalled for, since this kind of narrative is ultimately one in value with great fiction or the stories of those whose travels have been in places that defy articulation in the language usually at our disposal; men like T. E. Lawrence – and we should probably best call them poets, though some become even more than that. Edith Wyschogrod defines hagiography as "a narrative linguistic practice that recounts the lives of saints so that the reader or hearer can experience *their imperative power*."[5] Dostoevsky admitted in a letter written in 1867 that "nothing is more difficult" than "to portray a wholly good man." It cannot be done in theory, but only in practice, in the narrative fiction of a "real" person, in short, in a novel. The good man has thus to be imagined and constructed precisely in order that he may be "realized," and so it is in the lives of those semi-mythical figures who actually did, inconceivably, disappear into the desert, beyond the boundaries of the utterable. Of such people Pierre Delooz has written:

> Most saints were once real people, about whom objective facts may be estab-
> lished: their sex, their place of birth, and particularly of death . . . But beside
> the real saints are what we may call the *constructed* saints. All saints are more

or less *constructed* in that, being necessarily saints *for other people*, they are remodeled in the collective representation which is made of them.[6]

Nor does this construction cease, but continues in the texts that tell the stories: they live in their narratives, which continue to be read and appropriated. The scullery maid of the *Lausiac History* is forever disappearing into the desert and forever imprinting herself as an absence on the reader. Wyschogrod gives us also the example of the twelfth-century story of Mary the Egyptian,[7] a narrative of youthful pleasure, conversion, and calling to "spend the rest of [her] life in the desert." There she lives for forty years, naked like an animal, and when she dies her body does not decay. At last a lion of the desert digs her grave in ground which is too hard for human labor to excavate. That is it. Her silent life teaches little or nothing, but in the act of reading it provokes puzzlement and a demand to be taken seriously. Her legend is indeed well described by Wyschogrod as a "proto-novelistic discourse"[8] that has a harshness which claims no validity by any external standard and no possibility of reenactment – hers is not a life actually to be *lived* – but it makes its excessive demands in ways that are socially disruptive and destabilizing. In the words of Jean-François Lyotard, the legend of Mary the Egyptian "is working without rules in order to formulate the rules of what *will have been*."[9] Her utter degradation in the wilderness is a descent into pain that ensures only the loss of meaning, for, as Elaine Scarry has pointed out, pain is that condition which is finally singular and incommunicable and yet is a universal condition. No one can know *my* pain, and yet in its absolute form it is recognized as universal.[10] Truly an impossible *imitatio Christi*, Mary's life does not take on the character of a myth, which, as Lévi-Strauss has suggested, functions in the manner of a scientific hypothesis,[11] but a legend that, with all its extravagance, has a plausibility that is possible and therefore followable, even in its impossibility.

Let me give you an example of what I mean from recent and actual history. Charles de Foucauld (1858–1916) was indeed a true desert father whose life of failure and hiddenness in the French Sahara has given rise to the "legend of Father de Foucauld."[12] Born a French aristocrat, a cavalry officer and adventurer, de Foucauld was converted and drawn to the desert as a priest and a solitary life of extraordinary asceticism among the Tuareg people, among whom he was eventually assassinated. During his desert ministry he converted no one and attracted not a solitary follower, despite dreams of starting a community – and was almost crushed by his failure. He was, quite literally, lost in the desert, a small man hidden with Christ. But he was also a tireless writer, a man of words who devoted his formidable energies to compiling a massive dictionary of the Tuareg language and a collection of their poetry, "to make the Tuareg people live again!"[13] He was a silent and unheard man of words, who in his lifetime was "nothing" but whose legend has provoked a vast and worldwide spiritual family of Little Brothers and Sisters, and not least also, a family of readers of his words. Yet in his life he was lost, and only thus was the pretext for the construction of the fable that presents the unrepresentable.[14] He himself characteristically put it in these terms, his life centered on the liturgy and the sacrament which is the material presence of the wholly and immaterial "other":

> Before the Blessed Sacrament, one feels oneself so really in the presence of Being, even though everything created seems, according to all evidence, to touch nothingness.[15]

With the language of Being we are linked, in this unlikely desert place, with the work in the twentieth century of philosophers, theologians, and mystics – Heidegger, Tillich, Bonhoeffer, even Don Cupitt and Thomas Merton. They make a strange community. But with them we *begin* with writing – writing all the way down. Along with mystical texts of the desert and Western Christianity, with the Buddhist tradition, if no others, they acknowledge that "the idea of a truth beyond words is too paradoxical to be self-consistently stated."[16] And so, after the saintly, sandy monk Foucauld, we move on to the *enfant terrible* of English theology in the later part of the twentieth century, Don Cupitt. An Anglican clergyman beyond the pale, Cupitt first attracted my attention years ago with his book *Taking Leave of God* (1981). This strange, seemingly godless theologian took his title from a sermon by the German mystic Meister Eckhart: "Man's highest calling is when, for God's sake, he dares to take leave of God." That is, he dares to take leave of the security blanket of God and the foundationalisms of the tradition, and to go out into the desert prepared to meet and speak of nothing. In this book, Cupitt wrests theology from its "foundations," leaving it, with all that follows upon it, struggling for a new language and new articulation. How can we speak or write of God after we have taken our leave of "him"? Cupitt has this in common with de Foucauld: he is a tireless writer, and he writes not to please the academic community, but to be heard and read, if frequently misunderstood. He is prepared to stand on Matthew Arnold's Dover Beach watching the Sea of Faith withdraw until we are seemingly left "as on a darkling plain"[17] with the mindless conflicts of the world or with nothing except language; and "there is no meaningfulness and no cognition prior to language."[18]

The point, however, is that this is all right. It is perfectly all right. For in his book *Mysticism After Modernity* Cupitt emphasizes that mysticism, no more than any other religious experience, cannot constitute a claim to disappear beyond or behind language into some special kind of supernatural or higher way of knowing. It is not a going *beyond*, but a going *into* language and its demanding realism. Cupitt therefore sees Christian mysticism as a theological humanism, "seeking to escape from and to undo absolutism."[19] Far from being an escape into some ecstatic and unverifiable direct experience of God, it is profoundly realistic and even political. Cupitt affirms:

> The mystic is a religious anarchist and utopian, who speaks for an ancient tradition of protest against religious alienation. The mystic tries to undermine the Law, and to create religious happiness by melting God down.[20]

The result of this is a radical freedom and a spirituality that is an autonomous and willed human self-transcendence, a true disinterestedness that is a journey experienced as a movement into unknowing.[21] This is only possible in the abandonment of a literal religious language and an embracing of an expressive use of religious language, a poetics that is not an imposition upon God, but a waiting upon God. This is also the embracing of a true autonomy that *dares* to set out into the unknown and to a place of absolute judgment. Thus Cupitt can plead:

> If you judge my view atheistic please acknowledge also that it has an approximately equal claim to be judged orthodox.[22]

There is no better place to experience this than in the desert. The desert is most truly utopian, not in any bourgeois sense and with more than a trace of the *dystopian* and the irony that lurks in all utopian visions, from Sir Thomas More to the catastrophe that is Aldous Huxley's *Brave New World*. It is a utopia, and thus also a dystopia, not merely anticipated but outside time itself and of all time, a genuine no-place that is yet truly *there*. The desert wanderer, in whom our mystical traditions begin, seeks a utopia beyond the city walls of culture knowing that the earliest cities were cities of the dead.[23] Among nomadic peoples the only fixed place was the tomb and the necropolis antedates the city of the living. And so Abraham wanders, finding a fixed place only in death, and in their earliest creed, the Children of Israel confessed, "My father was a wandering Aramean" (Deuteronomy 26:5). Only in death does one sleep next to one's ancestors in the city of the dead, which is the beginning of the modern metropolis, which, "with all its affluence and all its bursting pride of apparent life, is a center for death."[24] From this center of power, saints, travelers, and mystics leave in a political gesture that is profoundly present in Lawrence and Thesiger, as well as Antony and Evagrius. In the desert Antony first dwells in a tomb, his fortress, only to rise again full of health and vigor and move on. And what he and his fellow travelers find emerges in words, for truly in the beginning was the creative word, and before that there was nothing. Cupitt writes of St. John of the Cross, in exile in his prison cell:

> St. John of the Cross did not first have a language transcending experience, and then subsequently try to put it into words. On the contrary, the very composition of the poem was itself the mystical experience. The happiness is *in the text*; it lies in the fact that John, in prison, has been able, through the imagery of the poem, to make religious happiness out of the conflicting forces bearing upon him and the personal suffering that he is undergoing. *Writing* is redemption; religious experience is self-expression in religious art. Mysticism is mystical writing: that is, it is writing and only writing that reconciles conflicting forces and turns suffering into happiness.[25]

The point, of course, is that John is *actually* suffering, incarcerated in his tiny cell, barely able to move, and it is precisely this suffering that enables him to embark on the ascent of Mount Carmel. The ladder for his feet is language. Let us take John's own words first, before we follow in our own way (in English).

Canción de la subida del Monte Carmelo
En una noche oscura,
   con ansias en amores inflamada,
   ¡oh dichosa ventura!,
   sali sin ser notada,
   estando ya mi casa sosegada.

A oscuras y segura
   por la secreta escala, disfrazada
   ¡oh dichosa ventura!,
   a oscuras y en celada,
   estando ya mi casa sosegada.

En la noche dichoas,
   en secreto, que nadie me veía,
   ni yo miraba cosa,
   sin otra luz y guía
   sino la que en el corazón ardía.

Song of the Ascent of Mount Carmel

1 In a dark night, inflamed by love's desires – oh, lucky chance! – I went out unnoticed, all being then quiet in my house.
2 In darkness and safe, by the secret staircase, and disguised – oh, lucky chance! – in darkness and by stealth, all being then quiet in my house.
3 On that lucky night, in secret, since no one saw me nor did I see anything, with no other light or guide except the light that was burning in my heart.[26]

How similar is this to the flight of St. Antony, except that he flees *towards* his tomb, there to remain for twenty years! But the text makes no distinction between interior and exterior. Notice, too, how experience becomes layered in the text. John, in his ascent to the unknown, leaves the house clandestinely, a lover secretly seeking the beloved. It is a love poem. He takes the opportunity offered, his "lucky chance" or venture, and, by good fortune, is seen by no one. He is utterly alone, as he must be, not daring to light a torch lest he is discovered, guided only by the inner light of his passion. Finally, safe in the fortress of the Beloved, he can forget himself utterly in the paradise garden: interior/exterior; erotic/spiritual – all are one.

> Quedéme y olvidéme,
>   el rostro recliné obre el Amado
>   cesó todo, y dejéme,
>   dejando mi cuidado
>   entre las ezucenas olvidado.
>
> I remained and I forgot myself, I laid my face against the Lover, everything stopped and left me, leaving my cares forgotten among the lilies.

In the politics of mysticism, Cupitt moves from St. John of the Cross, to Meister Eckhart, Mallarmé, and Joyce,[27] and from thence, across oceans and back, to the Rothko Chapel and Heidegger. It is a goodly company, although conversation cannot be easy. But let us allow Eckhart to take the lead, for whom God is both simple and *actus purus*.[28] Where then is God to be found but in the *desert absolu*,[29] the Paneremos, represented in unbounded brilliant light that is even beyond all categories and distinctions of color, for its brilliance deconstructs the spectrum itself. Here (for it is become a place) we are beyond even difference, a condition found in Eckhart's play on the words God, Being, and Nothingness. The writer plays in the garden. Yet language is nothing but difference, and the play of differences. *Esse est deus* is Eckhart's formula (at this point Heidegger enters the conversation), a literary move described by Cupitt:

Be-ing, life, the outpouring play of secondariness in the Now moment: that is as close as language, or we, can ever get to God. Eckhart is clear that be-ing's self-outpouring is its own ground.[30]

Eckhart's formula, in other words, acknowledges the kenosis or self-emptying of God in the outpouring of secondariness in the place where silence and language meet. It is a pure poetics, Total Presence, an impossible incarnation. It is the answer to Augustine's question about time in the *Confessions*: it is the secret to J. W. M. Turner's two great paintings on the Deluge once in the Tate Gallery, that strangely no longer exist, or at least are lost and therefore cannot be actually seen except in the "secondariness" of reproductions. To all intents and purposes, they are nowhere. But in them, existing still beyond existence, the colors that clothe objects and constitute the promise of the rainbow are taken up into the pure light that embraces and *is* all of them at once, absolutely beyond our seeing.

The mystics do not claim to write this poetry themselves. St. John of the Cross insists that it writes itself, it is the "silent music" (*musica callada*) that comes with the angels at the "time of the rising dawn."[31] It is a language that emerges out of nothing, out of the darkness of night, and thus speaks from nowhere. It is a radical language without referent, which, in de Certeau's words:

> display[s] a passion for what *is*, for the world as it "exists," for the thing itself (*das Ding*) – in other words, a passion for what is its own authority and depends on no outside guarantee . . . An ab-solute (un-bound), in the mode of pain, pleasure, and a "letting-be" attitude (Meister Eckhart's *gelazenheit*) . . .[32]

This profound realism opens up in the world as it "exists" spaces of utopia, dream, and writing, made possible only by a retreat from society itself. These spaces of writing are ever waiting in the expectation of a dialogue that is yet a dialogue realized in the writing itself, so that Angelus Silesius discovers here that

> The [Divine] Writing is writing, nothing more. My consolation
>   is essentiality,
> And that God speaks in me the Word of Eternity.[33]

In saying nothing, this writing permits saying, and in not meaning it allows the "I" to become meaningful. It is the pure kenosis of the word. Thus, de Certeau concludes his essay "Mystic Speech":

> Because it is always *less* than what *comes* through it and allows a genesis, the mystic poem is connected to the *nothing* that opens the future, the time to

come, and, more precisely, to that single work, "Yahweh," which forever makes possible the self-naming of that which induces departure.[34]

In the mystic poem "time" becomes, and is, truly realized in past, present, *and* future, which are all one, unlike our measurement of time as linear, which has only a past and a present, the future as yet unknown and merely anticipated.

When Jesus is thrown violently out into the desert, driven by the Spirit, he encounters the Satan who is the demon of his own self. Truly, he meets himself, and in his "Temptations" he overcomes the "I" so that it becomes possible to offer himself wholly to the "other." He becomes an empty space waiting on inscription that is entirely one with the empty space of the wilderness. It is a condition of negative capability, but far beyond anything imagined by John Keats when he invented that phrase.[35] Rather, it is a capability where a meeting takes place between the "I" in the wilderness, the mystic poem, and that "new humanism" described by Thomas Merton and to be found in twentieth-century Christian theologians from Bonhoeffer to Tillich, and that is being rediscovered in theological thinking today.[36] It is where Merton meets Don Cupitt in a radical theology that is as old as the hills, described by Merton as

> The tendency . . . no longer to regard God as enthroned "out there" at the summit of the cosmos, but as the "absolute future" who will manifest Himself in and through man, by the transformation of man and the world by science orientated to Christ.[37]

For others, this "Christ" is simply the Other, found in the immensity of vast open space for which we yearn in our contracting world, yet it is an immensity that invades the tiny cell of St. John of the Cross, and the prison cell in Berlin of Dietrich Bonhoeffer in 1945, prompting in him exactly the same question and challenge to the "I" seeking release into the Other, and stability in the place of wandering. In this Bonhoeffer was no different from T. E. Lawrence, except Lawrence never escaped from himself, however many times he reinvented this after his Arabian campaigns. Bonhoeffer is different. He writes in poetry:

> Who am I? This or the Other?
> Am I one person today and tomorrow another?
> Am I both at once? A hypocrite before others,
> And before myself a contemptible woebegone weakling?
> Or is something within me still like a beaten army
> Fleeing in disorder from victory already achieved?[38]

Defeat must in the end be recognized as victory. Somehow the terms of this new humanism are rarely palatable within the settled cultures of religion, though finally accepted only to be inevitably forgotten and lost again. What a furore there was in England in 1963 on the publication of Bishop John Robinson's little book *Honest to God*, yet it was a text, though admittedly a poor one, in this same tradition, and it simply gave people too much space. We fear wide open spaces, yet at the same time we long for them. Like Kafka's K. or those governed by Dostoevsky's Grand Inquisitor, we fear too much freedom, its responsibilities, its threat, its *unknown*. Bishop Robinson's call to focus upon a "depth at the center of life" was a reminder, too, that in the desert if you spend all your time gazing at the beauty of the stars you will break your foot against the rock that lies in the way before you.

And so we come finally to Thomas Merton. Like Wilfred Thesiger and many others who went before him in the nineteenth and twentieth centuries, Merton was a photographer who was acutely conscious of both the beauty and danger of this rock, and of the desert text. In the penultimate year of his life, Merton wrote (he might almost have been writing of de Foucauld):

> I have been summoned to explore a desert area of man's heart in which explanations no longer suffice, and in which one learns that only experience counts. An arid, rocky, dark land of the soul, sometimes illuminated by strange fires which men fear and peopled by specters which men studiously avoid except in their nightmares. And in this area I have learned that one cannot truly know hope unless he has found out how like despair hope is.[39]

For Merton, the true contemplative is one who has penetrated the desert of his own silence and there risked his mind in the wilderness that is beyond language yet found only in language.[40] And it is in the wilderness, the landscape which is the "geographical unconscious" of the solitary, contemplative mind, that God fashioned his people and brought "her" back there like a lover, to "allure her . . . and speak to her tenderly" (Hosea 2:14).[41]

Merton is the most autobiographical of writers and all his writing is essentially a diary and creation of his life. In this he often compares himself to Henry David Thoreau and his wilderness reflections. Yet at the same time he is genuinely and deeply aware of a profound but necessary "ingrained irrelevance" of the self, born of his thirst for solitude which became stronger with the passing years.[42] This he categorically denies is to be likened to Plotinus' "alone with the Alone," but rather it is a recognition of the Alone that is utterly solitary insofar as nothing is apart from it, and yet nothing can be with it, since it is a solitude that can only realize itself in a fusion of freedom and unfreedom.[43] It was this that Merton sought in his wanderings. It is the expression that he says he cannot translate, *le point vierge*, the vanishing point which is the point of nothingness and absolute poverty (completely understood by Charles de Foucauld).

Yet it is also here that Merton is at his most "wordy" and his most literary, engaging most readily with the poets. For if he looked back to Henry David Thoreau, he also liked to offer the reclusive Amherst poet Emily Dickinson as an exemplar of the solitary life, one who found and explored her solitude in language. His Master's thesis at Columbia University was on "Nature and Art in William Blake," in whom he found an ideal that was both mystical and supernatural. Through Blake he realized a natural analogue between artistic experience and mystical experience.[44] Like the theologian Thomas Altizer after him, as we shall see in chapter 10, Merton recognized in Blake a rebellion against naturalism in art and in the moral order. From Blake (again, as in Altizer) it was a natural move for Merton to James Joyce and Gerard Manley Hopkins, the subject of his unfinished doctoral dissertation and with whom he shared an admiration for the Greek philosopher Herakleitos.[45] Throughout his writings, like all true poets, Merton is sociably conversing with other writers and other texts, and not only in the Western traditions, but from Hinduism and especially Zen Buddhism. For deserts are sociable places and places of meeting, and there is nothing more sociable than texts, endlessly sharing their wisdom in silent, wordy exchanges.

At the same time Merton was profoundly visual, a fine photographer and fascinated by calligraphy – and as we shall see later, the desert has always been a place that draws the artist and the camera. In an essay on Zen,[46] Merton celebrates the fact that Zen teaches "nothing" – it does not teach, it points. It makes us look at what we too often fail to see, for it is not about "anything," it merely is. It is the same massive imperative as Merton feels in the woods surrounding his hermitage at the Abbey of Gethsemani in Kentucky:

> All this wild area is the geographical unconscious of my hermitage. Out in front, the conscious mind, the ordered fields, the wide valley, tame woods. Behind, the unconscious, this lush tangle of life and death, full of danger, yet where beautiful things move, the deer, and where there is a spring of sweet pure water buried.[47]

In his looking and his deep engagement with the natural world Merton becomes a writer – the wilderness a form of words – so that his writing *was* his hermitage and inner mountain as much as the breeze-block cabin near the Abbey.[48] And, looking back to the hagiography and the legends of the saints that we considered earlier in this chapter, Merton is the first to acknowledge that the true hermit eventually must become an impossible legend, "or, more likely, is totally forgotten."[49] Only when the traveler has been utterly consumed by the desert, has become a mere trace in the memory and therefore a legend dismissed by its own impossibility, outrageousness, and pointlessness, does the paradise that is Merton's endless theme become possible. It is as impossible as the truth that was at the heart of his life, as of the Desert Fathers long before. The self-emptying of God as the Divine is lost in the final obscurity of matter and its being.

As we turn now to more worldly, but no less wordy, travelers, I am led by way of transition to the more "mundane" wanderings of the poet Kathleen Norris, and her book *The Cloister Walk* (1997). As a child she had been asked to paint a picture of heaven. Her effort was a terrible failure:

> The newsprint cracked under all the layers of paint I had applied, in an attempt to get the image dark enough. It wasn't until I stumbled across Gregory of Nyssa in my mid-thirties that I discovered that my childhood image had a place within the Christian tradition.[50]

Text speaks to text across time and space. She was contemplating Jeremiah 13:16: "When you look for light, he turns it into gloom, / and makes it deep darkness."

Notes

1 Belden C. Lane, *The Solace of Fierce Landscapes: Exploring Desert and Mountain Spirituality* (New York: Oxford University Press, 1998), p. 78; see also Art Spiegelman, *Maus, Book II: A Survivor's Tale* (New York: Pantheon, 1991).

2 Thomas Merton, "Marxism and Monastic Perspectives." A talk delivered on the day Merton died, December 10, 1968, in Bangkok. *The Asian Journals of Thomas Merton* (New York: New Directions, 1975), p. 343.

3 Thomas Merton, *Conjectures of a Guilty Bystander* (1966), in Lawrence S. Cunningham (ed.), *Thomas Merton: Spiritual Master* (New York: Paulist Press, 1992), pp. 158–9.

4 See Lawrence S. Cunningham's introduction to *Thomas Merton: Spiritual Master*, pp. 36–7.

5 Edith Wyschogrod, *Saints and Postmodernism: Revisioning Moral Philosophy* (Chicago: University of Chicago Press, 1990), p. 6 (emphasis added).

6 Pierre Delooz, "Towards a Sociological Study of Canonized Sainthood in the Catholic Church," in Stephen Wilson (ed.), *Saints and Their Cults:*

Studies in Religious Sociology, Folklore and History (Cambridge: Cambridge University Press, 1983), p. 195.

7 Wyschogrod, *Saints and Postmodernism*, pp. 9–10. See also Phyllis Johnson and Brigitte Cazelles, *Le Vain Siècle Guerpier: A Literary Approach to Sainthood through Old French Hagiography of the Twelfth Century* (Chapel Hill: University of North Carolina Press, 1979), pp. 278–81.

8 See above, chapter 3, p. 33.

9 Jean-François Lyotard, *The Postmodern Condition: A Report on Knowledge*, translated by Geoff Bennington and Brian Massumi (Mineapolis: University of Minnesota Press, 1984), p. 81.

10 See Elaine Scarry, *The Body in Pain: The Making and Unmaking of the World* (New York: Oxford University Press, 1985).

11 Claude Lévi-Strauss, *The Savage Mind* (Chicago: University of Chicago Press, 1966), pp. 16–22.

12 Jean-Jacques Antier, *Charles de Foucauld (Charles of Jesus)*, translated by Julia Shirek Smith (San Francisco: Ignatius Press, 1999), p. 331.

13 Ibid, p. 316.

14 See Wyschogrod, *Saints and Postmodernism*, p. 13.

15 Quoted in René Bazin, *Charles de Foucauld* (Paris: Librairie Plon, 1921; translated 1923), p. 450.

16 Don Cupitt, *Mysticism After Modernity* (Oxford: Blackwell, 1998), p. 10.

17 Matthew Arnold, "Dover Beach" (1867), line 35.

18 Cupitt, *Mysticism After Modernity*, p. 11.

19 Ibid, p. 31.

20 Ibid, p. 56.

21 See Don Cupitt, *Taking Leave of God* (New York: Crossroad, 1981), p. 164.

22 Ibid, p. 93.

23 See Lewis Mumford, *City in History: Its Origins, its Transformations, and its Prospects* (New York: Harcourt, Brace, Jovanovich, 1961); and Cunningham, *Thomas Merton: Spiritual Master*, pp. 127–8.

24 Cunningham, *Thomas Merton: Spiritual Master*, p. 128.

25 Cupitt, *Taking Leave of God*, pp. 74–5.

26 J. M. Cohen (ed.), *The Penguin Book of Spanish Verse* (Harmondsworth: Penguin Books, 1956), pp. 179–81.

27 The link between Eckhart, Mallarmé, and Joyce is also made by John Caputo in "Mysticism and Transgression: Derrida and Meister Eckhart," in Hugh J. Silverman (ed.), *Continental Philosophy III: Derrida and Deconstruction* (New York: Routledge, 1989), pp. 24–39.

28 See Cupitt, *Taking Leave of God*, p. 100.

29 This is a term to be found in the tourist *Guide Bleu*; see below, chapter 6, p. 74, discussing Michael Pailin's *Sahara*.

30 Cupitt, *Taking Leave of God*, p. 100.

31 St. John of the Cross, *Cantico espirituel*, Stanza 13/14. Quoted in Michel de Certeau, "Mystic Speech," in Graham Ward (ed.), *The Certeau Reader* (Oxford: Blackwell, 2000), p. 203.

32 De Certeau, "Mystic Speech," p. 189.

33 Angelus Silesius, *Le Pelerin cherubique*, translated by Eugene Susini (Paris: PUF, 1964), p. 170.

34 De Certeau, "Mystic Speech," p. 205.

35 John Keats defined "negative capability" as "[being] capable of being in uncertainties, mysteries, doubts without any irritable reaching after fact and reason." He was a true Romantic, but he was neither a mystic nor a desert traveler!

36 For example, in the "theological humanism" that is being explored by David E. Klemm, William Schweiker, Maria Antonaccio, and others.

37 Thomas Merton, "Contemplation in a World of Action" (1968), in Cunningham, *Thomas Merton: Spiritual Master*, p. 384.

38 Dietrich Bonhoeffer, "Who am I?", translated by J. B. Leishman, in *The Cost of Discipleship*, revd. edn. (New York: Macmillan, 1959), p. 15.

39 Thomas Merton, "A Letter on the Contemplative Life" (1967), in Cunningham, *Thomas Merton: Spiritual Master*, p. 424.

40 Ibid, p. 426.

41 Merton, "Contemplatives and the Crisis of Faith", in Cunningham, *Thomas Merton: Spiritual Master*, p. 428.

42 The best study of this is Richard Anthony Cashen, *Solitude in the Thought of Thomas Merton* (Kalamazoo, MI: Cistercian Publications, 1981).

43 See Merton, "Learning to Live" (1967), in Cunningham, *Thomas Merton: Spiritual Master*, p. 363. He is reflecting at this point on Nicholas of Cusa.

44 Merton, *The Seven Storey Mountain* (1948), in Cunningham, *Thomas Merton: Spiritual Master*, p. 91.

45 In 1960, Merton wrote an essay entitled "Herakleitos the Obscure."

46 "A Christian Looks at Zen" (1967), first published as a preface to John C. H. Wu's book *The Golden Age of Zen* and reprinted in Merton's *Zen and the Birds of Appetite* (New York: New Directions, 1968).

47 Merton, *A Vow of Conversation: Journals 1964–1965* (1988), in Cunningham, *Thomas Merton: Spiritual Master*, p. 208. As Merton rather ruefully points out in a footnote, the spring of sweet pure water turned out to be anything but that, and caused him to be extremely ill! It is a timely reminder that we need to keep our feet on the ground.

48 See Cashen, *Solitude in the Thought of Thomas Merton*, p. 19.

49 Merton, *Conjectures of a Guilty Bystander* (1966), in Cunningham, *Thomas Merton: Spiritual Master*, p. 139.

50 Kathleen Norris, *The Cloister Walk* (New York: Riverhead Books, 1997), p. 39.

6

The Literature of the Desert, I

Travelers and Poets

I have only a measly ant
To think with today
Others have pictures of saints
Others have clouds in the sky.

Charles Simic, "October Morning"[1]

Surely some revelation is at hand;
Surely the Second Coming is at hand.
The Second Coming! Hardly are those words out
When a vast image out of *Spiritus Mundi*
Troubles my sight: somewhere in sands of the desert
A shape with lion body and the head of a man,
A gaze blank and pitiless as the sun,
Is moving its slow thighs, while all about it
Reel shadows of the indignant desert birds.
The darkness drops again; but now I know

That twenty centuries of stony sleep
Were vexed to nightmare by a rocking cradle,
And what rough beast, its hour come round at last,
Slouches towards Bethlehem to be born?

W. B. Yeats, "The Second Coming"

With Yeats' poem "The Second Coming" the twentieth century begins with the bloodbath in Europe and in Ireland, and the nightmare of the desert. The Sphinx, as in Flaubert, is a ghastly monster, awakened from its stony sleep, that slouches towards the *Parousia* in a terrible inversion of the Christian hope for Christ's second coming. The Jesus of Mark's Gospel, looking back to the Book of Daniel, foretells in chapter 13 the time of chaos, or war and rumor of war that will precede the end, which is the coming of the Son of Man "in clouds with great power and glory" (verse 26). For Yeats, however, in a young century already steeped in blood, the desert yields not the Son of Man but the horror, the heart of darkness; a place not of indifference, but of malign terror.

In the mythic imagination of the poet the desert is becoming the Waste Land, and worse. The centuries of the Christian church have awakened the nightmare, the demons that the Fathers fought, and the desert has become *us*. What is always represented in its otherness from the order of the city and society is now realized as the anarchy of that society. In the twentieth century nightmare the desert enters the city and invades Christian orthodoxy. Yet still the sands and the unknown heart of the desert remain "out there," the same beyond that was known to Antony: a beyond yet unknown to us and necessary for our being.

Thus, in spite of Yeats' nightmare and the Waste Land, the literature of the desert – of saints and travelers, of poets and even, perhaps especially, of charlatans – remains as it has always been: a place of romance. Physically the harshest places on earth, deserts also defy our sense of reality, its proportions and the boundaries we set on our lives and experience. Even when desecrated by oil pipelines and the detritus of human folly, they are places of dreams and fantasy. When the fabulous Queen of Sheba traveled to visit King Solomon (1 Kings 10:1–10), probably from northern Arabia,[2] she brought with her the riches of the desert: "camels bearing spices, and very much gold, and precious stones." From the Bible derives much of the imagery of the Desert Fathers, in their way inveterate romantics, as have been all who have followed them. Charles de Foucauld is remembered for his seven years between 1909 and 1916 as a priest living in the solitude of the North African desert, but we should not forget that he had first explored it as a young and idealistic French cavalry officer whose dreams were transformed into a religious vision which led him to seek in the desert the perfection of a "life hid with Christ in God" (Colossians 3:3).[3] The religious quest and the romance of the desert are never that far apart. The traveler Sir Richard F. Burton (1821–90) wrote ecstatically of seeing the Ka'aba in Mecca:

> It was as if the poetical legends of the Arab spoke truth, and that the waving wings of angels, not the sweet breeze of the morning, were agitating and swelling the black covering of the shrine. But, to confess the humbling truth, theirs was the high feeling of religious enthusiasm, mine was the ecstasy of gratified pride.[4]

In the literature of the desert such things are not far apart. Here normal categories are suspended; here notions of time and space change and disintegrate beyond the imagination of an Einstein; here is both and at once hell and paradise. In the words of the filmmaker and reporter Raymond Depardon:

> Moda [in Chad] is both paradise and hell. It was like Eden at a given point in time . . . I recall staying there, waiting for a plane, letting the days go by without feeling rushed. I remember having had the impression – which I have hardly ever had before in my life – of having nothing to do, and feeling like I was in another time dimension. I slept well. I was happy.[5]

Here, again, we find the experience of "nothingness" – of there being nothing to do, though perhaps that is the most important of all our doings. In this utopia, all reality is a kind of virtual reality, and to travel here is to be consumed and either utterly fulfilled or utterly destroyed. As Guy de Maupassant wrote, "Travel is a kind of doorway by which we leave reality to enter into a previously unexplored reality that is like a dream."[6] Like the invisible cities of the fiction of Italo Calvino or the haunted cities of Michel de Certeau, which are places "to be other and to move toward the other,"[7] the desert can only be a virtual reality, a place not to dwell in but to pass through propelled by subjective desire, even though the journey may take a whole lifetime. Here, and not in the noisy gaming arcade or in exchanges with the computer screen in cyberspace, is the paradox of a "true" virtual reality realized. Here is that unchanging, strange city where the monks who followed St. Antony "came forth from their own people, and enrolled themselves for citizenship in the heavens."[8] Its absolute antithesis is the "modernity" of Daniel Defoe's *Robinson Crusoe* (1719). Crusoe's response to solitude and the wilderness (not, indeed, a desert, but an island that is beyond the boundaries of human civilization, and therefore "nowhere"), is to cultivate it and make of it a city governed by sense, reflection, and reason, a place not exposed to but heavily guarded against the unknown "other," of which Crusoe lives in perpetual fear.

However, the romance and the lure of the desert lie ultimately and precisely in its total and inescapable and fascinating *otherness*. This is an absolute otherness that negates and exposes every construction and defense of human civilization and culture. Theology's insistent vertical lines and metaphors are flattened by the desert horizon, while the foul underbelly of cities and culture – the urban wastelands, the post-industrial ruins, the desolate parking places designed for waiting but where no one dare wait for fear of violence[9] – is a bizarre human distortion of true wilderness, a place of wreck and detritus. Jean Baudrillard makes the point well, emphasizing, like Thoreau before him, the necessity for American society of the wilderness and deserts of the American Southwest. They are necessary *religious* reminders to a society whose cities have become urban wastelands that are themselves almost uninhabitable.

> The grandeur of deserts derives from their being, in their aridity, the negative of the earth's surface and of our civilized humors. They are places where humors and fluids become rarefied, where the air is so pure that the influence of the stars descends direct from the constellations. And, with the extermination of the desert Indians, an even earlier stage than that of anthropology became visible: a mineralogy, a geology, a sidereality, an inhuman facticity, an aridity that drives out the artificial scruples of culture, a silence that exists nowhere else.
>
> The silence of the desert is a visual thing, too – a product of the gaze that stares out and finds nothing to reflect it. There can be no silence up in the mountains, since their very contours roar. And for there to be silence, time itself has to attain a sort of horizontality; there has to be no echo of time in the future, but simply a sliding of geological strata one upon the other giving out nothing more than a fossil murmur.[10]

In this silence and horizontality, the gaze is directed again to the vanishing point of all true perspective. It is towards that point that all desert travelers move, just as the Fathers moved ever deeper into the Egyptian desert, until their journey became entirely an interior one in every sense. They reached what desert travelers call *desert absolu*, though mystics have another word for it. Ultimately, it is all one. Even so prosaic and commercial a journey as Michael Palin's trip across the Sahara Desert, constructed and packaged for television and glossy publication, cannot altogether avoid this place that is no-where. Palin writes:

The camel train moves into a spectacular desert today. "*Desert absolu,*" as my *Guide Bleu* describes it. The *krim-krim* grass, acacia scrub, even the ubiquitous desert melon bushes, whose fruit is tempting but inedible, have all disappeared. This is landscape reduced to its barest essentials, a rippling, rolling, shadeless surface purged of every living thing.

The immense emptiness quietens everyone. Progress is slow and steady, although such is the lack of distinctive landmarks it sometimes feels as if we are walking on the spot.[11]

Here movement ceases to have significance – space and sound are absorbed. For Palin, as for all desert travelers, this world stands as an insistent "virtual" reality in contrast to the world of the city and culture. As he puts it, for him, "life in the desert is a diversion and the blazing skyline of New York is the reality."[12] It is a myth which has endured in the West since late Christian antiquity, described by Peter Brown inasmuch as "it delimited the towering presence of 'the world' from which the Christian must be set free, by emphasizing a clear ecological frontier. It identified the disengagement from the world with a move from one ecological zone to another, from the settled land . . . to the desert."[13]

The choice of words is significant. "Ecology" has become for us today a crucial word, as the post-industrial parody of the wilderness, its wasteland, threatens, in all its destructiveness, the fragile emptiness of deserted places. At the same time, at least in North America, the "frontier" is the line that is always being pushed back, across the desert, beyond which is the fabled country – the new promised land – of California and the West Coast with its City of Angels. The biblical language, and the tragedy, of that myth are found everywhere in works like John Steinbeck's *The Grapes of Wrath* (1939). Yet, for others, the paradise lies not beyond the desert, but *within*. It is a different form of romanticism, the romanticism of the interior place, not the land beyond viewed from Pisgah Height where Moses at his death sees the fertile country of Canaan, flowing with milk and honey, when the Lord says to him, as in a mirage: "I have let you see it with your eyes, but you shall not go over there" (Deuteronomy 34:4). And so Moses dies and vanishes, buried in the land of Moab, opposite Bath-peor, in a grave which remains unknown even to this day.

In the early years of the twentieth century, men like John C. Van Dyke in the United States were beginning to recognize the ecological necessity of preserving the interior desert. A rich son of the Eastern seaboard, Van Dyke is variously regarded almost as a desert saint and as a charlatan. His most famous book, *The Desert: Further Studies in Natural Appearances* (1901), purports to be the record of a journey into the great trackless wastes of the

American Southwest, yet is to some degree a fraud, full of factual errors. In short, it is a fiction, just as the literature of the Fathers is fiction; the desert in words that are, in the end, not so much about the desert as about ourselves.[14] And yet, at the same time, the word and the physical presence of place cannot finally be separated. In the desert, fiction and reality are merged, for as Van Dyke says, "This is a land of illusions and thin air. The vision is so cleared at times that the truth itself is deceptive."[15] He is the true desert romantic, who knows, deceiver that he is, that here even truth itself is a deception yet nonetheless still true. Throughout his book he returns to the theme of illusion:

> The Anglo-Saxon in us insists that there can be only one truth, and that every-thing else must be error . . . The reality is one thing, the appearance quite another thing; but why are not both of them truthful?[16]

Perhaps precisely *because* he is to some degree a charlatan, a dreamer, and a romantic, Van Dyke is a true desert traveler, living between word and rock, each having their own truth. Just as words and texts are necessary vehicles, as all mystics know well, carrying us to the silence that is the fullness and conclusion of all language, so the desert is a place of crossing where we do not dwell, but at the same time there is nothing beyond. The land beyond the Pisgah heights remains always a mirage, unattainable for God's true prophet. For John C. Van Dyke, the wilderness is a place of endless jour-neys, crossed by the animals who dwell and do not dwell there, and by the human traveler who cannot survive long there, but cannot survive long else-where, so that "practically there is no life of any kind that is native to the place."[17] But the life which it gives can only be described in a way that is somehow analogous to the Christian language of resurrection, impossibly uttered beyond the empty tomb. It was for this life that the Fathers trained their bodies in their fierce asceticism. As an aesthetician, Van Dyke trans-lates this into the terms of a modern romanticism which can, even like the early journeys of those who took a little time out from the world of the city and sought out the ascetics of the Egyptian desert, degenerate into mere tourism. Yet the basic impulse remains. In his later book, *The Grand Canyon of the Colorado* (1920), Van Dyke writes simply, "Was there ever a time in human history when a return to Nature was so much needed as now?"[18] As we saw in chapter 3, the desert is the "counter-world," the necessary other that allows us to be what we are, its silence the fullness of our being. A profound theological commentary on this world is offered in the words of the theologian Thomas J. J. Altizer, to whom we shall return at some length in chapter 10:

The real ending of speech is the dawning of resurrection, and the final ending of speech is the dawning of a totally present actuality. That actuality is
immediately at hand when it is heard, and it is heard when it is enacted. And
it is enacted in the dawning of the actuality of silence, an actuality ending all
disembodied and unspoken presence. Then speech is truly impossible, and as
we hear and enact that impossibility, then even we can say: "It is finished."[19]

The drawing together of this language and the reality of the silent desert
lies at the very heart of this book. The people who have crossed the ecological frontier have always been to some degree fools, madmen, saints, or
charlatans – or all these at once and all touched with a certain genius. They
have also been tellers of stories and spinners of words. Edward Abbey, whose
"cowboy" fiction we shall consider briefly in the next chapter, is another
such, a modern solitary who goes out into the wilderness, there mingling
myth and reality. Abbey's book describing his own desert residence, *Desert
Solitaire: A Season in the Wilderness* (1968), is both passionate and extra-
vagantly idealistic, knowing the need for opposites:

I want to be able to look at and into a juniper tree, a piece of quartz, a
vulture, a spider, and see it as it is in itself, devoid of all humanly ascribed
qualities, anti-Kantian, even the categories of scientific description. To meet
God or Medusa face to face, even if it means risking everything human in myself.
I dream of a hard and brutal mysticism in which the naked self merges with
a non-human world and yet somehow survives still intact, individual, separate.
Paradox and bedrock.[20]

Only here can we see things as they are in themselves, as the ruthless and
inhuman environment breaks down the epistemology of the Enlightenment.
Here nothing is "half-created" by the human mind, but we are confronted
with an absolute, the limit. In this essentially "mystical" encounter we lose
everything in order to gain ourselves. And it is so even for the touchy, ornery
Edward Abbey.

Abbey writes in anger as tourism and commercial greed threaten his
solitary world. It is a constant theme of twentieth-century desert travel
writing. If once the desert was the vast, impregnable "other" threatening
our civilized world of city and farm, now it is recognized to be fragile and
physically frail, disappearing under the blows of mineral exploitation and
tourism. Words and images that once were one with the sand and rocks,
their imaginative reaches like the shimmering mirages conjured by the
desert heat, now threaten to be mere windows insulating us as we gaze com-
fortably at that which we cannot know with our bodies. The writings of the
inveterate English traveler Sir Wilfred Thesiger constitute a kind of elegy

for a world that is disappearing, and with it something essential to our humanity. Like Van Dyke, Thesiger is a romantic, but there is a new edge and realism to his sense of loss. In his book *The Marsh Arabs* (1964) he records and celebrates an ancient way of life that has been systematically and brutally destroyed by the regime of Saddam Hussein in Iraq. Where once time had stood still, a few short years have drained the marshes and introduced them into the ephemeral events of "history." Hospitality is replaced by brutality, sharing by possession. What Saddam began, the rough army boots of the Western powers have completed, a tragedy we shall return to in a brief reading of Dominique Sigaud's post-Gulf War novel *Somewhere in a Desert*.[21] But it is during his earlier travels in the "Empty Quarter" of Southern Arabia that Thesiger comes closest to the universal experience and literature of the desert. He writes of his journeying:

> Hour after hour, day after day, we moved forward and nothing changed; the desert met the empty sky always the same distance ahead of us. Time and space were one. Round us was a silence in which only the winds played, and a cleanness which was infinitely remote from the world of men.[22]

Here once more are the great themes: the dissolution of time and space; the horizontality which allows theology to be at once present and unstated; the wind; the purity. Later on he quotes T. E. Lawrence in *The Seven Pillars of Wisdom* on the same subjects. Towards the end of *Arabian Sands*, Thesiger addresses the question, why does he go out into the Arabian desert? It was for no practical or measurable purpose. He is an indefatigable writer, though words are always inadequate, and he ends up telling stories, just stories, which alone reach into the heart of things.

> No, it is not the goal but the way there that matters, and the harder the way the more worthwhile the journey.[23]

Thesiger is a traveler, a romantic, and an outsider with a streak of masochism in him that prefers the harder to the easier way. But he is also an ascetic who is profoundly aware of the peoples who have passed his way since biblical times. His fellow travelers are not settled, city dwellers, but nomads:

> Only in the desert, they declared, could a man find freedom. It must have been this same craving for freedom which induced tribes that entered Egypt at the time of the Arab conquest to pass on through the Nile valley into the interminable desert beyond, leaving behind them the green fields, the palm groves, the shade and the running water, and all the luxury which they found in the towns they had conquered.[24]

Thesiger is, in many ways, the true heir of T. E. Lawrence. Yet Lawrence remains unique, a cultivator of solitariness that is relieved only in the exercise of his true vocation, which is that of a writer. The desert was the perfect environment for the development of his determined eccentricity,[25] the asceticism that, like that of the Fathers, was often bizarre, and the creation and recounting of the "myth" of his life. Jeremy Wilson begins his massive "authorized biography" of Lawrence, published in 1989, with an admission of the centrality of romance and enigma in Lawrence's life.[26] As much as any desert saint, Lawrence has become for us a "legend," and in his own writings he is the legend's prime maker, behind which he slips away in retreat from both publicity and himself. The legend then exists on as many levels as the text of *The Seven Pillars*, and between these levels Lawrence himself disappears, torn apart by the desert which grounds the story and ultimately defeats him. He is no St. Antony and for him anonymity becomes the mask of tragedy. Wilson succeeds as his biographer because he is canny and self-effacing enough to emphasize the story "rather than . . . the manner in which it is told."[27] But the result, it must be admitted, is somewhat lifeless (for the life of Lawrence is always elsewhere and always outside this "authorized" account), and to tell the story thus was not an option open to Lawrence himself. His tragedy was that he became the fiction that his writing created, but the desert never finally absorbed him. He was odd, haunted by his illegitimacy, but that oddity was also his genius. He writes in *The Seven Pillars of Wisdom*:

> I had learned to eat much one time; then to go two, three, or four days without food; and after to over eat. I had made it a rule to avoid rules in food; and by a course of exceptions accustomed myself to no custom at all.[28]

Lawrence never allows himself or his body to fall into "customary" habits. That is part of his asceticism, and his attempt to foil himself. What happens, however, is that his narration of the Arab Revolt and the desert campaign of 1917–18 is increasingly consumed by his own sense of deceit and of himself as an actor for whom the taking of Damascus from the Turks was not a culminating victory but merely an endpoint to one project. On more than one occasion in the later chapters of *The Seven Pillars*, he writes of himself as falling apart and of the sense of being different persons at war with one another. Increasingly, he became "decentered," and that defeated him in the end. It was no self-emptying into the claims of any "other," but rather a fragmentation and a loss of self – simply a falling apart:

> Now I found myself dividing into parts. There was one which went on riding wisely, sparing or helping every pace of the wearied camel. Another hovering above and to the right bent down curiously, and asked what the flesh was doing.

The flesh gave no answer, for, indeed, it was conscious only of a ruling impulse to keep on and on; but a third garrulous one talked and wondered, critical of the body's self-inflicted labor, and contemptuous of the reason for effort.[29]

This is of a time just after Lawrence's devastating experience of torture and rape at Deraa in November 1917. He was a man truly and inescapably haunted by his own demons, and they were very real. Yet as he wrote in a letter of December 23, 1922 to Edward Garnett, his pretences were not ineffective: "my war was a decent imitation of soldiering, and my politics chimed in well with the notes of politicians."

In the end, *The Seven Pillars* is indeed a narrative on many different levels, a story told of which there is not just one truth but appearance and reality, both of them in their way truthful. In his way, Lawrence is no different from the charlatan Van Dyke, no different from any other desert traveler. Here is the deeply romantic beginning of *The Seven Pillars* in the standard text of 1935 (the 1922 edition was privately published in Oxford and only eight copies were ever printed):

> Some of the evil of my tale may have been inherent in our circumstances. For years we lived anyhow with one another in the naked desert, under the indifferent heaven. By day the hot sun fermented us; and we were dizzied by the beating wind. At night we were stained by dew, and shamed into pettiness by the innumerable silences of stars. We were a self-centered army without parade or gesture, devoted to freedom, the second of man's creeds, a purpose so ravenous that it devoured all our strength, a hope so transcendent that our earlier ambitions faded into its glare.[30]

But there is also the suppressed opening chapter, that begins very differently:

> In these pages the history is not of the Arab movement, but of me in it. It is a narrative of daily life, mean happenings, little people. Here are no lessons for the world, no disclosures to shock people.[31]

Both of these are true, the story embracing all, and both are also fictions, mere words, and yet they are magnificent. Lawrence revised and rewrote his text, often as many as nine or ten times, and, paradoxically, as the writing is refined so it becomes closer to the sand of the desert; the more literary so the more real, and the "story" becomes "true." There is an extraordinary passage written of a time of comparative failure in the campaign, when Lawrence was, unsuccessfully, trying to cut the Yarmuk Valley Railway near Amman, and rapidly losing confidence in his tactics. Yet even in his defeat he was realizing an important truth. In his description of his Arab companions he comes as close as he ever does in his narrative to the spirit of the desert and its hauntings. He has recognized the spirit of negativity, its overturnings and its enemies, in a manner that the Desert Fathers themselves would have recognized:

> To be of the desert was, as they [his companions] knew, a doom to wage unending battle with an enemy who was not of the world, nor life, nor anything, but hope itself; and failure seemed God's freedom to mankind. We might only exercise this our freedom by not doing what it lay within our power to do, for then life would belong to us, and we should have mastered it by holding it cheap. Death would seem best of all our works, the last free loyalty within our grasp, our final leisure: and of these two poles, death and life, or, less finally, leisure and subsistence, we should shun subsistence (which was the stuff of life) in all save its faintest degree, and cling close to leisure. Thereby we would serve to promote the not-doing rather than the doing. Some men, there might be, uncreative; whose leisure was barren; but the activity of these would have been material only. To bring forth immaterial things, things creative, partaking of spirit, not of flesh, we must be jealous of spending time or trouble upon physical demands, since in most men the soul grew aged long before the body. Mankind had been no gainer by its drudges.
>
> There could be no honor in a sure success, but much might be wrested from a sure defeat. Omnipotence and the Infinite were our two worthiest foemen, indeed the only ones for a full man to meet, they being monsters of his own spirit's making.[32]

This is "high" literature and self-consciously so, yet its terms will, by now, be familiar to us in our literary journey from the Fathers. As Lawrence once wrote to Ernest Altounyan, "Writing has been my inmost self all my life, and I can never put my full strength into anything else." More than anything he was a writer and a friend of writers, and the composition of *The Seven Pillars* was as costly to him as the desert campaign itself: he called it his "millstone,"[33] an inevitable, brilliant failure and at the same time "a triumph" – which is its subtitle, perhaps ironic. Nor should one forget Lawrence's other literary works: *The Mint* and above all his translation of the *Odyssey*, and his vast correspondence, much of it with the leading literary figures of the time.

Lawrence drove his body to the limits in the desert, but essentially lived through words (which became his legend), and in *The Seven Pillars* his harsh and relentless honesty lies in his sincerity in the exposing of his own hypocrisy, a deceit painfully and explicitly exposed in the writing of the notorious chapter 80 of *The Seven Pillars*, in which he is captured by the Turks, tortured and raped. Here Lawrence's writing is at its most raw, its most honest and its most self-absorbed. Here is his temptation faced and finally yielded to, and never after this does he recover the purity that the desert imposes and requires. Indeed, this is a turning point not only in his desert campaign, but also probably in his life.[34] In this episode, in his own words, "the citadel of my integrity has been irrevocably lost."[35] For him, there could now be no "interior mountain" into which he can retreat, no space, but only the splintering of place, so that from this moment he becomes a figure of tragedy, and he knows it. On the last page of the book he asks General Allenby in Damascus for "leave to go away." "In the end he agreed; and then at once I knew how much I was sorry."[36] Lawrence never returned to the desert, and never found himself again. Some years later, seeking anonymity in the ranks of the RAF, he wrote to Sir Hugh Trenchard, Chief of Air Staff, in January 1922, "I like being private. People wouldn't understand."[37]

And yet he remained ambitious as a writer, and even considered starting a private press, for it was in written words, honed on his own experience in the desert, that he expressed the sharpest and cruelest of insights into the harsh spirituality of the desert, his piercing portrait of the "desert Arab" in *The Seven Pillars* (which I will interweave with a discussion of Jim Crace's novel *Quarantine* in the next chapter),[38] being repeated in his 1921 introduction to C. M. Doughty's *Travels in Arabia Deserta*:

> The creed of the desert is an inheritance. The Arab does not value it extremely. He has never been either evangelist or proselyte. He arrives at his intense condensation of himself in God by shutting his eyes to the world, and to all the complex possibilities latent in him which only wealth and temptation could bring out. He attains a sure trust and a powerful trust, but of how narrow a field! His sterile experience perverts his human kindness to the image of the waste in which he hides. Accordingly he hurts himself, not merely to be free, but to please himself. There follows a self-delight in pain, a cruelty which is more to him than goods. The desert Arab finds no joy like the joy of voluntarily holding back. He finds luxury in abnegation, renunciation, self-restraint. He lives his own life in a hard selfishness. His desert is made a spiritual ice-house, in which is preserved intact but unimproved for all ages an idea of the unity of God.[39]

One senses here that Lawrence is giving the reader a self-portrait, an exploration of his own complex and harsh relationship with the desert that finally defeats him and that he ultimately forsakes. And in his characterizing of the desert Arab, Lawrence is also describing something close to the roots of "Christian" desert spirituality – but far deeper than any creed, though a creed might become an instantiation of its mystery. It is no accident that William Dalrymple in his travels *From the Holy Mountain* in the 1990s finds the worship and liturgy of the odd, scrawny Christian hermits he encounters in the deserts of Lebanon, Syria, and Israel closer to Islam than anything we in the West would recognize as Christian. Perhaps it is part of the desert's indifference to our varieties of response to its imperative. In the end, all these are one, though different.

The same character that Lawrence describes is found in the odd assortment of wanderers and misfits who inhabit the pages of Sven Lindqvist's book *Desert Divers* (1990). They are all writers, mostly novelists, most of them French – Antoine de Saint-Exupéry, Eugène Fromentin, Pierre Loti, Isabelle Eberhardt. In another age these wanderers in the Sahara might have been saints, diverting their eccentricities into the lonely struggles of the dwellers in the interior, though one of them, Charles de Foucauld, did. Learning from them as the disciples of earlier ages learned from Antony and Pachomius, Lindqvist, an inveterate romantic, begins to understand the training and asceticism that the desert requires for survival and through which alone one finds *quies*.[40]

> How many muscles has a human life? You're sure to use most of them automatically, without experiencing them. Particularly in long-term relationships, developing a routine is labor saving, and thus enervating. The best part of suddenly encountering solitude is that it provides training: you discover your life when you have to start using its long-since forgotten and atrophied muscles.[41]

There is something of the same discovery in Saint-Exupéry's classic text *Wind, Sand and Stars* (1940), in which he recounts the story of his survival while lost in the Libyan Desert for three days near the ancient monastic settlement at Wadi Natroun, a feat only made possible by his steadfast "indifference" to the indifferent landscape, and later relived in words.[42]

Almost half-way through *Desert Divers*, Lindqvist introduces his reader to the Saharan poet Yara Mahjoub. He is unable to write. He carries his poems – hundreds of them – inside him. Without his poetry, he says, he falls ill.

Poetry is part of the fabric of the desert, as much a part as sand and rock. The Egyptian Jewish writer Edmond Jabès, in his book of dialogues *From the Desert to the Book* (1980), recalls how, as a young man growing up in Cairo, he "would often stay for forty-eight hours all alone in the desert. I wouldn't take any books, only a blanket. A silence of that order makes you feel the nearness of death so deeply that it becomes difficult to bear any more of it."[43] Like the Christian Fathers of old he crossed the ecological boundary between the city and the desert, so that later, as a writer – a poet, philosopher, and perhaps even theologian – the desert functioned at many complex levels as a metaphor in all his poetry. Perhaps even more than that: for Jabès, book and desert, sand and letter become absolutely inseparable, the desert and its truth reconstituted in each word of the text:

We saw later how the book was but the letters of each word and how this alphabet, re-used thousands and thousands of times in different combinations, slipped through our fingers like grains of sand. Thus we became aware of the infinite presence of the *desert*.[44]

Jabès' Jewish understanding of text and letter, and of letters as garments of Torah, permeates his sense of the book, and this sense is linked to the notion of place, and this place is both realized and negated in the desert. For as he once wrote (with Emmanuel Lévinas), "There is No Trace But in the Desert,"[45] a trace that is at once indicative and nothing, the trace of the place of God. It is found only when we leave the familiar sites for the unknown place of the desert and its mirage. In the desert there are no highways, but only traces to be discerned by the eye alert to the magnitude of the smallest things and merest dustings.

> Thought in infinite regress, writing of the abyss. At the edge. But if the trace is in me, beats within me? Every impulse of my body is a recorded, counted trace, multiplied by fever – by love, pain, delirium. The trace is tied to being, to essence, as to the emptiness with which it perhaps resonates.[46]

For Jabès, the desert, where all his writing begins and ends, must be a real place, "a matter of the concrete experience you have of it."[47] It represents also the metaphor of the void, for it is empty – there is nothing there. Finally, it is inescapably biblical in all its connotations. To go out into the desert alone makes writing possible, and finally impossible. For Jabès, in contrast to the color and sensuality of the city,

> In the desert one becomes other: one becomes the one who knows the weight of the sky and the thirst of the earth; the one who has learned to take account of his own solitude. Far from excluding us, the desert envelopes us. We become the immensity of sand, just as we are the book when we write.[48]

In his prose poem *Intimations: the Desert* (1976), Jabès the Jew meditates upon the desert as the place of origins and future, the place to which the Jew sets out for a renewed word that is his origin, and that origin is an abyss that wholly absorbs him.[49] But above all he explores the link between the word of God spoken in the desert and his "creature" who hears the word and becomes its root. For the word spoken in the desert is deprived of roots in the sand, but becomes instead a book of "inconsumable fire," like the burning bush of Moses' theophany (Exodus 3–4). God's word, spoken in the desert, is itself a wanderer and a nomad, like any other desert dweller, and finds its echo only in the word of a wandering people. Jabès is playing with parables – but his language is more than that. (True parables, perhaps, are always more.) In the desert that has become the book of God's word we have only "the book of this thirst, the devastating fire of this fire reducing all books to ashes at the threshold of the obsessive, illegible Book bequeathed to us."[50] The book of the desert is and consumes all language, and the end of our reading is to read that which cannot be read but from which all words and writing flow. It is to be one with the Divine.

Rosemarie Waldrop, Jabès' translator, has written about his battle with publishers for the blank spaces on the pages of his books.[51] Much of the selected poems in English, published under the title *if there were anywhere but desert* (1988), is blank paper. How do we read these words? Our eye traverses the empty spaces of the paper, and the book can be "read" in an hour. Otherwise, there is nothing there.

Empty space – which is meaningless.

We prefer cities of words, and densely populated pages.

But Jabès is no minimalist. Exiled from Egypt, he remains haunted by the desert: he dreams of the desert. A desert traveler in words, he knows its harsh, ultimate demands. His writing is an ultimate challenge and an acknowledgment: "he lays siege to silence."[52] It is a reaching out to the unreachable centre, Lançon's desert of signs.

Jabès the Jew. Late in life he reads the Kabbalah, and he also reads Arabic literature. Who will guide us? Handelman, Derrida, Lévinas, Celan – critics and poets. We seek explanation. But Jabès writes his book: *The Book of Questions, The Book of Resemblances, The Book of Limits, The Book of Margins* – a library of books without genre ("neither novel nor poem, neither essay nor play"),[53] seeking to speak what cannot be spoken. Jabès the diaspora Jew. The Book that is finally the unspoken to which all speaking points, the unspeakable name of God – who is only a metaphor – "Man does not exist. God does not exist. The world alone exists through God and man in the open book." (*Return to the Book*)[54]

Jabès is forever writing towards the book of silence. Writing in the desert – or words. Mysticism? But Jabès is no mystic, nor a religious writer.[55] God is only a metaphor. His transcendence is empty – there is nothing there. God's freedom is – *not to be*.

Jabès said, "the origin is not behind, but before us."[56] In our end is our beginning.

"this passing away of one's own *into* the properties of the Book, at once an extinction and a vivification."[57]

Jabès *is* a religious writer: Jabès is *not* a religious writer. I do not understand his writing. But Jabès' books are not obscure, someone once said: "They only become unreadable when one is looking for certainty. Their readability is dependent on the deferral of meaning."[58]

This Jabès is forever writing the Book; a traveler in books. He is always dreaming of the desert where there is no color, but where all colors are present at once, and each color is present as a possibility. Where there is nothing, everything is possible. "We pile up images and images of images until the last, which is blank, and on which we will agree" (Edmond Jabès to Serge Fanchereau).[59]

"Like the hidden God of classic Jewish theology, the text exists only by virtue of its absence" (Paul Auster).[60]

> Toujours cette image
> de la main sur le front,
> de l'écrit rendu
> à la pensée.
>
> Tel l'oiseau dans le nid,
> ma tête est dans le main.
> L'arbre resterait à célébrer,
> si le desert n'était partout.
>
> (Always this image
> of hand on forehead,
> of writing restored
> to thought.
>
> Like a bird in the nest,
> my head rests in my hand.
> I would now celebrate trees,
> if there were anywhere but desert.)[61]

Jabès writes in aphorisms, and it is right therefore to meet him in the shards and fragments of language. Born in Egypt, in exile in France (which he made his home), he wrote endlessly from his dreams, and can only ever be understood in the blank, white spaces of page that his letters make visible. As Rosemarie Waldrop acknowledges, "the writer/translator kills and is killed, writes and is written."[62] The word kills: the writer kills God even as she or he identifies with Him as creator. Jabès is another Moses, lamenting the impurity of the words written on the Tables of the Law, searching for the word that he lacks (O Wort, du Wort, das mir felht!),[63] whose lack is its presence.

The word kills. " 'It cannot name something without removing that thing's presence,' says Maurice Blanchot, following Hegel, 'a sign that death speaks when I speak.' And writing kills the word even while giving it life . . ."[64]

What did you go out into the desert to seek? (Matthew 11:7). Jabès, wandering in a desert of signs (Daniel Lançon).[65]

"The experience of the desert is both the place of the Word – where it is supremely word – and the non-place where it loses itself in the infinite" (*The Book of Margins*).[66]

The mysticism and obsessiveness of Jabès' poetry can be found also in the poetry of the Arab-Islamic imagination. Born of a place where almost nothing can take root in the unyielding dryness of sand and rock, the words of this poetry provide the roots which give life and sustenance. As Mounira Khemir has written, the Arabic language flourishes through the roots of words and their etymology. Even when they fall silent, like seeds in the dry earth awaiting rain, they wait for the poet to bring them back to life, breaking through their hard, protective, and grainy kernels – seeds that can easily be mistaken for sand or dirt.[67] In the desert the truth is always complex and paradoxical, and so it produces a poetry in Arabic that can say one thing and its opposite at once, for the truth is finally inexpressible. In such poetry, time is also complex and described by a number of different terms, and its sense of place is, in a way, exactly the opposite of that of the West. Arabic poetry is not a "desertion" of the wilderness, but an entering into it, and into its secret and mysterious life that is often hidden in wells that are buried deep below the surface. For in the desert is a secret life, waiting to be found, and the true poetry of the desert reflects this in its signs and textures. Hence, as in Jabès' writings, we can understand the importance of the *trace*, the absolute necessity of reading the signs and traces in the desert that indicate water and life. The desert traveler must be an interpreter of signs in the sand, and the book, too, is a place of interpretation, words like grains of sand bearing the merest traces of life and truth – if we read them aright.

The book and the desert. From Edmond Jabès and from the Islamic world we learn a new importance of the book and the text that is quite unknown to most of us. The Qur'an is not a text exactly, as we might understand it, and that it cannot be translated from the Arabic is not so much a thing forbidden as ontologically impossible.[68] For the Qur'an is not to be interpreted, appropriated, internalized. Rather, as Gerald Bruns puts it,

As a recitation the Qur'an surrounds us with itself, fills the space we inhabit, takes it over and ourselves in the bargain. The whole movement of reading as an appropriation or internalizing of a text is reversed. Here there is no grasping and unpacking and laying the text bare. On the contrary, reading is participation. To understand the Qur'an is to disappear into it.[69]

The desert and the book. To understand the desert we have to disappear into it, like St. Antony, like every traveler who relinquishes comfort and security and risks all to find nothing. We must become as unknown and mysterious as the English Patient, a helpless and unreadable figure in Ondaajte's novel, yet full of a mysterious power.[70] We must become solitary and as the mystics. In pre-Islamic Arabic poetry we begin with lost worlds and abandoned ruins, and the poem literally, and literarily, recreates a world into which we enter. "It is not about simulation but rather description."[71] Just as the desert is the utopia, is no-place, so too is the world of the book. It is only a poem, and here there are traces, and the effacement of traces (as the wind sweeps the sand), but even the effacements are signs in their nothingness. This is a poetry that matches the desert as described by Mounira Khemir:

> The desert encompasses the mystery of a pure, ineffable presence, the place where the souls of the dead are as important as those of the living. It is a place for men thirsting for the absolute and for mysticism based on an intuitive knowledge.[72]

The garden is the recurring image and center of this poetry. In the Bible the loss of the paradise garden is the first great bereavement in human experience – banishment from the lost, the mythic, garden where rivers flow and fruit hangs in plenty. We go into the desert to seek the garden, or the Kingdom of Heaven. Here the real, the mythic, the mystical, all become one. But it is also the place of betrayal. For the garden that is at the heart of the desert is an ideal place, and to dwell here is no longer to be of this world. It was for citizenship in this garden that the followers of St. Antony perfected their asceticism and were lost to the world. This same garden (perhaps) in the 1,001 stories of the *Arabian Nights* is a place of meditation between earth and a world of light. We cannot even imagine such a garden, for to us a garden is merely a place where nature is brought to order and shape.[73] But the model for the Arab garden is the oasis, described in the Qur'an as "a paradise made of gold and silver, where the rivers, trees and fruits are made of precious stones"[74] – in the desert there are no greater riches than rivers and fruit.

In the sura of Mary, the oasis comes to the aid of the Virgin:

> The [a voice] called to her from below: "Grieve not;
> your Lord has made a rivulet gush forth right below you.
> Shake the trunk of the date-palm tree,
> and it will drop ripe dates for you.
> Eat and drink, and be at peace. If you see any man,
> tell him: 'I have verily vowed to fast to Ar-Rahman
> and cannot speak to anyone this day.'"[75]

Elsewhere the image of the garden is also the image of the labyrinth, for in the desert we are lost, as in the poetry, as we search. Here we may meet fellow travelers. Here is a place beyond representation, where there is silence. It is the same silence that the Fathers sought in *quies*, or "rest," that is the perfection of freedom.[76]

In this chapter we have traveled with a strange and heterogeneous collection of pilgrims and poets. There have been saints and sinners, philosophers and madmen, poets and charlatans. Yet there is a curious unity in this rag-bag company, undiminished by differences of time and culture or even religion. It is a unity that lies at the very heart of this book. It also bound together the unlikely communities of the Fathers of the early church in Egypt. It is a unity that made traveling companions of William Dalrymple of the late twentieth century and John Moschos and Sophronius some fourteen hundred years before. Dalrymple, in his own writing, ceases to be a commentator, throws off the protective mask of the tourist or journalist, and becomes a fellow traveler, discovering that though politics change (perhaps not that much), in the desert time ceases to flow, and the ancient themes are recovered, even for him.

> So, as the sun sank down behind the date palms of the oasis, I thought of Moschos standing on this hillside amid these tombs at the end of the world, fretting about the heretics and brigands on the road ahead, checking in his bag to make sure his roll of notes and jottings was safe, then turning his back on this last crumbling outpost of the Christian Empire, and tramping on over the dunes to catch up with the tall, ascetic figure of Sophronius.
> I left them there, and wandered back down the hill alone.[77]

Notes

1 Charles Simic, *Unending Blues* (New York: Harcourt, 1986), p. 48.
2 Sheba was probably a north Arabian principality mentioned in an eighth-century Assyrian text. See John Barton and John Muddiman (eds.), *The Oxford Bible Commentary* (Oxford: Oxford University Press, 2001), p. 240.

3   See Andrew Louth, *The Wilderness of God* (Nashville, TN: Abingdon Press, 1991), pp. 17–35.

4   Sir Richard F. Burton, *A Personal Narrative of a Pilgrimage to Al-Madinah and Meccah* (1893), excerpted in Robyn Davidson (ed.), *Journeys: An Anthology* (London: Picador, 2002), p. 361.

5   Raymond Depardon, "Deserts," in *The Desert*. Fondation Cartier pour l'art contemporain (London: Thames and Hudson, 2000), p. 14.

6   Quoted in Paul Virilio, "The Twilight of the Grounds," in *The Desert*, p. 115.

7   Italo Calvino, *Invisible Cities* (1972), translated by William Weaver (London: Vintage, 1997); Michel de Certeau, *The Practice of Everyday Life*, translated by Steven Randall (Berkeley: University of California Press, 1984), pp. 108–10. See also Graham Ward, *Cities of God* (London: Routledge, 2000), p. 231.

8   *The Life of St. Antony*. A Select Library of Nicene and Post-Nicene Fathers of the Christian Church, 2nd series, vol. 4, St. Athanasius: *Select Works* (Edinburgh: T. & T. Clark, 1991), 14, p. 200.

9   See the discussion of the video art of Bill Viola in chapter 8, pp. 116–17.

10 Jean Baudrillard, *America*, translated by Chris Turner (London: Verso, 1988), p. 6.

11 Michael Palin, *Sahara* (London: Weidenfeld and Nicolson, 2002), pp. 187–8.

12 Ibid, p. 189. Compare this description with Rufinus' remarks on the "utter desert" of Scetis in the *Historia Monachorum*. See above, chapter 3, p. 34.

13 Peter Brown, *The Body and Society: Men, Women, and Sexual Renunciation in Early Christianity* (New York: Columbia University Press, 1988), p. 216. See also above, p. 27.

14 See Peter Wild's critical introduction to John C. Van Dyke, *The Desert* (Baltimore, MD: John Hopkins University Press, 1999), pp. xxviii–xxxi.

15 Van Dyke, *The Desert*, p. 2.

16 Ibid, p. 109.

17 Ibid, p. 54.

18 John C. Van Dyke, *The Grand Canyon of the Colorado: Recurrent Studies in Impressions and Appearances* (1920), quoted in Roderick Nash, *Wilderness and the American Mind*, 3rd edn. (New Haven, CT: Yale University Press, 1982), p. 189.

19 Thomas J. J. Altizer, *The Self-Embodiment of God* (San Francisco: Harper and Row, 1977), p. 96.

20 Edward Abbey, *Desert Solitaire: A Season in the Wilderness* (London: Robin Clark, 1992), p. 6.

21 See below, pp. 97–9.

22 Wilfred Thesiger, *Arabian Sands* (1959) (Harmondsworth: Penguin Books, 1991), p. 32.

23 Ibid, p. 278.

24 Ibid, p. 328.

25 The phrase is from Edward W. Said, "A Standing Civil War," in *Reflections on Exile and Other Literary and Cultural Essays* (London: Granta Books, 2001), p. 37.

26 Jeremy Wilson, *Lawrence of Arabia* (New York: Atheneum, 1990), p. 1.

27 Ibid, p. 16.

28 T. E. Lawrence, *The Seven Pillars of Wisdom* (1922), quoted in Said, "A Standing Civil War," p. 35.

29 *The Seven Pillars of Wisdom*, ch. 81 (London: World Books, 1939), vol. 2, p. 461.

30 *The Seven Pillars of Wisdom*, vol. 1, p. 27.

31 Quoted in Said, "A Standing Civil War," p. 35.

32 *The Seven Pillars*, ch. 74, vol. 2, pp. 421–2.

33 Jeremy Wilson, *Lawrence of Arabia*, p. 672.

34 Ibid, p. 461.

35 *The Seven Pillars*, ch. 80, vol. 2, p. 456.

36 *The Seven Pillars of Wisdom*, ch. 122, vol. 2, p. 683.

37 M. Brown, *Letters of T. E. Lawrence* (London: J. M. Dent, 1988), p. 192. See also, Wilson, *Lawrence of Arabia*, p. 664.

38 See chapter 7, pp. 000–0.

39 T. E. Lawrence, introduction to C. M. Doughty, *Travels in Arabia Deserta* (London: Jonathan Cape and the Medici Society, 1921), quoted in Davidson, *Journeys*, pp. 364–5.

40 See chapter 3, pp. 100–1.

41 Sven Lindqvist, *Desert Divers*, translated by Joan Tate (London: Granta Books, 2002), p. 35.

42 Antoine de Saint-Exupéry, *Wind, Sand and Stars*, translated by Lewis Galantière (New York: Harcourt, Brace, 1940), pp. 173–236. See also Stacy Schiff, *Saint-Exupéry: A Biography* (New York: A. A. Knopf, 1994), p. 262; Belden C. Lane, *The Solace of Fierce Landscapes* (New York: Oxford University Press, 1998), p. 186.

43 Edmond Jabès, *From the Desert to the Book: Dialogues with Marcel Cohen*, translated by Pierre Joris (Barrytown, NY: Station Hill Press, 1990), p. 14.

44 Edmond Jabès, *The Book of Resemblances 2. Intimations: The Desert*, translated by Rosemarie Waldrop, quoted in Jim Harold (ed.), *Desert* (Southampton: John Hansard Gallery, 1996), p. 47.

45 Edmond Jabès, *The Book of Margins*, translated by Rosemarie Waldrop (Chicago: University of Chicago Press, 1993), pp. 160–70.

46 Edmond Jabès (with Emmanuel Lévinas), "There is No Trace But in the Desert," in *The Book of Margins*, translated by Rosemarie Waldrop (Chicago: University of Chicago Press, 1993), p. 161.

47 Jabès, *From the Desert to the Book*, p. 14.

48 Ibid, p. 16.

49 See *From the Book to the Book: An Edmond Jabès Reader*, translated by Rosemarie Waldrop (Hanover, NH: Wesleyan University Press, 1991), pp. 166–7.

50 Ibid, p. 167.
51 Rosemarie Waldrop, *Lavish Absence: Recalling and Rereading Edmond Jabès* (Middletown, CT: Wesleyan University Press, 2002), p. 74.
52 Ibid, p. 104.
53 Paul Auster, introduction to *if there were anywhere but desert: The Selected Poems of Edmond Jabès,* translated by Keith Waldrop (Barrytown, NY: Station Hill Press, 1988), p. ix.
54 Quoted in Waldrop, *Lavish Absence*, p. 133.
55 Ibid, p. 127.
56 At a colloquium on his writing, quoted in Waldrop, *Lavish Absence*, p. 126.
57 Robert Duncan, "The Delirium of Meaning," afterword to *if there were anywhere but desert: The Selected Poems of Edmond Jabès,* translated by Keith Waldrop (Barrytown, NY: Station Hill Press, 1988), p. 111.
58 Richard Stamelman, Professor of Romance Languages at Dartmouth College, quoted in Waldrop, *Lavish Absence*, p. 84.
59 Serge Fanchereau, "Interview," *Instants*, 1 (1989), pp. 212–13.
60 Paul Auster, "Interview with Edmond Jabès," *Montemora*, 6 (1979).
61 Jabès, *if there were anywhere but desert*, pp. 98–9.
62 Waldrop, *Lavish Absence*, p. 61.
63 See above, p. 18.
64 Waldrop, *Lavish Absence*, p. 61.
65 Daniel Lançon, *Jabès l'Egyptien* (Paris: Jean Michel Place, 1998), p. 275.
66 Jabès, *The Book of Margins*, p. 172.
67 See Mounira Khemir, "The Infinitive Image of the Desert and its Representations," in *The Desert.* Fondation Cartier pour l'art contemporain (London: Thames and Hudson, 2000), p. 58. See also chapter 1, above, p. 3.
68 See Gerald L. Bruns, *Hermeneutics Ancient and Modern* (New Haven, CT: Yale University Press, 1992), pp. 125–7.
69 Ibid, p. 126.
70 See chapter 7 for a discussion of Michael Ondaatje's *The English Patient*.
71 Mounira Khemir, "The Infinitive Image," p. 60.
72 Ibid.
73 We might compare with this image the idea of garden in Psalm 136 or in the Qur'an, chapter 55 (The Merciful).
74 Mounira Khemir, "The Infinitive Image," p. 61.
75 *Al'Quran*, sura 19, Mary, verses 24–6, translated by Ahmed Ali (Princeton, NJ: Princeton University Press, 1994), p. 301.
76 This discussion of poetry and the text is also perhaps not so far from what Roland Barthes describes in his work *The Pleasure of the Text* (1971), where he writes: "what the text says . . . is the ubiquity of pleasure, the atopia of bliss." See *Barthes: Selected Writings* (London: Fontana, 1983), p. 412.
77 William Dalrymple, *From the Holy Mountain: A Journey in the Shadow of Byzantium* (London: Flamingo, 1997), p. 454.

7

The Literature of the Desert, II

Novelists

Deserts possess a particular magic, since they have exhausted their own futures, and are thus free of time. Anything erected there, a city, a pyramid, a motel, stands outside time. It's no coincidence that religious leaders emerge from the desert. Modern shopping malls have much the same function. A future Rimbaud, Van Gogh or Adolf Hitler will emerge from their timeless wastes.

Some of the best American thrillers have been set in the desert – *The Getaway*, *The Hitcher*, *Charley Varrick*, *Blood Simple*. Given that there is no time past and no future, the idea of death and retribution has a doubly threatening force.[1]

These words of J. G. Ballard ring entirely true – except, perhaps, the reference to the shopping mall. Wastelands, indeed, and productive of tyranny, they are hardly creative in any other sense. But my concern in this chapter is with the modern novel of the desert as it reflects, as we shall see, the harsh, beautiful amorality of the true wilderness. There time ceases to be – there is literally no time – and so the narratives that operate only within the narratives of temporality cease to be effective. A new kind of narrative begins to emerge, on the edge of language and experience, yet profoundly literary, as if the desert exists, if it exists at all in human possibility, only in the medium of word and artistic image. And as travelers meet and cross in the desert, so words meet and cross in a strange communality that stretches across the limits of literature, texts addressing new and fictional texts with respect but without deference even to the most ancient sacred word across the millennia of human history. For poets, words, for artists, images, are the drifting sands of the desert that is yet ever the same. In the shifting mirages of the desert and its literature we learn that here, and only here, is the trace – the absent presence that draws us on. Edmond Jabès, as we saw in the last chapter, writes of the trace in the desert that is tied to being itself and to every impulse in the body, felt and amplified by the fevers of pain and love. The trace is the very stuff of fiction.

The first of the "desert" novels we shall consider in this chapter begins, like Wordsworth's *Prelude*,[2] in a purely artistic moment, yet one which recovers the "fictional" life of St. Antony in all its theatricality, and is later given authenticity when its author himself visited Egypt in 1849. Gustave Flaubert's *La Tentation de saint Antoine* was not published until 1874, but it has its origins in his childhood imagination, given definition when Flaubert visited Geneva in 1845 and saw Bruegel's painting of the temptation of St. Antony. The image and Flaubert's dramatic prose return us to the desert hermitage of Antony. The opening words of the book set us, as on a stage, physically within the saint's dwelling.

> C'est dans la Thebaide, au haut d'une montage, sur une plate-forme arrondie en demi-lune, et qu'enferment de grosses pierres.
> La cabane de l'Ermite occupe le fond.[3]

There is a paradox here. This most stylized and self-consciously intellectual of books still somehow reaches back through its histrionics to the mystery of Antony himself. It is a kind of meeting of opposites. For here, as Michel Foucault has put it, "Saint Antony [is] able to triumph over the Eternal Book in becoming the languageless movement of pure matter."[4] Like Antony himself, this fictional representation finally absorbs the Book, to himself become the Book in pure "being."[5]

Sitting before his cabin, the saint remembers former temptations and fights new ones of lust and intellectual doubt. Like all desert dwellers, he is of all time and none. As in the ancient *Life of St. Antony*, his temptations and terrors come as beasts and visionary monsters. At one moment towards the end of the book, on the other side of the Nile, the Sphinx moves and

Plate 1 *Pieter Bruegel,* The Temptation of St. Antony *(ca. 1560). National Gallery of Art, Washington, Samuel H. Kress Collection, Image © 2003 Board of Trustees.*

approaches him, only to be himself beset by the green-eyed Chimera, both the mythic beast slain by Bellerophon and a grotesque, wild fancy of the brain. They argue, vile and lustful. Each, like the monsters of old, is a temptation to the saint. The Chimera boasts, using the desert dream of the paradise garden, "I seek for new perfumes, for vaster flowers, for pleasures never felt before. If I perceive in any place a man whose mind reposes in wisdom, I fall upon him, and strangle him."[6] The Sphinx counters, "All those tormented by the desire of God, I have devoured."[7] As always, it is the wise and God-seeking who are most oppressed. The monsters leave Antony, but their breath has created the desert fog that blurs his vision. *The Temptation* looks back to both classical and Renaissance theater, to Goethe's *Faust* and Gothic fiction of the eighteenth and nineteenth centuries, and is, at the same time, a philosophical treatise. It also looks back to the long tradition of art that visualizes Antony, especially when assailed by seductresses, and was regarded by many as scandalous in its day. In Flaubert, Antony's visions are, indeed, perverse and sometimes sordid, yet at the same time deeply theological – he is approached in turn by the great heretics from Arius to Sabellius, their arguments made in the political language of the church councils. He wavers upon the verge of pantheism[8] – Flaubert was not that far from the soul of the Desert Father for whom the Divine was all things, and nothing.

Indeed, with all its gothic and extravagant display of learning, Flaubert's static masque of human consciousness (the book had a profound impact on Freud) remains remarkably within the desert tradition. As the Devil returns time and again in different guises,[9] Antony laments "those who cross the desert meet with animals surpassing all conception."[10] Nor was this for Flaubert himself merely a literary observation, for he also crossed the deserts of Egypt. When he visited the great desert near the Red Sea in May 1848, he described his experience of the merging of the physical desert into the fantastic, and its fearful effect on him:

> The dust-cloud grows and comes straight at us . . . It is reddish and pale red; now we are in the midst of it. A caravan passes us coming the other way; the men, swathed in *kufiyehs* [head-cloths] (the women are thickly veiled) lean forward on the necks of their dromedaries; they pass very close to us, no one speaks; it is like a meeting of ghosts amid clouds. I feel something like terror and furious admiration creep along my spine . . . it seemed to me that the camels were not touching the ground, that they were breasting ahead with a ship-like movement, that inside the dust-cloud they were raised high above the ground, as though they were wading belly deep in clouds.[11]

Compare this real and disorientating experience with the description of imagined desert travel by the young Flaubert, only twenty-one, in his early Romantic novel *Novembre*:

> Oh, to be bending forward on a camel's back! Before you a deep red sky and deep brown sand, the flaming horizon stretching ahead, the undulating ground, the eagle hovering above your head, in one part of the sky a flock of rosy-legged storks passing over on their way to the cisterns. The ship of the desert lulls you; the sun makes you close your eyes, bathes you in its rays.[12]

The youthful imagination is far less dramatic and haunted, less fantastic than Flaubert's actual encounter with the desert itself as he describes it in later life.

The desert haunts many literatures. It holds its secrets in the vastnesses of the Australian interior, in the words of Patrick White's novel *Voss* (1957), where the dying explorers scratch a moment of time on its timelessness before they are extinguished and become bones, their deaths "an event in time such as these relics of human life seldom experienced now."[13] In the deserts of North America, however, the Native American fiction of Leslie Marmon Silko finds in their timelessness not oblivion but rather a liturgical sense of recovery of self and a return to roots that almost parallels the journey to the lost utopia of Paradise of the Fathers, so that finally in the wilderness

> Every evil
> which entangled him
> was cut
> to pieces.[14]

For Silko, this is a journey back to a primal innocence.

A different kind of innocence lies in the writings of Antoine de Saint-Exupéry (1900–44). Aviator extraordinary, adventurer, desert traveler, inveterate romantic, Saint-Exupéry was, like Charles de Foucauld, a French aristocrat. His turn of mind and spirit was utterly different, and yet they bore some strange similarities. Both men were writers whom the Sahara fed and nurtured. Saint-Exupéry's journeys and dramatic escapes are transformed in his writer's imagination into the stuff of fiction. Like others before him, he becomes larger than life. At the same time, while in charge of the remote desert airfield at Cape Juby in the French Sahara, he would write repeatedly of his "monk's cell" and his "monkish" life.[15] At the end of his life he owned a typescript of Teilhard de Chardin, which was initially credited to him.[16]

Saint-Exupéry's descriptions of his journeys, above all in *Wind, Sand and Stars* (1939), become fiction, compared by Stacy Schiff with the novels of Joseph Conrad.[17] Hardly an apt comparison, for perhaps Saint-Exupéry's only work to have fully stood the test of time is the brief children's story *The Little Prince* (1943), a story born out of a desert limit experience.

> So I lived my life alone, without anyone that I could really talk to, until I had an accident with my plane in the Desert of the Sahara, six years ago. Something was broken in my engine. And as I had with me neither a mechanic nor any passengers, I set myself to attempt the difficult repairs all alone. It was a question of life or death for me: I had scarcely enough drinking water to last a week.
>
> The first night, then, I went to sleep on the sand, a thousand miles from any human habitation. I was more isolated than a shipwrecked sailor on a raft in the middle of the ocean. Thus you can imagine my amazement, at sunrise, when I was awakened by an odd little voice.[18]

The Little Prince has something of the naivety and the wisdom of the Fathers. In his way, Saint-Exupéry has heard the voice which speaks out of nothing. There is something in him of the charlatan, like John C. Van Dyke, yet the drive to fictionalize and to tell stories, paradoxically, finds echoes of the universal literature that is our concern. For Saint-Exupéry is another lover of the wilderness: "at once a desert and a paradise, rich in secret hidden gardens, gardens inaccessible."[19]

Saint-Exupéry finally fell victim to his own rhetoric in his posthumously published *Citadelle* (1948) (*The Wisdom of the Sands*), an interminable meditation on wisdom by a fictional desert chieftain. Yet even here, at its heart, lies the desert that the writer knew, and a mystical sense that looks back, in some way, to the Fathers themselves. The desert prince contemplates an aged laborer among his people and reflects:

> . . . escaping by a miracle from his old gnarled flesh, he was growing ever happier, more and more invulnerable. More and more imperishable. And dying, knew it not, his hands full of stars.[20]

In the final pages of *The Wisdom of the Sands* we return precisely to *The Lives of the Desert Fathers* in the company of the two old gardeners, friends who have been parted for years. One of them, miraculously, receives a letter from his long-lost friend, which contains only the words: "This morning I pruned my rose-trees." He replies, in turn, "This morning I, too, pruned my rose trees."[21] It is enough, a true desert economy of language that expresses a deep community in profound silence. It is why Saint-Exupéry remains part of our company.

In one of the most remarkable and beautiful novels of the desert of recent years, Michael Ondaatje's *The English Patient* (1992), the North African desert becomes in a quite different way an invented world, both physical and imaginative.[22] From Herodotus in the fifth century BCE to the "sunburned, exhausted" explorers of the nineteenth century, the desert burns itself upon the European imagination and then is brought to new life by the wars of the twentieth century, which were fought among its rocks, creating new mysteries of loss and identity. In the burnt, anonymous body of the "English Patient," time and place disintegrate and offer possibilities of salvation to the shell-shocked survivors of war as they begin to rebuild their lives. Although most of the novel is actually set in Italy, it is the desert and its secret of the "English Patient" which dominates the lives of all the characters. On this charred, unrecognizable body is imprinted the desert's unreadable text that somehow holds the key to the restoration of these lives that have been shattered and divided by war. Yet this "English Patient" is also threatening, perhaps quite other than human, a counterfeit or charlatan, yet still powerful in sickness. In a way he is another desert mirage, burnt by fire; another devil.

A more recent war, the Gulf War in Iraq, is the context of the French writer Dominique Sigaud's novel, *Somewhere in a Desert* (1998). The specific and still-raw events of the war are dissolved in the deliberate vagueness of the title – it does not matter where the body of this fallen soldier is found, or even in which desert. All deserts are alike in the imagination – unreal places of loss and restoration, and yet at the same time this is a novel about a very real and specific place, and a real moment in historical time. Here, somewhere, place and placelessness/time and timelessness intersect. Sigaud's theme, as in other war writers and poets before her, is the pity of war and war as the true wasteland of human loss, wrought by human stupidity. At the beginning of the novel the war with Iraq has already ended. The body of an American soldier lies in no-man's land – somewhere, a stretch of indeterminate sand across the Iraqi border between the Allied front and a Saudi village. The soldier has been "lost" in the war, but his body is found, by accident, by a villager, Ali ben Fakr, four days after the war has ended. It is dead, yet not dead, for the body speaks to the villagers as they watch over it. In the desert there is neither time nor place, neither life nor death – it is beyond all these things. It speaks first to Ali ben Fakr's wife:

> Nour al-Koutoubi steps back. She turns and looks away, far away; far beyond the dunes which, all around, stretch out as far as the eye can see, farther than the vastness of night and the sky; she is looking for something, some fixed point, something to remind her of the order of things: that life and death are separate and distinct and she can never know the ties that bind them. She feels a terrifying loneliness, the earth seems to shift, she wants to cry, to scream, the gates of hell slam shut behind her; her face and hands already disintegrating; she falls to her knees, blinded by the darkness, she crumples and the man beside her speaks: "Don't be afraid."[23]

Somewhere in a Desert is the story of the death of John Miller, of the recovery of his body by his wife Mary, and of his journey from time to timelessness. As in *The English Patient*, or even *The Seven Pillars of Wisdom*, the war between nations is a mere backdrop for the even more momentous events that take place in the desert – the negotiation between life and death, between time and eternity. For men go out into this wilderness to fight, or to find God, but all are erased by the abrasions of sand that erode the order of things and the distinctions between living and dying. Sigaud's novel ends at a time before its beginning, at the very moment of the soldier's death, that poetic moment of which no one can speak directly, for it cannot be recalled in time, on the border between time and not-time. It is the one moment of universal experience, perhaps the greatest in our lives, and yet we have no language to describe it and are allowed no reflection to conceptualize it. For John Miller, the soldier, death is an end, and, like all desert wanderers, he is alone. Death is an end – and yet "he" continues to speak, uttering the words "Don't be afraid":

Alone, John Miller remembered the men he had known, the faces of the women, of old men and children he had met, eyes turned towards the sea or to some dry riverbed. He thought about who they were and what they wished to be, all the while feeling the coldness creep over him. He was surprised that he could feel it still and died shortly after, his last thought: part regret that he had not the strength to walk farther; part longing to live everything over; pain that this longing had not come sooner and amazement that it should end like this.[24]

Jim Crace's novel *Quarantine* (1997) recounts another death in the desert. When Jesus, before the start of his ministry, goes out into the Judean wilderness, does he die there? Is the Christian story a myth built upon a crazy youth who somehow worked miracles and brought reconciliation, but died young in an excess of zeal? Or, unlike the soldier in Sigaud's novel, does he survive his trial in the desert, purified to face even greater trials yet, between time and eternity, the finite world and infinity? But who is the "real" Jesus, hidden in the narratives of the gospels, or, perhaps, in the pages of Crace's fiction?

Quarantine revisits and converses with the biblical story of the temptations of Jesus in the desert where Jesus goes – or is sent – for a time of preparation before the work of his ministry can begin. The novel sees no reason to adhere closely to the gospel narratives or to the religious tradition that treasures them, yet it has uncanny resonances with scripture, and with the stories of the Desert Fathers, as well as other modern texts and films concerned with the desert. Crace is not a theologian, nor does he write directly in the traditions of Christian desert spirituality or theology. Yet his fiction oddly echoes patterns familiar in those traditions (the desert, like literature, is always full of echoes), and provides a new, sometimes uncomfortable starting place for religious thought and reflection from within the universal experience of what it is to be human in encounters with those crazy outsiders "by whom the world is kept in being." That precisely describes the function of Crace's adolescent "Jesus."

"Quarantine," by the definition of the *Oxford English Dictionary*, is the period of time, originally forty days, during which persons who might spread a contagious disease (especially travelers and strangers) are kept isolated. In Crace's novel, four individuals – one woman and three men – go out into the Judean desert to fast and pray, that they might somehow find healing and find themselves. They are afflicted, or believe themselves to be afflicted, by various conditions: infertility, cancer, and madness. A little way off a merchant, Musa, and his pathetic wife Miri, are left in the desert by their caravan, struggling with a terrible fever that has attacked Musa. All, then, require healing. But there is a fifth pilgrim, idealistic, a youth from Galilee called Jesus, who has come to "encounter god or die, that was the nose and tail of it. That's why he'd come. To talk directly to his god. To let his god provide the water and the food. Or let the devil do its work. It would be a test for all three of them."[25] This Jesus works miracles – but there are always miracles in the desert, as it suspends normal categories of human experience. The Desert Fathers worked miracles, just as the Jesus of the gospels works miracles of healing, for that is what happens in the desert. It is quite usual. The gospels certainly have no monopoly in this respect. And in the desert there is nothing – no god and no real devil – only Musa the merchant, who is a sadist, rapist, and manipulator of lives lived in the caves on the very edge of human existence, where a drink of water is worth a fortune. And this is not the Jesus we know from the gospels of Mark or Matthew, for this Jesus actually dies in his cave, or so it seems. He is not like the Fathers who lived for years on almost nothing, and yet emerge from their tomblike fastnesses full of strength and vigor. This Jesus, this fictional Jesus and his obsession with an indifferent god,

> was all surface, no inside. His leaf had fallen finally. He was a dry, discarded page of scripture now . . . This was his final blasphemy. He begged the devil to fly up and save him from the wind. He'd almost welcome the devil more than god. For the devil can be traded with, and exorcized. But god is ruthless and unstable. No one can cast out god. It was too late. Jesus was already standing at the threshold to the trembling world which he had sought, where he would spend his forty everlasting days. So this was death. So this was pain made powerless. So this was fruit turned back into its seed.
>
> Jesus was a voyager, at last, between the heavens and the earth.[26]

Crace's novel, like the desert itself, as always, confuses interior and exterior. What is it about – a parable of the soul, or a narrative of seven crazy lives fighting for survival, forgiveness, and power? Is it a religious book, a book about religion, and an intertext of the gospel narratives, with which it travels and plays? What is remarkable is its capacity to evoke in the mind, and inside the mind of the reader, the harsh place of the desert, a real place of scrubland, heat, and unforgiving rocks, which is yet a place of retreat from the lives of the characters in towns and villages, with families and practical everyday concerns. It is a place to be entered into, an interior where battles are fought with the self against real devils, and there is nothing, for all is negation – even, and especially, its pitiless God. The book is remarkable for its unity with the great tradition of desert literature, from the Pentateuch onwards. All such texts tell stories of crazy people. When Crace's Jesus dies there is nothing, or almost nothing, that is dreamed of in the desert – "no god, no gardens, just the wind."[27] T. E. Lawrence knew that wind also, as did Elijah on Mount Horeb. In a famous passage in *The Seven Pillars of Wisdom* (1935), Lawrence is led to a ruin in North Syria, dating from Roman times, where, at an opening in the wall, he and his companions

> drank with open mouths of the effortless, empty, eddyless wind of the desert, throbbing past. The slow breath had been born beyond the distant Euphrates and had dragged its way across many days and nights of dead grass, to its first obstacle, the man-made walls of our broken palace. About them it seemed to fret and linger, murmuring its baby-speech. "This," they told me, "is the best: it has no taste."[28]

The wind, *ruach*, spirit. It carries nothing and is nothing: the still small voice heard by prophet, soldier, and madman. And for Lawrence, the desert provokes in its dwellers an extreme form of the religious life.

> His sterile experience robbed him of compassion and perverted his human kindness to the image of the waste in which he hid. Accordingly he hurt himself, not merely to be free, but to please himself. There followed a delight in pain, a cruelty which was more to him than goods. The desert Arab found no joy like the joy of voluntarily holding back. He found luxury in abnegation, renunciation, self-restraint. He saved his own soul, perhaps, and without danger, but in a hard selfishness.[29]

This is a description of desert religion (it matters not *which* religion it is – it probably never does),[30] which echoes throughout all the texts we have been considering in this book, but especially in *Quarantine*. How can Lawrence's cruel Arab be likened to the saintly Christian Fathers of the fourth century? Because even in the highly tempered and romanticized accounts we have of their lives, they, too, could be rough and cruel. Essentially people of community, at the same time, in these fictionalized lives where we read of them, they are wanderers and solitaries with no abiding city;[31] indeed, they are people who seek not to abide, or eccentrics who seek escape or cleanness.

So what I suggest as regards *Quarantine* is a curious kind of reversal. The accounts of the Desert Fathers lead us through the literary traditions of scripture, to the larger traditions of desert literature in poetry and fiction. This is not to dispute their "truth," but it does raise the question, what does it mean for fiction to be true, and might a different fiction, different typologies, different metaphors, reveal a different yet still coherent and valid truth which does not contradict difference? This desert literature is a tradition of miracle, or deep religiosity born of life lived on the edge of bodily possibility between flesh and spirit, or mirage and vision, of loneliness and community, of harshness and necessary kindness, of a yearning for water springs and gardens, of wandering and meeting, of *praxis* and *theoria*. Such things link Antony, Evagrius, Macarius, and Patermuthius with Jim Crace's strange, wild, group of travelers and mystics, also obsessed with sex, water, and purity. The difference is that the one is a necessary fiction that validates the desert through the eternal consolations of Christian theology and belief, while the other, in a modern novel, delicately deconstructs such consolations, blurring their definitions and clarity in the heat haze of a different vision which just might, but does not inevitably, invalidate what has gone before. For in the desert nothing is lost – its dry heat and sand are the best of preservatives – but to gaze into its sun is not to see but to be blinded to our world, like the Roman general Regulus, whose punishment was to be forced to gaze into the pure light of the sun until it blinded him, or perhaps Saul blinded on the desert road to Damascus.[32]

At the beginning of *Quarantine* (and we should never forget that this is a purely literary experience – the heat we feel is pure fiction, and inside our heads) the reader is introduced to the merchant Musa and his dutiful wife Miri, abandoned in the desert by the caravan who are fearful of fever. For

> a devil had slipped into his open mouth at night and built a fire beneath the rafters of his ribs. Devils were like anybody else; they had to find what warmth they could or perish in the desert cold. Now Musa had provided lodging for the devil's fever.[33]

The devil of sickness is inside Musa, or Musa *is* the devil. Or is he just a grasping, unscrupulous merchant and desert brigand who will exercise his power over whatever helpless victim falls in his path – a monster of greed and sexual appetite? Is there, finally, any difference? When Pier Paolo Pasolini realized the narrative of Matthew 4:1–11 in the film *Il Vangelo secondo Matteo*,[34] he portrayed Satan as this Musa, a grubby, ordinary man who catches people foolish enough to travel in desolation at their weakest and most dependent. The demons of the Desert Fathers would come to their victims bearing succulent food and drink, while they sought ascetic purity. So does Musa to the desolate travelers, for "there's nothing like a desert water-hole for making good, brief neighbors out of animals that have nothing much in common other than a thirst."[35] But neighbors soon quarrel and become jealous and Musa is an expert in the policy of divide and rule. Only the strange, idealistic Galilean Jesus (with the crazy idealism of youth) keeps himself apart, a stubborn child who will neither drink nor sleep the more thirsty and tired he becomes (like that other selfish, selfless, decentered prophetic figure, T. E. Lawrence, he is "different"). Jesus miraculously heals

Musa of his fever by his touch. For Crace (like Pasolini or scripture) neither avoids nor explains the miraculous in the desert. By the end of the story, Jesus has followed to the letter the ascetic discipline of the Fathers.

> His fast had made him ready. Perhaps he'd served his thirty days just to be equipped for the wind. Quarantine had been the perfect preparation for his death. His body was quiescent and reduced; dry, sapless, transparent almost, ready to detach itself from life without complaint. A wind this strong could pluck him like a leaf, and sweep him upwards to the palaces and gardens that angels tended in the stars.[36]

He was ready to be the rider in the chariot, to fly to the Paradise Garden that all desert dwellers dream of. And in the end does he die pointlessly in the cave, while the others, more sensible, have fought their battles with Musa and return to their homes and normality a little wiser and more human at the end of their quarantine of forty days? It is Musa, the defeated devil, though a survivor in this world, who sees the final vision, after the body of Jesus has been buried, dead and done with.

> Musa looked towards the distant scree again. He told himself this was no merchant fantasy. His Gally was no longer thin and watery, diluted by the mirage heat, distorted by the ripples in the air. He made his slow, painstaking way, naked and bare-footed, down the scree, his feet blood-red from wounds, and as he came closer to the valley floor his outline hardened and his body put on flesh.
>
> Musa raised his arm in greeting, but there was no response.[37]

Like St. Antony, like Lazarus, like another Jesus, Jesus here seems to emerge from his tomb in bodily splendor, though with the marks of wounds on his feet. Or is this simply an emptiness? Is this just a mirage upon mirage – a double miracle of desert seeing? Certainly, this young lunatic had somehow effected a justice, god knows how, for the travelers are shriven and the devil is defeated, though he survives, unrepentant, to fight another day.

Quarantine is a fiction. Like all literature, it plays with other texts and fictions which have influenced it, consciously or unconsciously. It is desert literature, neither outside nor inside, and it tells a story which is another rewrite of an ancient story: story within story. As fiction it delicately unpicks the interpreted lives of the desert saints, who themselves followed the fictions of the gospels,[38] and find their way to us through the more prosaic John Cassian, St. Benedict, and the long story of Western monasticism. We are not asked to believe this story except in the literary sense of the willing suspension of disbelief, yet its effect is strangely familiar to those of us accustomed to the Christian narratives of repentance, temptation, asceticism, resurrection, and forgiveness. Perhaps we spend our time in the make-believe world of this fiction because it is, again, the old story of one "by whom the world is kept in being," who acts irresponsibly for no possible good purpose or reason. It is a story of the work of grace.

But it is also a story of the devil. Like the god from whom he is often indistinguishable, the devil haunts every desert place in an endlessly repeated and always renewable story. Cormac McCarthy's novel *Blood Meridian, or The Evening Redness in the West* (1985), is a chilling, raw restatement of the myth of the American West, a lyrical evocation of the beauty, the indifference, and the inhumanity of the deserts of Texas, New Mexico, northern Mexico, and the Pacific states, that is amoral, apocalyptic – steeped in the surrealism and nightmare of Dante, de Sade, and the art of Hieronymus Bosch. It is specifically American, yet is also of all time and no place. The central character in the novel is given no name except "the kid," a lost, solitary orphan. His journeys, sometimes in violent company, often alone, are a pilgrimage through the desert that is both real and interior. Here is a description of part of his journey.

> It was a lone tree burning in the desert. A heraldic tree that the passing storm had left afire. The solitary pilgrim drawn up before it had traveled far to be here and he knelt in the hot sand and held his numbed hands out while all about in the circle attended companies of lesser auxiliaries routed forth into the inordinate day, small owls that crouched silently and stood from foot to foot and tarantulas and solpugas and vinegarroons and the vicious mygale spiders and beaded lizards with mouths black as a chowdog's, deadly to man, and the little desert basilisks that jet blood from their eyes and the small sand-vipers like seemly gods, silent and the same, in Jeda, in Babylon. A constellation of ignited eyes that edged the ring of light all bound in a precarious truce before this torch whose brightness had set back the stars in their sockets.[39]

The passage is at once biblical and of no time and place. It is a reminder of the words of Flaubert's St. Antony (repeated almost verbatim at one point in *Blood Meridian*), that those who cross the desert meet with animals that surpass all that we can conceive. It is a journey that is locked into the origin of all things, into the fabulous ruins of Babylon, into all the mythic and deadly beasts of the desert which haunt the imagination, of the pilgrimages of the Fathers seeking Nothing, of the quests of the age of chivalry. It is at once utterly real and beyond all realism. This world is everywhere haunted by the huge and grotesque figure of Judge Holden, who is all-knowing, utterly amoral, and indestructible. The kid first sees him at a revival meeting in Nacogdoches, Texas. He was "an enormous man dressed in an oilcloth slicker

. . . He was bald as a stone and he had no trace of beard and he had no brows to his eyes nor lashes to them. He was close on seven feet in height and he stood smoking a cigar even in this nomadic house of God."[40] The judge is a man like no other, larger than life yet with no beard or hair, and eyes that never close. He falsely and without compunction condemns the preacher, the Reverend Green, before the congregation, while the preacher vainly identifies him as the devil. But no one believes him.

The judge follows the kid throughout his pilgrimage. He notes down everything he sees in his pocketbook and collects specimens from nature, for, he asserts, "Whatever exists . . . Whatever in creation exists without my knowledge exists without my consent."[41] Like the Satan of Mark 1 and Matthew 4, who tempts Jesus in the wilderness, the judge seeks to claim and control all things, so that even the freedom of the birds is an insult to him. When one of the "pilgrims" notes that to cage them he would have to construct "a hell of a zoo," the judge smilingly agrees.[42] For, as always, the devil of *Blood Meridian* can be charming, the kid's greatest friend. Thus it always is. And in the physical world of the desert the judge needs no Bible, for, like the Desert Father or the Christian theologian who sees God's word in the two books of Scripture and Nature,[43] he reads God's words in rocks and sands. "He speaks in stones and trees, the bones of things."[44]

As in *Quarantine*, so in *Blood Meridian*, in the amoral world of the wilderness, god and the devil are never far apart, utterly different yet the same. Or, at least, they are often frequently impossible to distinguish. How can we know the one from the other? In this world beyond the cities of civilization and beyond any rule of law, everything is possible (p. 245), and nothing can finally be achieved. McCarthy's novel is soaked in meaningless bloodshed, a cruel deconstruction of the myths of the American West, for here there is no justice but that of the judge himself. It is a primeval world where new settlers find both paradise regained, and also the ancient horror. It is the world of T. E. Lawrence's cruel Arab. It is the world of every desert. For indeed, "those who travel in desert places do indeed meet with creatures surpassing all description" (p. 282). At the end of the novel, the kid, wounded and accompanied by one companion, an ex-priest, is relentlessly hunted across the desert spaces by the judge. He cannot be killed. For if the devil is no parable but a "naked fact" and "a man like all men" (p. 297), yet he cannot be faced down. He is nothing, but is yet all things.

Why does the judge, the devil, in the end take the kid? This is the deep tragedy of the novel, that relates it to *Oedipus Tyrannos* and *Hamlet*, and indirectly to the Passion narratives of the gospels. The kid is Satan's because, like all tragic figures, he is at heart a good man. He is the judge's victim, because he is not truly of the judge, and the judge knows it and crushes him. He dares to exist without the judge's consent. The kid is unlike the other murdering, soulless wanderers with whom he journeys.

> No assassin, called the judge. And no partisan either. There's a flawed place in the fabric of your heart. Do you think I could not know? You alone were mutinous. You alone reserved in your soul some corner of clemency for the heathen. (p. 299)

And so the kid dies, his death an unspeakable horror in the jakes, beyond all description in the novel. Like Kurtz in Conrad's *Heart of Darkness*, he alone has seen the horror, and it destroys him. On the edge of the possibility of human existence, he, like Christ on the cross before him, meets the judge of all and it takes him because he remains the only good man. A story of salvation, or a tragedy – is there any difference, finally? It is again the story of the necessary and inevitable death of God. And the judge? Like Musa, he lives to see another day, another dance. For, throughout the novel, the judge is a great dancer in the greatest dance of all, the dance of death. The novel ends with these words:

> He never sleeps, he says. He says he'll never die. He bows to the fiddlers and sashays backwards and throws back his head and laughs deep in his throat and he is a great favorite, the judge. He wafts his hat and the lunar dome of his skull passes palely under the lamps and he swings about and takes possession of one of the fiddles and he pirouettes and makes a pass, two passes, dancing and fiddling at once. His feet are light and nimble. He never sleeps. He says he will never die. He dances in light and in shadow and he is a great favorite. He never sleeps, the judge. He is dancing, dancing. He says that he will never die. (p. 335)

The very words themselves become the dance. But the judge is the demon of all desert travelers. He alone seems to offer relief and salvation. He is the great tempter. He is the figure of death. Grace and the devil are almost indistinguishable.

The American frontier has frequently been the occasion for a retelling of the ancient, ever-new story of the desert. It is the same story as we find in the Bible, in the Desert Fathers, in Lawrence, in the poetry of Jabès. It is ineradicably religious, though of no religion, a story of love and alienation. As a preface to *Blood Meridian*, McCarthy quotes some words of Paul Valèry:

> Your ideas are terrifying and your hearts are faint. Your acts of pity and cruelty are absurd, committed with no calm, as if they were irresistible. Finally, you fear blood more and more. Blood and time.

T. E. Lawrence would have understood these words. And they are now translated into new contexts, sometimes more banal because more familiar, but still terrifying nonetheless. Edward Abbey, a writer whom we have already encountered in chapter 6, is also a novelist, a writer of "westerns," though quite unlike Cormac McCarthy. But even in their slight pages, the echoes remain. In *Fire on the Mountain* (1962) a lone rancher in the desert hills of New Mexico, north of El Paso, battles for his land against the irresistible, demonic, smiling forces of the United States military as they seek to appropriate his wilderness in the interest of national "defense." Satan again. They come to save and destroy. The landscape is the same – a place of mirage, death, and slaughter, and also the paradise again, a paradise garden where the soul finds rest. In the words of the young narrator, Billy:

> Each time I gazed upon the moon-dead landscape and asked myself: what is out there? And each time I concluded: *something* is out there – maybe everything. To me the desert always looked like a form of Paradise. And it always will.[45]

Notes

1　J. G. Ballard, *The Atrocity Exhibition*, marginal note to the annotated edition (London: Flamingo, 1993), pp. 92–3.
2　See chapter 1, p. 2.
3　Gustave Flaubert, *La Tentation de saint Antoine*, 3rd edn. (Paris: Charpentier, 1875), p. 1.
4　Michel Foucault, introduction to Gustave Flaubert, *The Temptation of St. Anthony*, translated by Lafcadio Hearn (New York: Modern Library, 2001), p. xliv.
5　Flaubert, *The Temptation of St. Anthony*, p. 190.
6　Ibid, p. 181.
7　Ibid.
8　Ibid, p. 5.
9　There are many similarities between *The Temptation* and Bulgakov's great novel *The Master and Margarita.*
10　Flaubert, *The Temptation of St. Anthony*, p. 179.
11　Flaubert's travel notes of 18 May, 1849, in *Flaubert in Egypt*, translated and edited by Francis Steegmuller (Harmondsworth: Penguin Books, 1996), p. 180.
12　From Flaubert, *Novembre*, published posthumously in 1914. Quoted in *Flaubert in Egypt*, p. 178.
13　Patrick White, *Voss* (Harmondsworth: Penguin Books, 1983), p. 425.
14　Leslie Marmon Silko, *Ceremony* (Harmondsworth: Penguin Books, 1986), p. 258.
15　Stacy Schiff, *Saint-Exupéry: A Biography* (New York: Alfred A. Knopf, 1994), p. 14.

16 Ibid, p. 440.
17 Ibid, p. 306.
18 Antoine de Saint-Exupéry, *The Little Prince*, translated by Katherine Woods (New York: Harcourt, Brace, 1943), pp. 5–6.
19 Antoine de Saint-Exupéry, *Wind, Sand and Stars*, translated by Lewis Galantière (New York: Harcourt, Brace, 1940), p. 44.
20 Antoine de Saint-Exupéry, *The Wisdom of the Sands*, translated by Stuart Gilbert (New York: Harcourt, Brace and World, 1950), p. 29.
21 Ibid, pp. 346–7.
22 See the review of *The English Patient* by Eileen Battersby in the *Irish Times*.
23 Dominique Sigaud, *Somewhere in a Desert*, translated by Frank Wynne (London: Phoenix House, 1998), p. 30.
24 Ibid, pp. 123–4.
25 Jim Crace, *Quarantine* (Harmondsworth: Penguin Books, 1998), p. 22.
26 Ibid, p. 193.
27 Ibid.
28 T. E. Lawrence, *The Seven Pillars of Wisdom* (London: World Books, 1939), vol. 1, p. 38.
29 Ibid, pp. 39–40. See above, chapter 6.
30 See chapter 6, p. 82.
31 See Philip Sheldrake, *Spaces for the Sacred* (London: SCM, 2001), pp. 33ff.
32 See Jacques Derrida, *Memoirs of the Blind: The Self-Portrait and Other Ruins*, translated by Pascale-Anne Brault and Michael Naas (Chicago: University of Chicago Press, 1993). Regulus is the subject of a painting by J. M. W. Turner, who was fascinated by the idea of pure light that is the consummation of all color, and causes blindness. Its effect is pure darkness.
33 Crace, *Quarantine*, p. 2.
34 Pasolini's film is discussed in some detail in chapter 9.
35 Crace, *Quarantine*, p. 49.
36 Ibid, p. 191.
37 Ibid, p. 243.
38 I am consciously following here Douglas A. Templeton, *The New Testament as True Fiction: Literature, Literary Criticism, Aesthetics* (Sheffield: Sheffield Academic Press, 1999).
39 Cormac McCarthy, *Blood Meridian, or The Evening Redness in the West* (London: Picador, 1989), p. 215.
40 Ibid, p. 6.
41 Ibid, p. 198.
42 Ibid, p. 199.
43 See, for example, John Keble, "There is a Book who runs may read," in *The Christian Year* (1827), "The Sunday Called Septuagesima."
44 McCarthy, *Blood Meridian*, p. 118. Henceforth page references to *Blood Meridian* will be given in the text.
45 Edward Abbey, *Fire on the Mountain*. (New York: Avon Books, 1992), p. 2.

8

Artists

Georgia O'Keeffe, Bill Viola, and
American Abstract Expressionism

We move in this chapter from the written word to the visual image, from the desert as word to the desert as a place of looking and blinding, and of looking as a necessary act of grasping meaning and losing the sense of it. It may be, as I suggested in chapter 1[1](and Edmond Jabès, I suspect, would agree), that the experience of the desert is primarily auditory rather than visual, and much of this book is about written texts. Nevertheless, the human senses cannot finally be divided, and it has equally been my contention that the wilderness is a *real* place, yet imprinted on the imagination. It is a place where we must keep our eyes open, for the eye may be deceived, and our words then become false. We need also the artists to remind us what it is truly to "see." For all desert literature emphasizes the mirage – the image conjured by the place that is not there, yet is part of the place. In his poem "The Line of the Horizon" in *The Journey* (1985), Edmond Jabès writes:

To see, means to die; to watch, dying.
Wind and sand revel in worsting the eye, making it cry.[2]

The poem records, as Jim Harold has put it, "a bitter-sweet relation between the desert as a topographic site, the act of looking and the drive to understand existence."[3] If the grains of sand are words, they are also the grains of the photograph and the minute splashes of paint. The picture holds the eternal timelessness of the desert, but in its momentariness reflects also its endless shiftings – it is but a moment of time caught in the seeming eternity of the landscape. Our concern in this chapter will not be with the art to be found in the desert, but with art which is inspired and provoked by deserts, both external and interior. Yet on the rocks of Saudi Arabia there are inscriptions that curiously remind us that even this timeless place has been subject to change over millions of years. In January 1879, Lady Anne Blunt, the granddaughter of Lord Byron, and her husband Wilfrid crossed the Nafud Desert on their way to see the city of Hail. They realized that this "great bare space fringed by an ocean of sand and overlooked by a sandstone massif" was, in fact, the site of an ancient, prehistoric lake. In search of inscriptions, of words traced upon the rock, they admitted that they had "hitherto found nothing except some doubtful scratches, and a few of those simple designs one finds everywhere on the sandstone, representing camels and gazelles."[4] It was a place that had once teemed with life, a paradise garden indeed. What it once was has continued to haunt it and those who travel there. It is a new slant on an old, mythic theme. The Paradise *did* once exist, in fact! In 1952 the explorer and writer Harry St. John Philby made a survey of the rock art and inscriptions of south Arabia, but little of his work has ever been published.[5] The desert images remain, frozen in time and largely neglected, yet modern artists have begun to explore the desert in image and abstraction and the myths are reborn. Contemporary artists like Michael Heizer have also inscribed their art on the face of the desert, far from the quiet spaces of art galleries in cities and in a strange continuity that echoes the ancient art of cultures which are distant in both time and place. Heizer's great *Double Negative* (1969–70) is cut into the desert 80 miles outside Las Vegas and is deliberately barely accessible and difficult to find. It is a broken gash across the desert landscape which involved the displacement of 240,000 tons of rock and rubble. The two great trenches across a broken landscape that comprise *Double Negative* have been described by Mark C. Taylor as "the strangest of works":

Frustrating the expectations we have for the work of art, this negative not only inverts but *subverts* the opposites that support the edifice of Western religion, philosophy, and art: primitive/modern, nature/culture, permanence/change, one/many, purpose/chance, placement/displacement, completion/incompletion, active/passive, time/space, speech/silence, sense/nonsense, visible/invisible, appearance/disappearance, form/formlessness, figure/ground, presence/absence, being/nothing, positive/negative . . . Like a gift from some long-lost civilization, this overwhelming petroglyph cannot be decoded but must be read and reread without end.[6]

The life of Georgia O'Keeffe (1887–1986) parallels in a curious way the lives of the great Desert Fathers. She, too, moved out into the spaces of the desert as she withdrew from the life of the city (in her case, New York) and moved to the deserts of New Mexico, becoming what the *New York Times* called "an enigmatic and solitary figure in American art."[7] Fascinated by the dry bones of dead animals lying on the desert floor, she wrote:

> To me they are as beautiful as anything I know. To me they are strangely more living than the animals walking around . . . The bones seem to cut sharply to the center of something that is keenly alive on the desert even tho' it is vast and empty and untouchable – and knows no kindness with all its beauty.[8]

Indifference again: and in death there is most truly life. O'Keeffe's art strangely revisits Ezekiel's valley of dry bones (Ezekiel 37:1–10), perceiving in the dryness a life, although hers, I think, is not a particularly religious vision. Her art acknowledges the life in the emptiness and nothingness of the desert that is beautiful and deadly, without kindness. From the beginning, long before she withdrew into the desert, O'Keeffe's art began a journey from acute and precise observations of the particularities of nature and natural phenomena towards abstraction, a journey that the desert itself seems to provoke and embody. Increasingly reductive, her paintings embrace opposites, a visual *concidentia oppositorum*, of the utterly solid and the void, the surface and the abyss.

Married to a photographer, Alfred Stieglitz, she looked with the piercing truthfulness of the camera lens, yet also with its optical freedom. As early as 1917, Stieglitz asserted:

> The photographer's problem is to see clearly the limitations and at the same time the perennial qualities of his medium, for it is precisely here that honesty no less than intensity of vision is the prerequisite of a living expression. This means a real respect for the thing in front of him.[9]

In the desert, the eye learns this same honesty, its limitations and intensity, and above all the necessary respect for the object before it. O'Keeffe learnt

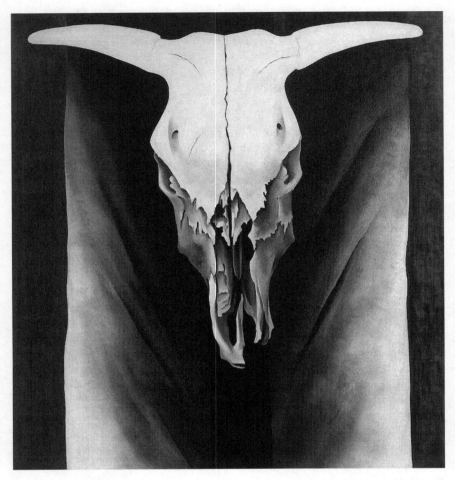

Plate 2   *Georgia O'Keeffe,* Cow's Skull: Red, White and Blue *(1931). The Metropolitan Museum of Art, New York, Alfred Stieglitz Collection, 1949. © ARS, New York and DACS, London 2004.*

to see with a desert vision long before she lived in New Mexico. Already as a young artist she was a romantic, like all desert dwellers, and her precise paintings of flowers taught her to slow down and see the vast in the minute particular, to find eternity in the moment. She wrote:

> That was in the twenties, and everything was going so fast. Nobody had time to reflect . . . There was a cup and saucer, a spoon and a flower, well the flower

was perfectly beautiful. It was exquisite, but it was so small you could not really appreciate it for yourself. So then and there I decided to paint a flower in all its beauty. If you could paint that flower on a huge scale then you could not ignore its beauty.[10]

O'Keeffe's art trains her to see the eternal in the particular and appreciate minute beauties in things as they are. In her own way she discovered the truth of Duns Scotus' sense of *haecceitas* or "thisness," which is also Gerard Manley Hopkins's poetic "inscape": the particularity of the being of each and every "thing." As in all desert experience, there is in O'Keeffe's art a deep sensuality that recalls the temptations suffered by the Fathers as they fought with the demons of sexuality and their own desires.

Her seemingly explicit sexual images in her flower paintings earned from the critic Lewis Mumford the comment that her art was "one long loud blast of sex, sex in youth, sex in adolescence, sex as gaudy as 'Ten Nights in a Whorehouse' and sex as pure as the vigils of the vestal virgin, sex bulging, sex tumescent, sex deflated."[11] Yet her discipline, her asceticism, as an artist actually reflects a passion, erotic indeed, but one that is very different from what Mumford sees. It is, indeed, a purity that fixes only upon the thing in itself, so that she replied indignantly to such comments, born of the decadence and obsession of the city: "You bring all your associations with flowers on my flower, and you write about my flower as if I think and see what you see what you think and see of the flower – and I don't."[12] She replies to Mumford with a simple negative, an absolute refusal. In her art, rather as in the poetry of the medieval woman mystic Hadewijch, the very real sensuality is profoundly transfigured. When she retreats into the desert in later life, her art is ready to respond to the demands of place as she moves from the vertical city skyline of New York, and so it begins to reflect the shift from the vertical to the horizontal that the landscape demands. She herself is also physically present in the art, both defining and defined by the place. Desert, artist, and art begin to merge in a seamless world in which all is united, exactly as the Fathers became, as it were, one with Christ and with all "Being," even in its utter otherness. O'Keeffe's art speaks of a Total Presence. There is an exquisite image, in a photograph by Stieglitz of 1930, of her hands probing the cavities of a horse's skull. It is both beautiful and terrifying – a portrait of life and death in a mutual caress, the hands lovingly and trustingly exploring the dry bone as if searching for the life that is no longer there, yet still a very real, though absent, presence.[13]

In 1979 the American video artist Bill Viola traveled to the Sahara and the result was his installation entitled *Chott el-Djerid (A Portrait in Light and Heat)*. Chott el-Djerid is a vast dry salt lake in the Tunisian Sahara where

Plate 3   *Georgia O'Keeffe*, Black Iris III *(1926). The Metropolitan Museum of Art, New York, Alfred Stieglitz Collection, 1949. © ARS, New York and DACS, London 2004.*

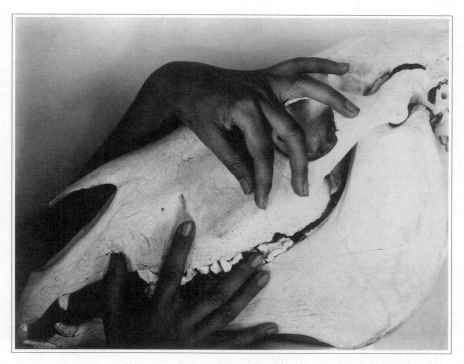

Plate 4   *Alfred Stieglitz,* Georgia O'Keeffe *(1930). The Metropolitan Museum of Art, New York, gift of Georgia O'Keefe through the generosity of The Georgia O'Keefe Foundation and Jennifer and Joseph Duke, 1997.*

mirages are conjured out of the burning, distorted light rays of the midday sun. Viola's intention was to photograph what was "not there" in these distortions, where physical objects appear to float above the ground, and sharp edges become ripples and vibrations. It was, Viola said, "like being inside someone else's dream."[14] Viola's remarkable video, which counterpoints images from the Sahara with images of the winter prairies of Illinois and Saskatchewan where intense cold induces similar experiences of disorientation, takes us again to the desert land of the Fathers – a place that is intensely real, yet also a place of dream – a utopia – which is neither wholly exterior nor interior. Indeed, it is the very intensity of its reality, the imperatives of its extremes of heat and light, that provoke the dream. In a note written on April 29, 1979, Viola comments:

> I want to go to a place that seems like it's at the end of the world. A vantage point from which one can stand and peer out into the void – the world beyond . . . There is nothing to lean on. No references . . .
>
> You finally realize that the void is yourself. It is like some huge mirror for your mind. Clear and uncluttered, it is the opposite of our urban distractive spaces. Out here, the unbound mind can run free. Imagination reigns. Space becomes a projection screen. Inside becomes outside. You can see what you are.[15]

The experience is precisely the opposite of the moment of death described by the poet Emily Dickinson as the instant when light fails and folds in and "I could not see to see."[16] Rather, it is the moment of the most intense life in the void of the self, when the self becomes nothing, the categories of perception and definition are utterly broken, and the verb "to be" stands alone. It is, as Viola says, the end of the world where we see what we are.

Viola visited this theme again in 1994 in the collaborative project *Deserts*, made with music by Edgard Varèse. Viola wrote in a note of January 24, 1992:

> Seeing *is* Being. Aspects of this approach can be observed in the experience of being in the desert. Standing in the vastness, two things happen. First, you feel insignificant – a tiny black speck on the surface of the earth that can be wiped off at any instant. But secondly, a part of you travels out along with that line of sight extending for 50 miles or more and becomes part of that landscape, perception as touching, as contact, becoming a perception.[17]

Viola is a visual artist who moves from image to word and back to image. In a sense, all his video installations are the result of words and the verbal interpretation of visual impressions; the desert *seen* as a place of language, and where language is fulfilled and transfigured. *Deserts* is as much as anything an interior experience born in the mind as a landscape of objects and sounds (Varèse's music). In his handwritten notes for the work Viola repeatedly uses the phrase "objects break surface" – objects freed from the laws of gravity move in the mind's eye like desert mirages and reassemble in a renewed vision. He identifies the following interwoven themes in desert imagery:

– Notions of wilderness and the untouched natural world.
– The "eternal landscape," the presence of an ancient, prehistoric, and post-future time and place.
– Desolate physical existence as an evocation of the "other world" of death, mortality, and non-being.
– The vast distances, extremes in scale, and severe minimalism as the basis of perceptual reorientation and reintegration.
– A physical description of the extremes of the human condition: loneliness, isolation, and solitude.
– Contemporary sites for the ancient and traditional role of the desert as the locale of vision and revelation.[18]

From non-being to being, the video installation translates the solitude of the desert into the inner mind lost in the barren wastelands of city streets, empty parking lots, and bare rooms. The viewer then becomes a modern St. Antony through a visual poetry that transforms desolation into mystery and revelation. It offers hope in the negativities of the "other world," as interiority becomes space illimitable, darkness visible.

Viola has learnt not only from the Sahara Desert, but also from the point where the desert meets the mystical vision of St. John of the Cross (1542–91). In the installation *Room for St. John of the Cross* (1983), he counterpoints the tiny box-like cell where the poet was imprisoned for nine months in 1577, without a window and without room even to stand upright, with a surrounding vision of vast, snow-swept mountains and the sound of rushing winds, which are the true habitation of the saint. From his cell St. John of the Cross reaches out to St. Antony in his interior mountain in the deep desert of Egypt, together realizing that

> In this nakedness the spirit finds its rest,
> for when it covets nothing,
> nothing raises it up,
> and nothing weighs it down,
> because it is in the center of its humility.[19]

At this moment, for St. John of the Cross, theology itself becomes possible again:

> This is the transformation: You will be so at rest in the hand of God that he will be able to teach you anything He desires, knowing that you will not complain, resist or argue. You will grow rich – that is, *rich in the presence of God!*[20]

But this is a journey whose end is also the complete abolition of both faith and doubt. What for St. John of the Cross is the vision of paradise can be, for others, an absolute negation and utter hell. Desert art then bears with the burden of a deep truth that requires that it moves always towards abstraction and the judgment which that move forces upon us. For in utter abstraction we no longer *know*, but can only *be* in a daring to be exposed to what is other and indefinable. In his 1979 video, Viola's figures of people or camels first dissolve into shapes and silhouettes, and finally merge into the abstract haze and mirage heat of the landscape. In a sense, we may say, some of the greatest desert art of the twentieth century is to be found in the pure abstractions of the artists of the New York School of the American Abstract Expressionists, painters and sculptors such as Jackson Pollock, Mark Rothko, and Barnett Newman, who have entered the desert of the mind and met there the intense physical challenges and judgments encountered by all desert travelers – and paid the price. They have moved beyond the epistemological traditions of the Enlightenment mind, beyond Kant (although they carry that burden too), to the spaces of mind as it meets the wholly "other" and is utterly lost. It is right, therefore, that they take their place in our present narrative.

At the beginning of his book *Memoirs of the Blind* (1993) Jacques Derrida insists:

> But skepticism is precisely what I have been talking to you about: the difference between believing and seeing, between believing one sees [*croire voir*] and seeing between, catching a glimpse [*entrevoir*] – or not. Before doubt ever becomes a system, skepsis has to do with the eyes.[21]

In the mirage world of the desert we are caught between seeing and not seeing, between seeing what is there and what is not there – and that instant in which doubt and revelation are equally and maximally present. The beginning of belief and the beginning of unbelief may be one and the same, and in that one instant there is both ecstasy and despair, utter sanity and utter madness.

When Jackson Pollock produced his great drip painting entitled *Cathedral* in 1947 he finally abandoned any suggestion of the mimetic for "all-over painting"; that is, an act of absolute and total immersion in art, another moment of Total Presence, controlled but, as Pollock put it, with no beginning and no end.[22] The painting offers us a profound space that refuses to be bounded by the space of the canvas, suggestive of infinity. There is no reason why the painting should not go on for ever, a deeply romantic, utopian no-place that is everywhere and nowhere. Like the great stained-glass windows of medieval cathedrals, Pollock's painting sheds light, refracts it, becomes a window to another world that we can but glimpse and cannot understand. Perhaps, rather, it *is* that other world: a world that is nothing but window. It is, indeed, a desert space, outside all establishments of religion – a mystical space between the finite and the infinite, its quality of the absolute removing it from the biblical and theological narratives of churches. Pollock's remarkable lines – thickening, thinning, ending in pools of darkness and space and making *that* space possible[23] – share an impulse with ritual and liturgy as fundamental acts of faith that are not even remotely mimetic. They are, rather, acts entirely in and for themselves, pure sacraments, and to look at them demands a total suspension of any articulation of belief, a blindness that is yet visionary and revelatory. In his own way, Pollock was a true desert dweller, restless, homeless and finally absorbed by it – another rider in the chariot.

Paintings like *Cathedral* or *Greyed Rainbow* (1953)[24] have been rightly compared in American culture to the "free jazz" of Ornette Coleman, which abandons prearranged structural limitations and allows the musicians an absolute spontaneity – an individuality in ensemble. The result is "difficult" only because it is an approach to pure music (rather as Jabès' poetry is "difficult" only because we too eagerly seek meaning):[25] that is, improvisation is not upon any "theme," but is entirely the music itself, a pure, spontaneous, and utterly present act of creation and a total improvising upon a ground of silence. It can be heard only when we stop listening for the reassurance of an underlying melody or theme – for there is none. There is only that which is not heard. A harsh, sometimes trackless, music, it can only be listened to by a gesture of resignation or giving, an acceptance of non-understanding (by which the listener begins to become a participant in its ritual, and therefore begins to "know"), and a recognition of its laws of hospitality. They are the ancient laws of the desert. As Coleman himself said:

> The most important thing was for us to play together, all at the same time, without getting in each other's way, and also to have enough room for each player to *ad lib* alone.[26]

Plate 5 *Jackson Pollock,* Cathedral *(1947). Dallas Museum of Fine Arts, Dallas, Gift of Mr and Mrs Bernard J. Reis. © ARS, New York and DACS, London 2004.*

This is, I believe, a pure music that is the sound equivalent of Pollock's art. Does the space of *Cathedral,* or indeed Coleman's music, prompt a re-vision of theological thinking after the act of seeing and hearing – the re-vision of a person once utterly blind or deaf? The space of the painting lies beneath and between the lines of the picture itself; in a sense, what is *not* there is more important than what is – what we see (and perhaps initially attempt to interpret in line and shading) interrupting and disturbing what is more deeply (not) seen in the visionary light beyond and within. We move from the attempt to interpret and articulate to a recognition that this is defeated by something far more profound that is yet still within language.

Space is offered yet more richly, uninterruptedly, and perhaps impersonally in the great canvasses of Mark Rothko.[27] When, at the very end of his life, Rothko executed the paintings that now constitute the walls of the Rothko Chapel in Houston, they were deliberately placed in a religious space (originally intended to be a Roman Catholic chapel) and today exist alongside a chapel containing Christian frescoes rescued from an ancient chapel in Cyprus – a timeless meeting of cultures in art. Rothko's paintings are much more precise and interesting than much of the sea of writing that they have provoked. True, they are clearly not of any particular religious tradition or confession: the Rothko Chapel deliberately extends hospitality to all and every faith, and none. But as Harris Rosenstein has noted,[28] as one looks at them, with an initial response of "there is nothing there," further patient looking and contemplation draws us into a more profound experience that is physical and eventually more than that. First one begins to realize and *feel* that these black surfaces are pulsating and textured in unique and shifting ways. Like the sands of the desert, they are at once still and endlessly moving, so that in them we tend to become disorientated. The movements of the eye become movements of the whole being; looking a journey that has no end, but is an end in itself. These paintings are truly "darkness visible," dark nights of the soul that are at the same time points of vision and enlightenment.

Of course, this does not work for everyone.[29] Judgment again. Such space must always be ambivalent and paradoxical, a place of meeting and encounter, of life and death. In the paintings of the Rothko Chapel and in other works of Rothko, the great blocks of color, quite unlike the mazy lines and junctions of *Cathedral,* do not spread beyond the canvas to infinity, but are themselves infinite. That is, the massive rectangles of color spreading almost, but not quite, to the edge of the canvas, are startling, deep and, most important of all, utterly devoid of the specific personality of the artist. Like St. Antony in the desert, Rothko has given himself up entirely to his art so that he becomes as nothing. That is what makes him so extraordinary.

For his yellows, blacks, and purples *are* space, the artist only reasserting himself in the smudged and sometimes torn lines dividing them from the actual edge of the picture. But to enter into the deep interior of the paintings is utterly to lose oneself and all the signposts of our being. Rothko's paintings of the 1950s, gestures of defiance against the depression that would eventually lead to his suicide, are precise and uncompromising in their utter refusal to entertain the distractions of any traditional narratives, themes, or even images, or to allow any vague religiosity to mar their immediacy and their ascetic beauty. Supreme of all these paintings is the great *Purple, White and Red* (1953) in the Art Institute of Chicago, a true descent into hell that is also and at the same time a resurrection.

The viewer of Rothko's paintings is denied the luxury of recognizing narratives, except perhaps in traces in the sometimes anxious boundaries that separate colors – those nervous moments when we shift from one state of contemplation to another. But these very lines actually accentuate the need to lose ourselves in the contemplation of that which cannot be of us, and cannot be *read* in any biblical or normative sense, but can only be seen in an utter absorption of outer and inner, object and subject. In the traditions of European Romanticism, Rothko has been compared to Caspar David Friedrich and J. M. W. Turner. In them, in the words of the critic Robert Rosenblum referring to a famous painting by Friedrich, "we ourselves are the monk before the sea, standing silently and contemplatively before these huge and soundless pictures as if we were looking at a sunset or a moonlit night."[30] As we gaze at these pictures, we become one with the monk who gazes at the sea or the illimitable desert, our attitude, like that of Rothko himself, one of Kantian detachment,[31] but more than that, with a disinterestedness or indifference that is akin to the religious contemplation of the infinite and the sublime. The image is a precise one. We are *of* the picture, and one with it, and yet remain *detached*, the gazer who merely stands looking. We are, then, both inside and outside the picture, and cannot be the one without being utterly the other. We become wholly ourselves only in the wholly other.

In the work of another artist of the New York School, Willem de Kooning, like Pollock and Rothko, we move from early mythic images to a pure abstraction, from the word spoken to the word which is beyond utterance. In his last works, de Kooning offers to the vision of the human condition not a familiar narrative of salvation but instead, in the 1980s when he was already dying, space and luminosity of line and color which, deeply romantic, draw the gaze through abstract forms that refuse mimetic interpretation to an absolute infinity of light. It is one with the desert light that both blinds and illuminates. Often inspired by an inner eye which draws not

Plate 6   *Mark Rothko,* Untitled *(1953). National Gallery of Art, Washington, gift of the Mark Rothko Foundation, Inc., image © 2003 Board of Trustees. © 1998 Kate Rothko Prizel and Christopher Rothko/DACS 2004.*

directly from nature but, as in reverie or contemplation which is the sanity and poise of true *quies*, and meditating inwardly on its dearly loved beauties, de Kooning's ethereal paintings clear the ground for a language which is so profound we have not yet articulated it, or perhaps have forgotten as in a dream; the language of a theology yet to be uttered. Derrida, again, provides a precise commentary on such art.

The blindness that opens the eye is not the one that darkens vision. The revelatory or apocalyptic blindness, the blindness that reveals the very truth of the eyes, would be the gaze veiled by tears. It neither sees nor does not see: it is indifferent to its blurred vision. It implores: first of all in order to know from where these tears stream down and from whose eyes they come to well up. From where and from whom this mourning or these tears of joy? This essence of the eye, this eye water?[32]

As in the shimmering, hazy landscapes of the late and mature Turner, the viewer's gaze is led through these paintings of de Kooning through color and form to what lies within – not behind – the painting, for the light is *in* the painting: not a God who has utterly died or disappeared, but one wholly present, yet as the merest trace, present though almost forgotten, as in the forgotten dream that continues to haunt us and eludes our grasp.[33] To follow the history of de Kooning's paintings is to move from scenes of violence to a final state of extraordinary light and color, simple, profound, and filled with infinite possibility. When he painted them de Kooning himself was near death.

Like all desert travelers, the artists of the New York School were outsiders and loners. They sought in their art to articulate an immediacy that was outside anything available to them in image, technique, or word. They were pioneers, treading ground that no one had trodden before them, though what they discovered was as old as the hills. It was the recovery of a lost memory. Intuitively, they etched an illegible text that undid earlier narratives in art and made new things possible. In their generation they too were men by whom the world is kept in being. Avoiding institution, as prophets have always done, these artists call finally for a renewal of faith to those with eyes to see, and to see fully. It was not the abandonment of faith, and such faith as they demanded involves risk and adventure – a going out to meet an unknown truth, yet a truth which we recognize as a prodigal returned after long separation. But we are the prodigals. In 1950 the artist Robert Motherwell wrote.

> The process of painting . . . is conceived of as an adventure, without preconceived ideas, on the part of persons of intelligence, sensibility and passion. Fidelity between what occurs between oneself and the canvas, no matter how unexpected, becomes central . . . The major decisions in the process of painting are on the grounds of truth not taste.[34]

These artists were realists, aware always of the demands of the physical elements which they encountered and worked with – and not a few of them paid dearly for it with their own lives. For art, like the desert, can be a cruel master. Barnett Newman, the painter of the magnificent *Stations of the Cross*

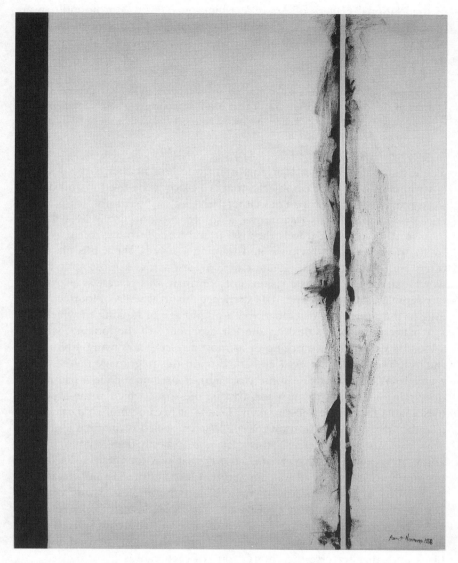

Plate 7   *Barnett Newman*, Stations of the Cross, I *(1958). National Gallery of Art, Washington, Robert and Jane Meyerhoff Collection. Image © 2003 Board of Trustees, © ARS, New York and DACS, London 2004.*

in the National Gallery of Art in Washington, DC, was profoundly aware of the space into which one enters in a work of art. He described this silent place in a description of a synagogue which he designed (it was never constructed – a no-place):

> My purpose is to create a place, not an environment, to deny the contemplation of the objects for the sake of that ultimate courtesy where each person, man or woman, can experience the vision and feel the exaltation of "His trailing robes filling the Temple."[35]

The distinction he makes is an important one. For neither is the desert an environment or a place of objects, that is a place to be lived in and defined from the perspective of living as either "hostile" or "beautiful." It is a place pure and simple, on its own terms, absolute. No one finally lives there as in an earthly city, but travels through it and in it, learning to survive only by the most arduous discipline and training – *askesis*. What this place then offers and demands is the greatest of *courtesies* – it is a most aptly chosen word – an insight into true vision. For Newman, this place was also a place of pilgrimage and journeying. To experience the great series of fourteen paintings of the *Stations* is to embark on a pilgrimage of looking in which subject matter and form vanish in the felt experience of the looking, which is a looking essentially at nothing or at most a trace – a drawing attention to the insight of blindness. As I embarked upon this pilgrimage myself during a visit to Washington, DC some years ago, it became for me a painful and uncertain meditation upon space, that is, the space which *is* the sheer and inescapable meaninglessness of pain. That is, it became more a participation in rather than a meditation on the *via dolorosa* which is the final journey to the Cross, just as the Desert Fathers, far more radically than anything I could know, devised a Christlike *modus vivendi* that was for them a dwelling in his luminous nature in all its pain and its glory.[36] Entering into its depths, yet robbed of the comforts of mimesis and the endless words which so saturate our "poor chattering Christianity,"[37] we share instead the silent, framed space of Newman's paintings, a space of suffering and pain offered to the inner eye undiluted by the sentiment of representation, beyond the stark black lines that traverse the empty "zip" of each canvas.[38]

It has been suggested that the artists of the New York School did not personally need religion in their lives, at least not as an institution or theology. I think this is profoundly true. Nevertheless, Jackson Pollock, Mark Rothko, and Barnett Newman all worked on "religious" projects – they by no means abandoned church, scripture, or theology. Pollock designed windows for an unbuilt chapel,[39] Rothko designed and executed his Chapel, and Newman not only painted his *Stations*, but also large abstracts with biblical titles – *Genesis* (1946), *Abraham* (1949), *Covenant* (1949), and *Joshua* (1950), among others. Such works constitute exercises in scripture and sublimity that prompt the possibility of religious language and theological thinking when, for many, they have become impossible. Barnett Newman put it most articulately in 1948 in a essay entitled "The Sublime is Now":

> The question that now arises is how, if we are living in a time without a legend or mythos that can be called sublime, if we refuse to admit any exaltation in pure relations, if we refuse to live in the abstract, how can we be creating a sublime art? *We are reasserting man's natural desire for the exalted, for a concern with our relationships to the absolute emotions.* We do not need the obsolete props of an outmoded and antiquated legend . . . We are freeing ourselves of the impediments of memory, association, nostalgia, legend, myth or what have you, that have been the devices of Western European painting. *Instead of making cathedrals out of Christ, man or "life," we are making them out of ourselves, out of our own feelings.* The image we produce is the self-evident one of revelation, real and concrete, that can be understood by anyone who will look at it without the nostalgic glasses of history.[40]

The Fathers of the desert would have understood well what Newman is saying here. They, too, were building cathedrals. Freeing themselves of all impedimenta, of everything that was holding them back, they ran the race to win absolutely.[41] And yet their vision was a universal one, concrete and utterly untheoretical. In their realization of *apatheia* they became what they sought, they made it out of themselves.

What I have suggested in this chapter, in the art of Georgia O'Keeffe, Bill Viola, and the painters of the New York School of Abstract Expressionists, is that we find an asceticism that takes us to a place, a space that invites the impossible possibility of absolute vision – that is, a vision in which faith and knowledge become utterly one. It is both an end and a beginning, and absolutely so. Through the infinitely complex and deeply romantic tracery of Pollock's *Cathedral*, we glimpse for ourselves the desert space which blooms in the hope of the forgotten dream which does not forget us.[42]

Notes

1 See p. 3.
2 Edmond Jabès, *From the Book to the Book: An Edmond Jabès Reader*, translated by Rosemarie Waldrop (Hanover, NH: Wesleyan University Press, 1991), p. 202.

3   Jim Harold, introduction to *Desert* (Southampton: John Hansard Gallery, 1996), p. 10.

4   Quoted in Peter Harrigan, "Art Rocks in Saudi Arabia," *Saudi Aramco World*, vol. 53, no. 2 (March/April 2002), p. 37.

5   Much of Philby's research remains in manuscripts in St. Antony's College, Oxford.

6   Mark C. Taylor, *Disfiguring: Art, Architecture, Religion* (Chicago: University of Chicago Press, 1992), pp. 272–3.

7   Quoted in Roxana Robinson, *Georgia O'Keeffe: A Life* (London: Bloomsbury Publishing, 1990), p. 481.

8   Quoted in Lisa Mintz Messinger, *Georgia O'Keeffe* (New York: Thames and Hudson, 1988), p. 72.

9   Beaumont Newhall, *The History of Photography*, revd. edn. (London: Secker and Warburg, 1964), p. 114.

10   Quoted in Edward Lucie-Smith, *American Realism* (London: Thames and Hudson, 1994), p. 89. Compare Julian of Norwich's vision of the hazel nut that is "all that is made," in *Revelations of Divine Love*, translated by Clifton Wolters (Harmondsworth: Penguin Books, 1966), p. 68.

11   Quoted in Roxana Robinson, *Georgia O'Keeffe: A Life*, p. 282.

12   Ibid.

13   See further, Lisa Mintz Messinger, *Georgia O'Keeffe*, pp. 72–6.

14   Bill Viola, *Reasons for Knocking at an Empty House: Writings 1973–1994* (London: Thames and Hudson, 1995), p. 55.

15   Ibid, p. 54.

16   Emily Dickinson, "I heard a fly buzz," in Thomas H. Johnson (ed.), *The Collected Poems of Emily Dickinson* (London: Faber and Faber, 1970), p. 224.

17   Bill Viola, *Reasons for Knocking at an Empty House*, p. 260.

18   Ibid, p. 262.

19   St. John of the Cross, quoted in Bill Viola, *Reasons for Knocking at an Empty House*, p. 117.

20   St. John of the Cross, "Living Flame of Love," in David Hazard, *You Set My Spirit Free: A 40-Day Journey in the Company of St. John of the Cross* (Minneapolis, MN: Bethany House Publishers, 1994), p. 163.

21   Jacques Derrida, *Memoirs of the Blind: The Self-Portrait and Other Ruins*, translated by Pascale-Anne Brault and Michael Naas (Chicago: University of Chicago Press, 1993), p. 1. This book was written on the occasion of an exhibition of the same name in the Louvre Museum, Paris in 1991.

22   See Irving Sandler, *The Triumph of American Painting: A History of Abstract Expressionism* (New York: 1970), pp. 110–11.

23   Frank O'Hara notes Pollock's "amazing ability to quicken a line by thinning it, to slow it by flooding, to elaborate that simplest of elements, the line – to change, to reinvigorate." Quoted in David Britt (ed.), *Modern Art: Impressionism to Post-Modernism* (London: Thames and Hudson,

1989), p. 265. His art reduces all to a minimum, and then begins to explore that condition in all its extraordinary complexity.

24 In the Art Institute of Chicago.

25 See chapter 6, p. 83.

26 Ornette Coleman, from notes to the LP *Free Jazz* (Atlantic SD1364, 1961).

27 See also chapter 1, pp. 6–7.

28 See above, p. 7.

29 See, for example, Graham Ward's dismissive commentary on the Rothko Chapel in *True Religion* (Oxford: Blackwell, 2003).

30 Robert Rosenblum, "The Abstract Sublime," *Art News*, vol. 59, no. 10 (February 1961); reprinted in Henry Geldzahler, *New York Painting and Sculpture: 1940–1970* (New York: E. P. Dutton, 1969), p. 353.

31 Neither the word nor the concept actually appears in the exploration of aesthetic experience in Kant's *Third Critique*. See Jacques Derrida, *The Truth in Painting*, translated by Geoff Bennington and Ian McLeod (Chicago: University of Chicago Press, 1987), pp. 39–40.

32 Jaques Derrida, *Memoirs of the Blind*, pp. 126–7.

33 See Peter Baelz, *The Forgotten Dream: Experience, Hope and God* (London: Mowbrays, 1975), written "not to establish a position but to explore a predicament," p. vii.

34 Quoted in Anthony Everett, "Abstract Expressionism," in David Britt, *Modern Art*, p. 266.

35 Quoted in Lawrence Alloway, *Barnett Newman: The Stations of the Cross* (New York: Guggenheim Museum, 1966), exhibition catalogue, p. 36.

36 See James Cowan, *Journey to the Inner Mountain: In the Desert with St. Antony* (London: Hodder and Stoughton, 2002), pp. 126–7.

37 This arresting phrase is from E. M. Forster's novel *A Passage to India* (1924).

38 The term "zip" is Newman's own, his name for the empty, biscuit-colored space that occupies almost the whole of each painting.

39 See A. E. Carmen, Jr., "The Church Project: Pollock's Passion Themes," *Art in America* 70.6 (1982), pp. 110–12.

40 Barnett Newman, "The Sublime is Now," *The Tiger's Eye*, no. 6 (December, 1948), pp. 51–3 (emphasis added).

41 1 Corinthians 9:24.

42 "It was hardly reasonable of Nebuchadnezzar to ask his wise men not only to interpret his dream for him but also to tell him what it was that he had dreamed. But he had a reason for his request. His spirit was troubled. He had forgotten the dream. The dream, however, had not forgotten him." Peter Baelz, *The Forgotten Dream*, p. viii.

9

Films of the Desert
Pier Paolo Pasolini, Wim Wenders, and Claire Denis

> Life and literature: Pasolini bound them tightly together to the point of
> confusing them, to the point that they cancelled each other out, and then, by
> a miracle, were reborn from their ashes entirely distinct, each with its own
> appearance, or were sublimated into a utopia similar to a negative theology.[1]

In David Lean's 1962 film *Lawrence of Arabia* we are only very tangentially
in the world of *The Seven Pillars of Wisdom*. As always with the desert,
however, there are continuities in the very landscape's capacity to evoke
extremes of emotion – deep love and profound hatred, the sense of living
on the edge and the endless journeys, the nomadic life. In the film, the desert
is a brooding, ubiquitous presence which defines every thought, every
action, and every relationship. It is also highly romanticized and contrived.
Yet still against its definition, human politics, the Arab Revolt, and the war
with Turkey are merely pretexts, a passing foreground to the greater events
beneath and within the mind of Lawrence himself.

The film begins in the green landscape of England and presents Lawrence as an enigma, a mystic even, laying a sheen over the complexities and rest-lessness of the real Lawrence who was, it would seem, a man born for the desert yet self-destructive, self-sufficient, at once solitary and sociable, restless and beset with demons, and without a real home. E. M. Forster sensitively caught the spirit of the man, describing Lawrence in the cottage he owned at Cloud's Hill, where he could "reject intimacy without impairing affection" (one thinks, perhaps, of the Desert Fathers in their cells, of the solitary Antony or Pachomius in community, or the Bedouin in their tents).

I don't know whether I'm at all conveying in these remarks the atmosphere of the place – the happy casualness of it; and the feeling that no one particu-larly owned it. T. E. had the power of distributing the sense of the posses-sion among all the friends who came there. When Thomas Hardy turned up, for instance, as he did one sunny afternoon, he seemed to come on a visit to us all, and not especially to see his host. Thomas Hardy and Mrs. Hardy came up the narrow stairway into the little brown room and there they were – the guests of us all. To think of Cloud's Hill as T. E.'s is to get the wrong idea of it. It wasn't his home, it was rather his *pied-a terre*, the place where his feet touched the earth for a moment and found rest.[2]

It takes one writer, or poet even, to recognize another. For it is, as we have seen, in the inextricable connection between his writing and his experiences in the desert that Lawrence most truly and mysteriously lives, and in this gap, this interstice, he is also lost. In other respects, like all true desert dwellers, he is a restless wanderer without a home except for the place where his dwelling is put for the night. There are few moments in the film which begin to capture this quality, but when they do the effect is profound.

As always, the desert is the "other," a place to be gone into from the established and ordered military buildings and machinery of Cairo. It is a place of wanderings and out of step with modernity, helpless against the violence of modern machines of war, until the spirit of those who travel within it, the warring Arab tribes, finds its focus in the awkward young English army officer. As Lawrence, played by Peter O'Toole, begins his journey across the desert, he is led by a Bedouin towards Prince Feisal's camp. He is utterly different from the Arab, utterly unsuited for survival in the desert. Light haired and pale skinned he comes from Oxfordshire. But even there he is an outsider, for, he tells his companion, people from his homeland are fat, unlike the lean and athletic nomads of the desert. But he is different, for he is thin and frail – almost like the pale Messiah of Ernest Renan's imaginings in his *Vie de Jésus* (1863). He is haunted by his illegitimacy, a man living on the borders and nowhere at home. As they rest and drink at a well, a rider comes to them out of the desert. As always, the desert is a place of meeting and journeying, a place to be entered into, and from which emerges mysterious strangers, demons. At first, in a long shot that is perhaps the most haunting moment of the film, the black dot appears to be hovering above the surface of the land. In the shimmering heat it looks like a mirage, seen and at the same time indecipherable. Only gradually does the black dot begin to take on the shape of a man mounted on a finely arrayed camel. The man, Sherif Ali ibn el Hussein, richly attired, brings death – Lawrence's companion is not of his tribe, the Harith, and should not have been drinking at the well. For Lawrence, it is different. He is welcome, the outsider and desert hospitality cannot deny him refreshment.

The scene has a mythic status: indifference to life – hospitality. Who, or what, is the mystery that emerges from the vastness of the desert? It is somehow more than a man. A mirage? Something in the mind's eye? A stranger who is both friend and foe? Or is it the inner self whom we meet in this lonely place? In Matthew 4:3 the Tempter comes and speaks to Jesus while he is alone in the desert. The Greek word is *peirazon*, from the verb meaning to make trial of, or perhaps even to seduce. Jesus is tested – by the Devil or by his own inner demons? In Pier Paolo Pasolini's film *Il Vangelo secondo Matteo* (*The Gospel According to St. Matthew*) (1964), Jesus is met by a dusty, rather shabby figure in another scene in which we watch as a dusty speck moves towards the figure of Jesus and towards the viewer, and gradually is transformed into a man, rather ordinary at close quarters, though in the desert nothing is ordinary. Yet Jesus, who is kneeling in prayer in the vast spaces of the wilderness, remains somehow strangely solitary. The film has caught something of the mystery of the hauntings of the Desert Fathers, as they struggled in their solitary encounters with this dark, ordinary figure. It is there also in the scene from *Lawrence of Arabia*.

But we may superimpose another similar scene on this moment in Pasolini's film. Alongside *The Gospel According to St. Matthew* another film was shot, a documentary made during a journey to Israel by Pasolini as he was preparing to make his film. The documentary is entitled *Sopralluoghi in Palestina* (*On Location in Palestine*). It was shot, not by Pasolini's cameraman, but by a news footage cameraman, the voice-over an improvised commentary by Pasolini himself. He was accompanied by Don Andrea, a priest of Pro Civitate Christiana in Assisi. Pro Civitate Christiana was founded in 1939, not to proselytize but to practice a social gospel of good works, "inspired by a sense of the sacred as self-sufficient." Beside him in the film, Pasolini is the Marxist "alight with the fire of the sacred."[3] There are some odd ironies about these two films, one a preparation for the other.

The documentary is now almost forgotten, while the gospel film itself is justly famous. *Sopralluoghi* was actually filmed in the Judean desert. *Il Vangelo* was filmed in Calabria with only the memory of the desert in Pasolini's mind. In Israel Pasolini saw the past in all its immensity and allure almost erased by the incursions of a modernity which he loathed. Yet here were still the memories and the traces which he sought, to be realized in *Il Vangelo* in the south of Italy with a miscellaneous cast drawn from various parts of Italy and (in the case of Christ) Spain. The analogy to the lost biblical reality in Calabria proved to be a clearer reality than the modern Israel – though there the dreams still lingered. Calabria became Pasolini's deep desert, his Paneremos, and at the same time his text upon which he inscribed his art. In Sam Rohdie's words, "artifice exhibited was the means to a hidden truth."[4]

And yet it was in the Holy Land itself that Pasolini "saw" the Jesus who was translated onto the film, shot in Italy, of Matthew 4 and the tempta-tion in the wilderness. Andrei Ujica records the genesis of the scene from a moment in *Sopralluoghi*:

> Pasolini and Father Andrea are riding in a Fiat across the desert, soaking up the pictorial simplicity of the Holy Land on a scale with the sublime as described in the scriptures. He is seen grappling with the gap between perception and memory. The car stops, the two men get out and take a few steps. Pasolini realizes that it would be impossible, in Italy, to reproduce the impression of the desert. There are similar landscapes in the region around Etna, but the impact of this sheer immensity, the vast horizon in particular, could not be conveyed.
>
> They get back into the car but don't start off right away. Pasolini is at the steering wheel, and Father Andrea in the front passenger seat. They grow silent. Pasolini turns around and his expression is riveted on the desert through the rear window. Jesus is there, praying, kneeling down, his arms raised towards the sky. What Pasolini sees is a scene from *Il Vangelo secondo Matteo*.[5]

Jesus, like his demon, emerges from the desert, but only in the mind of the watcher. He is there and yet not there. His presence in the wilderness is in the mind of Pasolini, schooled by the gospel text, and will be realized for us by an actor in an unreal desert that takes us back, uncannily, to the fiction of Matthew's text and to an encounter there recorded which perhaps took place, perhaps did not, two thousand years ago in the same Judean wilderness – but has become part of our spiritual mythology. The desert, as always, blurs our reality, but there we encounter the things of greatest reality. Sight and sound are internalized, and the filmmaker makes the film, the theolo-gian his or her theology. We see, and do not see, we hear, and do not hear. Ujica continues:

We continue with images from *Vangelo*. Jesus gets up and walks through the desert. He is silent but we hear what he is thinking . . . Then Jesus walks towards the sea and walks on the water.[6]

In the film, as in the desert, the "intemporal purity" of the landscape and the inner mind of the man become merged, inseparable, illustrating the "tautological perfection of God (God is perfect because he is perfect)." That tautology might, indeed, well describe Pasolini's own religion. A Marxist, he did not believe in God, but he was acutely sensitive to the sacred and its necessary presence in the world. It is as though his films – political statements, just as the gesture of Antony and his followers was also a political statement – are a reminder of those things by which the world is kept in being. Pasolini's Christ is an angry, passionate, loving figure, but an outsider. Sam Rohdie sums this up well:

> But [Pasolini] did believe in, and could identify imaginatively with, the belief of the people who believed in the Ascension and in Christ. It was this belief that created the magic event of Christ rising to heaven, since life as it was then was a sacred one in which miracles were believed to have occurred. Christ was not crucified once but repeatedly. The message of his sacrifice and resurrection was embedded in a popular world. That world, and Christ, had been and were being eliminated by the other world that had crucified Christ, hence the repetitiveness of the Crucifixion. The fathers who killed Christ had killed Oedipus, had tried to kill Pasolini's poetry. Christ crucified therefore was a revolutionary sign of the sacred against the profane of authority.[7]

In another film by Pasolini, taken not from scriptural myth but from the equally valid Greek myth of Oedipus, the desert remains a place of journey and encounter, but here with a violence that is resolved only in tragedy. Pasolini's script for *Edipe Re* (*Oedipus Rex*) (1967) was written before shooting began and contains scenes and dialogue which do not appear in the film itself, which was shot largely in the deserts of Morocco. Once again the script exists only in the mind of the author, to be translated back subsequently into a dramatic visual form that imprints itself upon our minds as we watch. Pasolini describes the road to Thebes:

> Oedipus is walking along the road that leads to far-off Thebes. He is alone, but not sad. He has resigned himself to his destiny: that of a man who can never go back, who must always press onwards, out into the wide world waiting for him . . . The road in front of him winds into the haze of the far-off horizon. A road without end, a road leading to a whole in the shape of a void. Dissolve.[8]

The void eventually takes a mundane shape. It is the carriage of his father, escorted by five soldiers and a slave, whom Oedipus kills in a bloody confrontation. In other respects, his solitary desert journey is that of the Fathers on an unending road leading them from all that is familiar to a void that will eventually take a shape, to be fought with until, for them, for Antony, Evagrius, Patermuthius, and others even more hidden, the void becomes the tautologous perfection of God. The real encounters are deep in the past, in the physicality of the desert, but translated, as John Cassian and others translated the authentic desert into the theology of Western monasticism. The filmmaker Pasolini makes his own synthesis and translation, which is then taken back into the visual narrative of the film as it impresses the Moroccan landscape onto our minds, taken up with the myth of Oedipus. He describes the inauthentic/authentic nature of his art, at the heart of which are the timeless rocks and sands of the desert itself:

> In a particular film . . . reality is dead and thrown back upon the past, where it is gathered or collected into an idea . . . the aestheticism and humor which I allowed to guide me were inauthentic and shameful, because they are typical of a bourgeois intellectual. But at the same time they were in fact authentic and real because they belonged to a man who is relating things already deep in the past.[9]

In such filmmaking Pasolini is engaged in a act of *anamnesis* or remembering. Yet he, too, remains a solitary. He begins one of his greatest poems, *Versi del Testamento* (*Lines from the Testament*), with words that describe all the desert travelers we have encountered:

> Solitude: you must be very strong
> to love solitude; you have to have good legs
> and uncommon resistance . . .[10]

The theme of inauthenticity/authenticity underlies Wim Wenders' film *Paris, Texas* (1984), which begins with a solitary figure walking through and out of the Mojave Desert, going, apparently, nowhere and out of a mysterious past. The German director has chosen Texas to symbolize the modern American "city," "a world of surfaces increasingly deprived of memory or self-reflection, where fantasy and reality have become so confused and the notion of self-identity so diluted that it no longer seems possible to tell one's story."[11] Here Travis, played by Harry Dean Stanton, searches for an authentic "memory," a forgotten dream located only in faded photography of a derelict piece of land in "Paris, Texas" – an ironic comment on the "real" Paris, France, for him an unattainable, almost unimaginable, ideal city. Paris, Texas is a utopia nearer home, though it does exist in the dust of Texas not far from Dallas, but also a place of origins, for it was here that Travis believes he was conceived. He has another faded photograph, of himself, his lost wife Jane, and their son Hunter – his family, another forgotten dream.[12]

Wenders, a lover of cities, has also admitted his passion for "empty landscapes like deserts."[13] His film *To the End of the World* concludes in the Australian desert at "an end" of the world that is both temporal and spatial. As a director, Wenders describes himself as "entering a landscape that a lot of previous explorers have been through and left their traces in, and you use a language and a grammar that others have used before you, in order to tell a similar kind of story."[14] He joins our company of travelers, also (like Pasolini) a writer for whom books speak together with a kind of music, "a choir of mankind."[15] But it is through the medium of film, and ultimately through the act of seeing, of "being there," that Wenders realizes his purpose of finding and offering *quies*, rest. He has said: "Films are there to take away fear, and create peace and serenity."[16]

Paris, Texas opens, in Wenders' own words, with the image of "a man leaving the freeway and walking straight into the desert."[17] For four years Travis endures his desert purgatory, lost to the world, walking without purpose, abandoning the roads that are highways to the American dream. He does not speak – he imposes on himself an ascetic discipline in a complete disappearance from the world, losing his name and his identity until tracked down by his brother, into whose family his son Hunter has been adopted. Wenders, however, has compared Travis's initial condition to a kind of autism, a refusal to acknowledge the world outside and a living entirely within himself. He goes on writing of

> How affection or love become impossible if you concentrate too hard on an image of yourself or of someone else. That happened in *Paris, Texas*, where Travis, the jealous guy, had too strong an image in his head of his young and beautiful wife, which finally got in the way of his actually seeing her. And I think the obverse of a love story – for *me* anyway – is always that problem when you don't see the other person any more, only the image you have of him or her. Or, more fundamentally, when you fall in love with an image – actually more of yourself than of the other person. That moment when they fall into that autistic narcissism spells the end of the love.[18]

It is from this hellish desert that Travis emerges, to embark on a journey that will repair his isolation and his family, but at the final cost of himself and an exit into another desert at the end of the film. In order to redeem, and to be redeemed, Travis must disappear.

Journeying is the central motif of the film. Travis refuses to fly with his brother to Los Angeles. For to fly in a modern jet plane is not to travel but to hang suspended in a moment of anonymous time between two places. He must cross the surface of the land and thereby recognize and respect its spaces.

When Travis is eventually taken back to the city, to his brother's home in Los Angeles (this brother, Walt, significantly makes billboard signs, huge advertisements for the world from which Travis has fled), he begins to rebuild his relationship with his son, Hunter. He is the "hunter," the seeker and guide back to Travis's lost wife and his own lost mother, and so together they embark on another journey, back to Texas and the recovery of the lost world of the family as they search for Jane. In Walt's house, Travis has watched grainy family home movies of himself and Jane in the halcyon days of their marriage. Like all desert journeys his is a voyage towards a utopia, a lost paradise, a "reconfiguration of a disordered place into a restoration of a pre-lapsarian paradise"[19] that is also the places of origins and lost innocence. But to be redeemed, the vision has to meet a reality – Travis's flight must become a journey *through* the desert and its hardships.

For Jane has to be found and rescued in a narrative which has overtones of the Orpheus and Eurydice myth. Travis must enter into the underworld, which here is the red-light area of Houston, where Jane is working in a peep-show club, an image or simulacrum of reality to satisfy the voyeuristic fantasies of paying customers, trapped in a system of one-way mirrors in which she can be seen but not see. But as we have discovered and as always, it is finally only in words that recovery is to be found. In this underworld it is in words and narratives that redemption becomes possible and paradise regained in a place of mirrors and reflections. When Travis finds Jane, the club allows him to see her, while she cannot see him. It is only when, using the telephone system that is the means of communication, he turns his back on her and tells their story (and in the film we see his face imaged upon and one with Jane's in the mirror), that they can begin to find each other, to remember and build on their memories. Wenders has commented in interviews that at this point in the film he abandoned the script and allowed the actors – Stanton and Kinski – to use their own words. They ceased to act, and became the characters they were portraying, and the result is a narrative of almost unbearable honesty and beauty as Jane begins to realize who this faceless "customer" actually is.

The great desert expanses of the opening scenes of *Paris, Texas* continue to dominate the film. Travis enters the desert, must leave it and then return again in order to find his "Paris" and repair the Trinity of his family.[20] The cityscapes of Los Angeles and Houston are the desert's opposite, crisscrossed by roads and the lights of airports, images of journeys that Travis cannot make, for his is a greater journey than can be attained by modern and ultimately alienating transport systems. Almost in the middle of the film, we see Travis walking across a flyover that spans a massive freeway in Los Angeles, and there meeting a mad prophet, speaking to the empty air as the cars rush past (as the script indicates) "like a voice crying in the wilderness." He preaches as if to the drivers, isolated and deaf in their cars and cabs:

> I make you this promise on my mother's head, or right here and now, standing on the very head of my mother, our Good Green Mother Earth, which anybody who wasn't born in a fuckin' sewer ought to know and understand to the very marrow of their bones . . . There is nowhere, absolutely nowhere in this godforsaken valley . . . Not one square foot will be a safety zone . . . You will all be extradited to the land of no return. You'll be flying blind to nowhere. And if you think that's going to be fun, you've got another thing coming.[21]

Like John the Baptist, the mad prophet speaks from the wilderness, a hopeless, homeless voice. Nor does Travis find a square foot to be a safety zone for his family. Paris, Texas, the place of origin, is no place and he never goes there, but in the desert he finds his forgotten dream. At the end of the film, through Travis, Hunter is reunited with his mother, released from the fetish images of the peep-show club by Travis' healing narrative of words. But it is a place that Travis himself cannot inhabit – like Orpheus, he cannot look back – and the film concludes with him driving away past a poster bearing the slogan "Together We Make It Happen." Like the mad scullery maid in the *Lausiac History*, he disappears into the wilderness and where he goes no one knows. He must be silent, without name or speech, the "excluded one [who] renders possible an entire circulation."[22] Travis is a wanderer, a desert traveler, one of those "by whom the world is kept in being," and through him the dream of "Paris" is actually realized for Hunter and Jane.

The desert in Claire Denis' film *Beau Travail* (1998) is not the place of journey so much as the edge, the border of the mysterious "other." The film is set in the northeastern African nation of Djibouti, where a company of the French Foreign Legion is stationed. The men have come from the cultured place of France, the "city" that is the equivalent of Los Angeles or Houston in *Paris, Texas*. But in *Beau Travail* the desert is not an interior (except at one crucial point in the film). Rather, the company is stationed at its edge, by the sparkling sea, which we see them crossing in boats, swimming or fishing in. They live on a border between the city and the desert. Socially, too, they live on a borderland. The film begins with a visit to a dance club in the town and the beautiful African girls who have adopted for them the music and dances of the West. But as legionnaires they live in a wholly masculine world, endlessly training, practicing the rigorous ascetic disciplining of the body through which alone, like all desert travelers, they can survive. Denis choreographs the training sequences like a ballet, or perhaps a liturgical dance: beautifully stylized and slow-motion images of the bodies of the men challenging and then becoming one with the desert sands. Asceticism can take more than one form.

Beau Travail is a reworking of Herman Melville's novella *Billy Budd, Sailor*, the tragedy of the Handsome Sailor who strikes the evil master-at-arms Claggart, described by Melville as "a man about five-and-thirty, somewhat spare and tall, yet of no ill figure upon the whole."[23] In the film, Claggart becomes the sergeant Galoup, the "perfect legionnaire," and this is his tragedy. For his perfection, like Billy Budd's, is flawed. Almost all of the script is a voice-over by Galoup. He is a man without personal attachments, utterly devoted to the routine of training, domestically self-sufficient. But then appears a handsome young recruit from France, Sentain, equally a man without attachments or family. He quickly attracts the jealousy of Galoup, not least in the face of the unit commander Forestier (the film's version of Melville's Captain Edward Fairfax Vere). Forestier, unlike Galoup, oversees his men like a father, yet with a distance and indifference that never once falters. Almost like the leader of a religious community, like the God of the desert, his care is utterly without sentiment – he is described by Galoup as a man without ideals. Eventually it is Galoup, in jealous rage and as an indirect way of inflicting his rage against Sentain, who administers an unduly harsh punishment on a soldier, and when he denies the suffering man water, Sentain lashes out at him with his fist.

Galoup's response is to take him into the heart of the desert and leave him to find his way back – with a damaged compass. Eventually, close to death beside a salt lake, Sentain is found by desert travelers (one is reminded again of St. Antony), and brought back to life by the African girl whom we had first seen in the disco at the beginning of the film. Now, however, she has abandoned her "Westernized" ways to become again herself, an African, a desert dweller. Throughout the film the world of the legionnaires is counterpointed with the indigenous world of the African women, and into this "lost" world Sentain disappears. He is never seen again by the French soldiers. Like the madwoman, like Travis, he disappears and becomes dead to the world. In effect he has become one with the desert utopia, with the perfect world that always lies within and beyond the desert, the world apart from the cities of people. Ironically, it is the world of perfection sought but never reached by the ritualistic ascetic training of the legionnaires. Sentain disappears, but he remains as a judgment on Galoup. For he must return to France, to the city of Marseilles, a man not fit to be a soldier and unfit to be a civilian. In a way like Lawrence, the desert has judged him. Like the Desert Fathers, he sought perfection, but he never forgot himself and it issued only in jealousy for the self's perfection, and not in selflessness. Obsessive to the last, we see him finally make his perfect soldier's bed, and then, the final scene, return to the world of the dance club, where he performs a solo dance that is a parody of the legionnaires' beautiful training "dances," a pastiche in the city of people of the aesthetics of the desert. At the beginning the legionnaires, himself included, are dressed in white. In his final dance he is dressed all in black and is alone. It is the dance of death, as he spins off the stage.

In the desert there is tragedy and there is salvation. *Beau Travail* attains what Melville describes as "the symmetry of form attainable in pure fiction."[24] In the art of film, as in the literature of the desert, word and image themselves become both the medium and the subject of the unutterable purity of the wilderness, an absolute purity that eventually takes Sentain into the "no-place" of its silent interior, a place that exists only in the mirage created by the effect of heat on sand and rock, and only in the words and images of those who speak and see what is beyond image and word. Such would be, in Wim Wenders' phrase, a perfect "act of seeing."[25]

Notes

1 Enzo Siciliano, foreword to Pier Paolo Pasolini, *Poems*, translated by Jonathan Galassi (New York: Random House, 1982), p. x.

2 E. M. Forster, quoted in Edward W. Said, *Reflections on Exile and Other Literary and Cultural Essays* (London: Granta Books, 2001), p. 33.

3 Sam Rohdie, *The Passion of Pier Paolo Pasolini* (Bloomington: Indiana University Press, 1995), p. 161.

4 Ibid, p. 163.

5 Andrei Ujica, "2 Pasolini, June 2000," in *The Desert*. Fondation Cartier pour l'art contemporain (London: Thames and Hudson, 2000), pp. 207–8.

6 Ibid.

7 Sam Rohdie, *The Passion of Pier Paolo Pasolini*, p. 164.

8 Pier Paolo Pasolini, *Oedipus Rex*, translated by John Mathews (London: Lorrimer Publishing, 1971), pp. 48–9.

9 Pasolini, "Why That of Oedipus is a Story," in *Oedipus Rex*, p. 10.

10   Pier Paolo Pasolini, *Poems*, selected and translated by Norman MacAfee with Luciano Martinengo (New York: Random House, 1982), p. 211.

11   Richard Kearney, *The Wake of Imagination* (London: Routledge, 1988), p. 324. See also J. Hillman, *Interviews* (San Francisco: Harper and Row, 1983), pp. 127–8.

12   The reference here is to Peter Baelz's 1974 Bampton Lectures, published as *The Forgotten Dream*. See above, chapter 8, note 42, p. 129.

13   Wim Wenders, *The Act of Seeing: Essays and Conversations*, translated by Michael Hofmann (London: Faber and Faber, 1997), p. 49.

14   Ibid, p. 183.

15   Ibid, p. 161.

16   Ibid, p. 194.

17   Quoted by D. Hounam in a review article on *Paris, Texas. In Dublin*, 214 (1984), pp. 10–11.

18   Wim Wenders, *The Act of Seeing*, p. 58.

19   Philip Sheldrake, *Spaces for the Sacred* (London: SCM, 2001), p. 42.

20   On the Trinitarian metaphor in *Paris, Texas*, see Kearney, *The Wake of Imagination*, p. 327.

21   *Paris, Texas* (Berlin: Road Movies, 1984), pp. 45–55.

22   Michel de Certeau, *The Mystic Fable*, vol. 1, translated by Michael B. Smith (Chicago: University of Chicago Press, 1992), p. 34.

23   Herman Melville, *Billy Budd, Sailor* (1924) (Harmondsworth: Penguin Books, 1970), p. 342.

24   Ibid, p. 405.

25   In his film *To the End of the World* Wenders has his character Dr. Farber, in the Australian desert, obsessed with making his blind wife "see," and with registering perfect images in her brain that bypass, so to speak, the refractions and distortions of the eye. Perfect vision would thus be not to "see" at all.

10

Desert Theology and Total Presence

The Poets William Blake and Yves Bonnefoy Meet Hegel and Tom Altizer

And so faith at once "decenters" us, for it disintegrates the experiential structures of selfhood on which, in experience, we center ourselves, and at the same time draws us into the divine love where we are "recentered" upon a ground beyond any possibility of experience.[1]

[The soul that] wants to go into the simple ground, into the quiet desert, into which distinction never gazed, not the Father, nor the Son, nor the Holy Spirit . . . this ground is a simple silence, in itself immovable, and by this immovability all things are moved, all life is received by those who in themselves have rational being.[2]

The quiet desert of Meister Eckhart has never quite left us, if only because it was known to Hegel, and has been repeated again in our own time by the theologian Thomas J. J. Altizer, who asserts in a brief commentary on the *Phenomenology of Spirit* (1807) that "the most important movement of his [Hegel's] dialectic, the negation of negation, was anticipated in a mystical form by Eckhart."[3] It is Altizer also who has recognized that the joy of solitude can only come from a profound decentering which is "a loss reversing every manifest or established center of our interior so as to make possible the advent of a wholly new but totally immediate world."[4] Every true desert traveler, as we have seen, experiences such decentering, though some, like T. E. Lawrence, it utterly fragments and destroys. It is no accident that the life of St. Antony has been equated by James Cowan in his book *Journey to the Inner Mountain* (2002), in some respects at least, with another seeker in deserts of the spirit, the Marquis de Sade – yet they are total opposites, and the one finds only destruction in passion, while the other is transformed by its denial.[5]

The themes of Altizer's writing are remarkably consistent over some forty years, though they are deepened through the development of a style that is both profoundly poetic and a real self-enactment of the word. His theological reflection is insistently dialectical, as must be the nature of all true theology, and such dialectics are the deep roots of the present book. Altizer's is also a style that is deeply scriptural, and therefore reverses all our attempts to make scripture absolute. In his book *The New Apocalypse*, first published in 1967, Altizer writes of Blake, Melville, and of America as holding the key to the future of theology. (He repeats his words, almost verbatim, in an essay of 1973 entitled "America and the Future of Theology"):[6]

> While *Moby Dick* fails to culminate in an apocalypse, if we incorporate this most prophetic of novels into the world of Blake's vision we must be prepared to see that an America which can become the murderer of God will enact the initial victory of the Apocalypse. Blake believed that Europe was hopelessly bound to a history that is past, and, to the true European, America must appear as a desert, and a desert shorn of the vegetation of history. But a desert can also be a gateway to the future.[7]

This cultural desert may again become the wilderness where we have our beginning and our ending and where is found our true self. In between there is the distraction of speech, against which, paradoxically, the poet writes and from which, in Altizer's vision, theology must flee, though clothed in language, towards a profound isolation which is its heart. In the same essay of 1973 he writes: "theology must cultivate the silence of death. To be sure, the death to which theology is called is the death of God."[8] In the same way for St. Antony, the purpose of the ascetical life was utterly to move beyond and at the same time into the heart of this earthly life in an absolute preparation for the death of self. Apart from this the Word becomes simply words in a babble of confusion which only the radical, apocalyptic Jesus can save us from in that pure *coincidentia oppositorum* that neither the church nor Christendom has ever acknowledged. This is most deeply pursued in Altizer's book *The Contemporary Jesus* (1997), which can be read, in some ways, as a working through of the central passage in his early essay "William Blake and the Role of Myth" (1965):

> Of course, Blake belongs to a large company of radical or spiritual Christians, Christians who believe that the Church and Christendom have sealed Jesus in his tomb and resurrected the very evil and darkness that Jesus conquered by their exaltation of a solitary and transcendent God, a heteronomous and compulsive law, and a salvation history that is irrevocably past.[9]

In this Blake was at one with the radical Christianity of the Desert Fathers. For him, like them, both space and time merged in the interior discovery of eternity, space being simply the form taken by the internal universe when it is seen as external,[10] so that in Blake's poetry the solid matter of rocks, caves, and all of the natural world both overwhelm us in their harsh reality and yet are also reborn in symbolic form, in a utopian vision. Eternity also becomes present in moments of real time, so that in the imagination of the poet, "the Ruins of Time builds [*sic*] Mansions in Eternity." In the reality of his imagination, Blake wrote in a letter of 1800 to William Hayley, "even in this world by it I am the companion of Angels."[11] In his poetry Blake is indeed like the Desert Fathers who, "while dwelling on earth . . . live as true citizens of heaven,"[12] and he in his verse, as they in their lives, could actually realize the apocalypse of the New Jerusalem in either the dark, satanic mills of England or the barren wastes of the eastern desert.

The absolute source of Blake's understanding of the Incarnation is to be found in the Greek term that has appeared throughout this book: kenosis or "emptying," whose verbal form occurs in Philippians 2:7, where Paul affirms that Christ "though he was in the form of God, did not count equality with God a thing to be grasped, but emptied himself, taking the form of a servant, being born in the likeness of men." In his self-emptying Christ becomes absolutely one with all humanity, so that in their asceticism the Fathers seek to become absolutely one with him in an essentially liturgical and universal celebration that barely even needs to refer to the name of Christ. Thus Blake writes in *Jerusalem*:

> We live as One Man; for contracting our infinite senses
> We behold multitude, or expanding, we behold as one,
> As One Man all the Universal Family, and that One Man
> We call Jesus the Christ, and he in us, and we in him . . .[13]

It is Altizer, above all, who has made the connection between Blake and the philosophy of Hegel as "the one thinker in Christendom who self-consciously and systematically created a kenotic form of understanding."[14] Remembering always the central claim of this book, that it is through the Fathers and Mothers of the desert that "the world is kept in being," we should now link this with Hegel's definition of *pure being* in the *Phenomenology of Spirit* (1807):

> But this pure being is not an immediacy, but something to which negation and mediation are essential; consequently, it is not what we *mean* by "being," but is "being" defined as an abstraction, or as the pure universal; and our "meaning," for which the true [content] of sense-certainty is *not* the universal, is all that is left over in face of this empty or indifferent Now and Here.[15]

It is this indifferent pure being to which we are drawn absolutely, towards a pure self-recognition in absolute otherness.[16] This is an absolutely kenotic movement, illustrated by Hegel in the proposition "God is being":

> "Being" is here meant to be not a Predicate, but rather the essence; it seems, consequently, that God ceases to be what he is from his position in the proposition, viz. a fixed Subject.[17]

To follow this pattern of self-negation is ultimately to be absorbed into universal pure being, a simultaneous realization and utter loss of self-consciousness as it finds itself only and entirely in the consciousness of the Other.[18] Nor, as Hegel points out, is this merely an individual self-consciousness, but it is universal, as the Spirit inspiring a religious community.[19] Indeed, it is only in the death of the individual center of consciousness that a universal consciousness, a true community, becomes possible.[20] This community is at once utterly self-absorbed and utterly emptied of self, a truly kenotic community for whom the specifics of the events of the gospel are fully merged into their universality. It is simultaneously itself and wholly other than itself in God. In Hegel's words, "This hard saying is the expression of the innermost simple knowledge of self, the return of consciousness into the deep night of I = I, that can no more distinguish or know anything outside of itself."[21] It is, indeed, purely tautological.

At this point, theology must turn towards the future in a move which lies at the heart of all liturgical celebration, and cultivate an isolation which – like that of the Desert Fathers – is deeply communal, and quite unlike the terrible solitariness of the "transcendent God" of Christendom. For in consigning God to transcendence, Christianity and its theology consigned God to an isolation, forgetting that transcendence can only be realized and fulfilled in immanence. Theology must also dare to move towards a poetics (one thinks here of Jabès) and yet one that has absorbed all speech into the silence that is the fulfillment and total presence of all language. In his book *The Self-Embodiment of God* (1977), Altizer describes this moment in this way: "Resurrection is the voice of speech only when that voice is actual as silence, only when the voice of speech has passed away into silence."[22] These words lie at the heart of the nature of prayer, and are realized as closely as anything in the silence experienced at the center of the eucharist which *is* the moment of resurrection even and only in the event of Christ's Passion, death, and descent into hell. But they are also the expression of a deep Christian poetics, a poetics understood by St. Antony and others, which recognizes the true poet as one who actually overturns the language which necessarily sustains the enterprise of theology and effects what Altizer calls a fully kenotic or self-emptying theology. We move here to the boundaries of a silence which, like Augustine in the *Confessions* (Altizer's "favorite theological book"),[23] opens our ears and eyes to the profound dichotomy and even deeper harmony between nature and grace. The true poet, with whom we have been traveling in many forms in this book, and who alone knows the depths of utter solitude, actually overturns theological discourse in a move or journey, repeatedly made and rarely heard, and makes possible the survival of a Christianity that is largely rejected by Christendom itself, and a future for theology. In philosophical terms probably only Hegel (whose huge shadow stretches across everything that Altizer has written) has given us the opportunity of a kenotic language that can project theology into a genuine future, though in a succession of poets and writers at least from Dante and Blake there is given us a true adumbration of it. In recognition of this I will employ the term "true poet," one who is a close companion to the desert travelers of this book. It also acknowledges Altizer's own writing as within this poetic tradition and as a poetics that yearns in its very language for a Total Presence which is, in fact, nothing other than true prayer – a voice of silence experienced as such an intensity that it is everything and nothing. Such Total Presence in Altizer's theology is a suspension which explains his profound acknowledgment of Dante's vision of Purgatory, the space (which is no place) where opposites meet and the possibility is held out of purification and redemption – the recovery of the paradise garden.

This moment of silence, wholly embodied in language, is a Total Presence in the meeting of opposites in which the true poet finds in utter solitude a pure vision. Of course, it is more than that, and can be found and deepened in other traditions. In the chapter entitled "The Buddhist Jesus" in *The Contemporary Jesus*, Altizer correlates the total *absence* of Buddhist *anatta* with the total *presence* of the Kingdom of God realized only in the absolute desolation of the crucifixion. *Anatta,* or selflessness, is at the heart of Buddhism (ultimately a child of the wilderness of North India), realized in nirvana as *sunyata* or absolute emptiness which is absolute freedom.[24] It is this tradition, in its complete opposition to theoretical or conceptual expression, that Altizer sets against the Christianity that has sought to burden with theological identity the elusive Jesus of Eckhart or Blake. Indeed, *The Contemporary Jesus* is dedicated to the memory of Albert Schweitzer, whose great work *The Quest of the Historical Jesus* ends with the "unknown" Jesus, the one who is finally anonymous. Altizer's "Buddhist Jesus" meets the Desert Fathers with their instinctive loathing of Arianism[25] that predates the Trinitarian resolution of the Council of Chalcedon and even the theological disputes of Athanasius himself, in their insistence on a dynamic (if ultimately heretical) monarchianism[26] and its identification of the Creator Father and the Son. Irresistibly, this desert theology reappears among the mystics and poets – Eckhart, Blake, Hegel – another unlikely company. Why so? Because, Altizer insists,

> Hegel and Eckhart refuse every final distinction between the eternal generation in the Godhead and the kenotic incarnation of Godhead or Spirit. Christian orthodoxy would condemn both Eckhart and Hegel as atheists because they refuse the absolute immutability of God, and do so precisely in knowing the ultimate self-emptying of God, a self-emptying that quite simply is the Incarnation.[27]

This insistence upon a *journey* and the refusal of immutability and the "lethal and pathological conflicts" of Christianity,[28] can only be the journey to the Cross, which is the absolute antithesis of the Buddhist journey to nirvana. In Altizer's words, "the crucified Jesus, and only the crucified Jesus, is the full and actual opposite of Gotama the Buddha."[29] And yet, it seems to me, in the journeying of the true desert wanderers, these two finally become one in a complete *coincidentia oppositorum*.

For the journey into the desert is to a death, and ultimately the desert *is* death (as we saw in Sigaud's novel).[30] Here alone is realized the Total Presence of the Kingdom of God, the true utopia, for in this death alone is the Kingdom known in its totality as absolute nothingness – the Kingdom of God *is* the

Kingdom of God only when it is not "being" the Kingdom of God.[31] We need to be clear, at last, about the true implications of such a utopia, such a paradise. It is nothing other than Christ's journey into hell that is a radical reversal of the Christian trajectory upwards, the journey of resurrection and ascension.[32] Christ's absolutely necessary descent into the desert of hell alone makes possible the actualization of the chiasmic language of scripture, which calls us to reverse the order of life and death, riches and poverty. In the apocalypse of Jesus's death alone does the heart of the desert become a place of life, not anticipated but realized in its full being.

At the same time this journey is itself *quies* or "rest," an absolutely empty *anatta* that is nirvana. This is seen in the perfect horizontal line of the desert horizon, the purity of utter immanence, unbroken and unending: while the death, as the Kingdom realized, is found only in the stillness of one place – the Desert Fathers knew well the value of staying still in their cells.[33] At the same time the stillness is still moving – always the journey. It is the still presence of the Kingdom as it is proclaimed by Jesus in his cry, "The Kingdom of God is *at hand*" (Mark 1:15). The Greek word translated here as "at hand" is *enngiken*: it is impossible to translate – a Greek perfect tense meaning wholly present and yet also arriving. It is a dynamic yet still presence that is the vertical line of transcendence, but an absolutely empty transcendence, a lavish absence,[34] that is realized in the "intersection of the timeless moment" of Eliot's "Little Gidding." It is a perfect coincidence of opposites – the transcendent utterly immanent, and the immanent perfectly transcendent. Totality is then present as absolute nothingness, even beyond the possibility of self-negation. As Altizer puts it:

> For if Gotama is Jesus, or Jesus is Gotama, then the Kingdom of God is the reversal of absolute nothingness, just as the self-negation of absolute nothingness is an absolute act of sacrifice and compassion.[35]

It is upon this vision that Altizer meditates in an unpublished essay in honor of Patrick A. Heelan, through the visual poetics of Vincent van Gogh, whose tragic last letter to his brother, written in July 1890, sums up the work of a true theologian and a poet in a cry of dereliction which is deeply Christocentric,[36] its final terrible question prompted by the moment when we truly "see" and seeing is utterly extinguished in the realization of St. Paul's words on "the image of the invisible God" (Colossians 1:15).[37]

> Well, my own work, I am risking my life for it and my reason has half foundered owing to it – that's all right – but you are not among the dealers in men so far as I know, and you can choose your side, I think acting with true humanity, but what's the use?[38]

This is the van Gogh whose last self-portrait, painted in Paris, Altizer has described as "the very face of death," yet a transfiguring embodiment in which life and death are truly indistinguishable, "for death in being truly embodied, thereby ceases to be death alone, ceases to be sheer nothingness, but becomes instead an embodied nothingness or an embodied death, and thus a death actually occurring."[39] Such deaths were seen in the desert, as of the monk Amoun, who "when he died, completely alone, Antony saw his soul borne up to heaven by angels."[40]

In these moments the task of the theologian is radically transfigured, for it has abandoned the language of theology as it has always been understood in Christianity, and finds itself in the deep experience of the poet, and beyond that in a vision in which, we might say, the invisible proceeds up into the visible; a necessary death which transforms consciousness in the loss of identity and self. In Altizer's words:

> True darkness can then be known as the fruit of compassion, and the actual death of an individual center of consciousness can then be celebrated as the self-annihilating presence of the universal Christ. Now the way "up" will be the way "down": an ascension to Heaven will be *identical* with a descent into Hell.[41]

The artist and the true poet have always known this intense, dark, and deeply consoling moment that is the end of all speech. It is consoling because it is also the moment when we recognize that Christ and Satan – the two figures who have equally haunted the travelers in this book, fearful because they cannot be distinguished – actually and fully become one. In his essay "Van Gogh's Eyes," Altizer traces this abysmal light back to the Scrovegni Chapel frescoes of Giotto, painted in about 1305, in which one of the most profound paintings is the Lamentation over the Dead Christ, a revolutionary work in the history of Christian art. Here everything is fixed upon the gaze, and above all the gaze of the grieving mother looking straight into the face of her dead son, taking her whole being from his eyes, which are themselves lifeless, yet full of life, in a moment of utter grief which leaves her "nowhere reflected but in the pupils of the eyes of God"[42] – and God is dead. Altizer claims that van Gogh was the first painter fully to envision the absolute darkness of the godhead itself – but Giotto also knows this darkness, as did Meister Eckhart who, in his great sermon "Qui audit me," affirms that "our greatest journey begins as we step away from God, leaving him for his own sake." Surely no one knows this more than the Mary of Giotto's fresco, or those who have lost themselves in quiet deserts, both Eckhart's and those of Egypt or North America – for they are the same, and it is of this same abyss that Altizer speaks in *Total Presence*, for only in this Total Presence does language

Plate 8   *Giotto di Bondone,* Lamentation over the Dead Christ *(1303–6). Scrovegni Frescoes in the Arena Chapel, Florence. Photograph AKG Images.*

move into silence, and only thus can the true language of Jesus himself be recovered. Only then does it become possible to think God without any conditions or distinctions, to think beyond Being without any pretence at an inscription of God or any description of him as Being. Only then can we realize how dehumanizing has been almost all theology in the Christian tradition, precisely because, as Ray L. Hart argues, of its futile preoccupation with God in a way that only God can be preoccupied with himself.[43]

Here indeed we truly discover the being of God when God is not being God. Giotto knows this, and so does van Gogh, though it cost him his life, and before that his sanity. But another modern poet, never referred to by Altizer, finds this again in a contemplation which is deeply religious yet utterly unmoved by the discourse that is the realm of the church and its theology.

The title of Yves Bonnefoy's most startling collection of poems is *Ce qui fut sans lumière* (literally, *That which was without light*, although the English translation is published under the title *In The Shadow's Light*). Bonnefoy is fascinated by the coincidence of darkness and light – of darkness *in* light and light *in* darkness. His poem "Dedham vu de Langham" is a profound meditation on the work of the landscape artist John Constable, and in particular his painting of September 1802, usually simply entitled *Dedham Vale*. What is the relationship between this landscape of lush English countryside and the desert which is our theme? In fact it is remarkable and complex. For Constable's painting is usually thought to be based on Claude's painting of *Hagar and the Angel* (Genesis 21:19), a biblical story which fascinates Bonnefoy. After the jealous rage of Sarah, Hagar and her child Ishmael are sent out into the Negev Desert at Beer-Sheva. Her water-skin empty, Hagar despairs, until God hears her crying and he opens her eyes "and she saw a well of water." In the desert, and in the depths of despair, God provides and brings life.

Thus we move from the desert, which is both a place of exile, but also divine refreshment, Constable's painting realizing, as it were, the garden that is at the heart of every true desert, and when we reach it, it is utterly familiar, yet we come to it as if for the first time. Bonnefoy realizes in words a picture which lies peacefully beyond language, capturing like so many of Constable's greatest works a moment in time which becomes eternal in the held image of the painting. (The original title of Constable's most famous painting, *The Haywain*, was *Landscape: Noon* – a visual "spot of time" and as much a painting of a moment as a pastoral scene). Words are absorbed into the silence of the image, yet the painter needs the words of the poet to capture the instant of vanishing into eternity, the vanishing point.

> On pourrait croire
> Que tout cela, haies, villages au loin,
> Rivière, va finir. Que le terre n'est-pas
> Même l'eternité des bêtes, des arbres . . .
>
> (You might think that
> The whole scene, the hedges, the distant villages,
> The river, was about to vanish. The earth
> Was not even the eternity of the flocks and trees . . .[44])

Then, as we move between word and image, Bonnefoy introduces from this silence the sound of music – another deep theme in Altizer's work – which resonates with a harmony found in the coincidence of opposites, a death into a new and creative life. Altizer has written in an unpublished memoir that music is the only art "in which the sacred is truly universal, and so much so that it is extraordinarily difficult to discover a genuine music which is genuinely profane." Bonnefoy, the poet, writes of Constable, the artist:

> Tu as vaincu, d'un début de musique,
> La forme qui se clôt dans toute vie.
>
> (You vanquished
> With the beginnings of a music
> The form which is the dead face of all life.)[45]

Thus music brings life, just as the word of the angel announces life to Hagar in the desert. Bonnefoy writes:

> Peintre de paysage, grâce à toi
> Le ciel s'est arrêté au-dessus du monde
> Comme lange au-dessus d'Agar quand elle allait,
> Le coeur vide, dans le dédale de la pierre.
>
> (Thanks to you landscape painter,
> The sky has paused above the world
> As did the angel above Hagar when she went
> With empty heart, into the labyrinths of stone.)[46]

In this wasteland, where the angel appeared to Hagar, which is also and thereby the lush Essex Vale of Dedham, the word moves into image in the silence which is the fullness of speech, and this is the birth of music. It is from this fertile wasteland that Altizer speaks in self-confessed isolation. For true theology is never, properly, merely written, but lived within, just as in the desert, in the overcoming of the distinction between being and non-being, the Fathers spoke little of Christ, for they lived utterly within him as a kind of *alter Christus*.[47] Altizer speaks with an intensity which comes as close as anything in contemporary writing to an apocalypse of the word, moving through language as only true poets have done. This apocalypse, just as all true mysticism is a liturgical event, resides at the heart of the liturgy, though a liturgy that is far from most contemporary liturgical practice within the church, which has forgotten the apocalyptic prayer which is most truly the language of Jesus. Altizer has acknowledged his own debt to the liturgical scholar Dom Gregory Dix, and in particular his great book *The Shape of the Liturgy* (1945), written in the darkest days of modern European history. Early in his account of the eucharistic prayer, Dix gives close attention to the words in 1 Corinthians 11:25: "Do this in remembrance [*anamnesis*] of me." Referring back to the earliest Roman tradition in Justin and Hippolytus, Dix writes of the active sense . . . of "recalling" or "re-presenting" before God the sacrifice of Christ, and thus making it here and now operative by its effects in the communicants . . . the Eucharist is regarded both by the New Testament and by the second-century writers as the *anamnesis* of the passion, or of the passion and resurrection combined.[48]

In the *anamnesis* of the eucharist, the moment of the Passion is not merely commemorated as an act in history, but is also realized actually within the utterance and present act of the eucharistic prayer. It is this presenting or "presencing" of the sacrament as an apocalyptic enactment (a ground underplayed in Dix's account of the liturgy) which is fully realized in the imagination of true poets in whom language becomes a genuine kenosis. It is why the life of the desert *is* liturgical even and especially in its solitariness, and why all the literature and art discussed in this book partakes of the quality of the divine, though for some this is defeat and utter, empty silence. For here, language is fully found only in a self-emptying and therefore in the silence which lies at the heart of the celebration of the sacrament, that is a reversal, in the death of God, of everything in an apocalyptic moment that is beyond anything realized within the church, its liturgies or its formularies. At the same time it is an absolutely scriptural and apocalyptic language which insists upon the chiasmic demand that in order to read scripture we must suffer its absolute reversals, so that reading itself is negated in the very rhetoric. Words negate words and reveal a purity that is beyond words. It is a pure poetics and why only a very few "true poets" like Blake have dared utterly to follow scripture – and have been almost universally misunderstood as a result. But it was Blake, in his "Memorable Fancy," who supped with the Prophets. Altizer finds this scriptural poetics most radically present in modern literature in James Joyce's *Finnegans Wake* (1939), truly a desert text that finds its rest in paradise. Altizer writes:

> If *Finnegans Wake* is our most imaginative text which is simultaneously a liturgical text, only here does our uniquely Western liturgy undergo a full imaginative metamorphosis, and even if the awe and sublimity of the Mass now passes into a cosmic ribaldry, there an ultimate transgression occurs, and one inverting and reversing the Eucharist, as the language of the Roman Rite becomes the very opposite of itself in *Finnegans Wake*.[49]

The *Wake* continuously enacts a death which is an awakening, a sacrifice which is deeply worshipful precisely in its glorious profanity, so that, finally, "I sink I'd die down over his feet, humbly dumbly, only to washup," and in this ending is the beginning, the rediscovery and recovery in the wilderness of the lost paradise, though we are still in Dublin, indeed in the pub, as the book concludes with the words, "A way a lone a last a loved a long the . . . riverrun, past Adam and Eve's . . ."

To washup – to worship; like the bishop in the ancient narrative who gave up all to go out into the Egyptian desert, and there serve as a simple laborer, becoming the servant of all. In *Finnegans Wake* the Fall of the opening pages is a reinvention of Blake's vision in which the Fall is all, and an absolute *felix culpa*, a fall into the recognition and the true moment of creation and an absolutely apocalyptic moment of reversal of all history.[50] It is the moment when the women rush from the empty tomb in astonishment and fear – because they *know* the truth of Christ's death (Mark 16:8).

It is precisely this moment which is disastrously refused by Paul Klee's "Angelus Novus" in the celebrated ninth of Walter Benjamin's *Theses on the Philosophy of History*, as it flees backwards into the future, driven by the storm which we have called progress.[51] This deeply liturgical moment is known only to those whom Altizer has called radical or spiritual Christians, those who, like desert travelers, like Blake or like the exile Joyce, celebrate a death which is also the genesis of God. This genesis can only be in, and can only be the absolute kenosis or self-emptying of, God, and always an *anamnesis* of the moment of dereliction, recognized in the words of the true poet: "My God, my God, Why have you forsaken me?" (in Mark or Matthew's gospel), or van Gogh's cry, his last written words before his suicide, "What's the use?" Here is the moment, recognized by the apophatic tradition, in which Jesus accomplishes his mission in failure; in the words of St. John of the Cross:

> This was the most extreme abandonment, sensitively, that He had suffered in His life. And by it, He accomplished the most marvelous work of His whole life surpassing all the works and deeds and miracles that He had ever performed on earth or in heaven.[52]

Here, too, we recognize Altizer's long obsession with the theology of Karl Barth, his cry for a "theology of freedom" that looks ahead and strives forward, and his acknowledgment of the apocalyptic Christ. In his book *Apocalypse and Genesis* (1990) Altizer affirms:

> Perhaps the deepest theological response to Nietzsche's vision of eternal recurrence was the *Church Dogmatics* of Karl Barth, the first theology which was a theology of the Church and only of the Church, and thus the first Christian theology which effected or intended a total disjunction or chasm between the Church and history, for it was the first theology created in full response to the historical realization of the death of God.[53]

Yet was it the first? Was not this chasm first opened up when people first crossed the border between the civilized world and the *desert absolu*, and began a radical journey into the death of self and the death of God? At the same time, Barth's journey is absolutely authentic, for the *Church Dogmatics* is a world that is entirely one unto itself, a pure vision in language that is as visionary as Barth's beloved Mozart, and in which words are as real and as demanding as the grains of desert sand. And the genesis of the *Church Dogmatics* is to be found in Barth's flight from the wreckage of Europe in the Great War of 1914–18, a human wasteland that is the antithesis of the purity of the desert, and from which Barth emerges in the writing of the *Romerbrief* through readings of the true prophets of modernity: Dostoevsky, Kierkegaard, Nietzsche, and the vision of Mathias Grünewald's "Crucifixion" in the Isenheim Altarpiece – the very rocks of language and image that carry him on his journey. But Barth begins with Abraham, the first great desert wanderer of the biblical tradition, who went out into the unknown, in faith.

> Jesus would not be the Christ if figures like Abraham, Jeremiah, Socrates, Luther, Kierkegaard, Dostoevsky remained, contrasted with Him, merely figures of past history, and did not rather constitute in Him one essential unity.[54]

History merges in an essential unity with and in Christ, who is incalculably more than the Christ of Christendom. Christianity ceases as Christendom in the realization of an absolute unity in the book, in Word. It is just as in Grünewald's painting of Christ on the cross, where the Evangelist points to the terrible figure hanging there while he holds the book – words are fulfilled and silenced in the perfect unity between the book and desert of Christ's desolation. It is a moment of absolute isolation, a *coincidentia oppositorum* that is at the same time a celebration and a true *anamnesis*.

That is, when we speak of the *celebration* of the eucharist, which is also the ultimate risk, we use the word in its primary sense of coming together and performing an action that is appropriate to the occasion.[55] Such festivities are found, paradoxically, only in the deepest solitude, in the deepest darkness where is affirmed the No which evokes a Yes, the last word of Joyce's great epic *Ulysses* – the word which finally brings us home after terrible wanderings. It is also, in *Ulysses*, a word of sexual fulfillment, reminding us that St. John of the Cross and Hadewijch in their mystical writings never avoided sexuality as a metaphor for *divine* love. Blake, in his "Memorable Fancy" in *The Marriage of Heaven and Hell* (1790–3), walks among the fires of hell, delighted with the enjoyments of Genius, which to Angels look like torment and insanity, for Blake, like Nietzsche, knew well the ecstasy of "liberation occasioned by the collapse of the transcendence of Being, by the death of God."[56] It is the moment known to Crace's Gally at the end of *Quarantine*. It was known to St. Antony on his mountain. It was known to St. John of the Cross. It is the dark mysticism of the desert.

Martin Heidegger once remarked "if I were to write a theology, which I am sometimes tempted to do, the term 'being' would not be allowed to appear in it . . . Faith does not need the thought of being, and if it needs it, it is no longer faith."[57] And yet it was said of the monks of the desert, in the *Historia Monachorum*, that it is by them that the world is kept in being. But being is not simply existence. By them the world was realized and sustained in its true being, precisely inasmuch as they entered into a solitude that was the utter abandonment of being, into a way of faith which Altizer calls "the nothing."[58] It was this silence, "a purely mystical silence [which] inactivates all movement and process and disengages all passion and will,"[59] that goes beyond historical and spatial particularity – most truly in this trackless wilderness we are "lost" and here alone realize a Total Presence. In Altizer's words:

> Already in the proclamation of Jesus, a total presence realizes and presents itself only by way of its negative assault upon all given or established identity, and it is the reversal of the center or ground of established identity which actualizes a total and final presence.[60]

To abandon "being" in the solitude of the interior mountain of the desert is to discover, by abandonment, a Total Presence. On December 26, 1910, Franz Kafka noted in his journal this power of being over him: "My interior dissolves (for the time being only superficially) and is ready to release what lies deeper."[61] Kafka is one with the crazy Jesus of Jim Crace's *Quarantine*, who, in his solitary death, "was all surface, no inside . . . He was a dry, discarded page of scripture now."[62] In going out into the desert, this Jesus (is he the Jesus of the gospels also?) realizes the pure moment of the identity of the word and the grain of sand: from sand to book, and from book to sand, and there is truly nothing outside this text. For there is truly nothing, and in a condition which costs not less than everything,[63] in the solitude of the end and the utter decentering of the being of self is "made possible the advent of a new but wholly immediate world."[64]

There is the final paradox. All our journeyings have brought us to an immediacy that is deeply hidden, so far beyond any interiority that it is all surface (as Maurice Blanchot once described Kafka's fiction, and as we shall see again in the chapter 11), that we fail to see that what lies at the heart of our common humanity is precisely "just what is most invisible and inaudible in our society."[65]

And so let us make our final journey into the wilderness.

Notes

1 Denys Turner, *The Darkness of God: Negativity in Christian Mysticism* (Cambridge: Cambridge University Press, 1995), p. 251.

2 Meister Eckhart, *German Sermon 48*, in *The Essential Sermons, Commentaries, Treatises, and Defense*, translated by Edmund Colledge and Bernard McGinn. Classics of Western Spirituality (New York: Paulist Press, 1981), p. 198.

3 Thomas J. J. Altizer, *The New Apocalypse: The Radical Christian Vision of William Blake* (Aurora: Davies Group, 2000), p. 63.

4 Thomas J. J. Altizer, *Total Presence: The Language of Jesus and the Language of Today* (New York: Seabury Press, 1980), p. 106.

5 See James Cowan, *Journey to the Inner Mountain* (London: Hodder and Stoughton, 2002), pp. 153–4. "In its own way, Sade's debauchee resembles Antony's recluse. 'He is thoughtful, concentrated in himself, and incapable of being moved by anything whatsoever', wrote Sade . . . For Sade, negation is power in man, and man's whole future depends on this negation being pushed to its limit . . . [But] while Sade might have seen the complete man as he who completely asserts himself and is destroyed, Antony saw the complete man as he who completely negates himself, and so 'self'-destructs."

6 See Thomas J. J. Altizer and William Hamilton, *Radical Theology and the Death of God* (Harmondsworth: Penguin Books, 1968).

7 Altizer, *The New Apocalypse*, p. 150.

8 Altizer and Hamilton, *Radical Theology and the Death of God*, p. 30.

9 Ibid, p. 182.

10 See Altizer, *The New Apocalypse*, p. 32. See also Bernard Blackstone, *English Blake* (Cambridge: Cambridge University Press, 1949), p. 230.

11 Quoted in Altizer, *The New Apocalypse*, p. 85.

12 *The Lives of the Desert Fathers*, translated by Norman Russell (Kalamazoo, MI: Cistercian Publications, 1981), p. 50.

13 William Blake, *Jerusalem* (ca. 1804–20), 38: 17–20.

14 Altizer, *The New Apocalypse*, p. 62.

15 G. W. F. Hegel, *Phenomenology of Spirit* (1807), in Stephen Houlgate (ed.), *The Hegel Reader* (Oxford: Blackwell, 1998), p. 81.

16 Ibid, p. 56.

17 Ibid, p. 66

18 See G. W. F. Hegel, *Phenomenology of Spirit: Self-Consciousness*, in Stephen Houlgate (ed.), *The Hegel Reader* (Oxford: Blackwell, 1998), p. 91.

19 See J. N. Findlay, "Hegel's Study of the Religious Consciousness," in Thomas J. J. Altizer (ed.), *Toward a New Christianity* (New York: Harcourt, Brace and World, 1967), p. 55.

20 See Thomas J. J. Altizer, *The Descent into Hell: A Study of the Radical Reversal of Christian Consciousness* (Philadelphia, PA: J. B. Lippincott, 1970), p. 213.

21 Hegel, *Phenomenology of Spirit*, quoted in Findlay, "Hegel's Study of the Religious Consciousness," p. 55.

22 Thomas J. J. Altizer, *The Self-Embodiment of God* (New York: Harper and Row, 1977), p. 95.

23 An acknowledgment made in an as yet unpublished memoir.

24 Thomas J. J. Altizer, *The Contemporary Jesus* (Albany: State University of New York Press, 1997), p. 162.

25 See above, chapter 3, p. 37.

26 The heresy that eventually became known as Sabellianism.

27 Altizer, *The Contemporary Jesus*, pp. 170–1.

28 Ibid, p. 161.

29 Ibid, p. 175.

30 See chapter 7, p. 98.

31 See further Robert P. Scharlemann, *Inscriptions and Reflections: Essays in Philosophical Theology* (Charlottesville: University of Virginia Press, 1989), "The Being of God When God is Not Being God", pp. 30–53, and "Being 'As Not': Overturning the Ontological", pp. 54–65.

32 See Altizer, *The Descent into Hell*.

33 "An Elder said: Just as a tree cannot bear fruit if it is often transplanted, so neither can a monk bear fruit if he frequently changes his abode." Thomas Merton, *The Wisdom of the Desert* (London: Sheldon Press, 1961), p. 34.

34 See Rosmarie Waldrop, *Lavish Absence: Recalling and Rereading Edmond Jabès* (Middletown, CT: Wesleyan University Press, 2002), p. 127; and above, chapter 6, pp. 84–6.

35 Altizer, *The Contemporary Jesus*, p. 183.

36 We should recall here Altizer's admiration for the theology of Karl Barth. See also Mark A. McIntosh, *Mystical Theology* (Oxford: Blackwell, 1998), p. 207: "In the language of mystical paradox, then, one might even say that Jesus is most divine (most fully enacting the eternal mission of the Son) and the Incarnation is most fully consummated exactly at Golgotha, when the aching physicality of his humanity is unlimited and the unknowing of himself and God is entire."

37 See also Jean-Luc Marion, *God Without Being*, translated by Thomas A. Carlson (Chicago: University of Chicago Press, 1991), p. 17.

38 Mark Roskill (ed.), *The Letters of Vincent van Gogh* (London: Fontana, 1983), p. 340.

39 Thomas J. J. Altizer, "Van Gogh's Eyes." Unpublished manuscript.

40 *The Lives of the Desert Fathers*, p. 112.

41 Altizer, *The Descent into Hell*, p. 214.

42 Austin Farrer, *A Celebration of Faith*, edited by Leslie Houlden (London: Hodder and Stoughton, 1970), p. 122.

43 Ray L. Hart, *Unfinished Man and the Imagination* (Atlanta, GA: Scholars Press, 1985), p. 38.

44 Yves Bonnefoy, *In the Shadow's Light*, translated by John Naughton (Chicago: University of Chicago Press 1991), p. 93.

45 Ibid, p. 93.

46 Ibid, p. 95.

47 This state the Pseudo-Dionysius called *atelis* ("Perfectionless"), and in Sufism it is called *fana* ("annihilation") or even more, *fana dar fana* ("the annihilation of the annihilation"), that is "beyond perfection." See Henry Corbin, *Creative Imagination in the Sufism of Ibn Arabi* (Princeton, NJ: Bollingen Press, 1969), pp. 202–3. See also Cowan, *Journey to the Inner Mountain*, p. 140.

48 Dom Gregory Dix, *The Shape of the Liturgy* (London: Dacre Press, 1945), p. 161.

49 Thomas J. J. Altizer, *The Genesis of God: A Theological Genealogy* (Louisville, KY: Westminster/John Knox Press, 1993), p. 133.

50 "In the light of Blake's vision, the fall is all, and, dialectically, the very fullness of his vision derives from the totality of its fallen ground: vision cannot reverse all things unless it initially knows them in a fallen form." Altizer, *Radical Theology and the Death of God*, p. 172.

51 Walter Benjamin, *Illuminations*, translated by Harry Zohn (London: Fontana, 1973), p. 249.

52 St. John of the Cross, *The Ascent of Mount Carmel*, II, vii, 11. Quoted in McIntosh, *Mystical Theology*, p. 207.

53 Thomas J. J. Altizer, *Genesis and Apocalypse: A Theological Voyage Towards Authentic Christianity* (Louisville, KY: Westminster/John Knox Press, 1990), p. 149.

54 Karl Barth, *The Epistle to the Romans*, translated from the sixth edition by Edwyn C. Hoskyns (Oxford: Oxford University Press, 1933), p. 117.

55 See P. F. Bradshaw, "Celebration," in R. C. D. Jasper (ed.), *The Eucharist Today* (London: SPCK, 1974), pp. 131–2.

56 Altizer, *Radical Theology and the Death of God*, p. 116.

57 Jacob Taubes, "On the Nature of Theological Method: Some Reflections on the Methodological Principles of Tillich's Theology," *Journal of Religion* (January, 1954), p. 21.

58 Thomas J. J. Altizer, *Oriental Mysticism and Biblical Eschatology* (Philadelphia, PA: Westminster Press, 1961), p. 189.

59 Altizer, *Total Presence*, p. 97.

60 Ibid, p. 99.

61 Quoted in Altizer, *Total Presence*, pp. 101–2.

62 See chapter 7, pp. 100–3.

63 See T. S. Eliot, "Little Gidding," discussed in chapter 11, pp. 167–9.

64 Altizer, *Total Presence*, p. 106.

65 Ibid., p. 104.

11
Conclusion
Meeting Point

The secret [of the Law] is nothing – and this is the secret that has to be kept well, nothing either present or presentable, but this nothing must be kept well.[1]

But, of course, as Derrida is foremost in recognizing, theology has never, ever, not dealt in the aporetic, the desert experience, the *via negativa*. Aporia infects the ecstasy of the believer.[2]

The tree is to the mast what the desert is to the city.[3]

Those who lose themselves in the deep desert discover the secret which Kafka's applicant in his parable "Before the Law" never appreciates. The law's secret is its nothingness. That is its ground, and only those who dare to go outside and beyond the law – to become outlaws in the Badlands – can hope to learn of its "mystical" foundations.[4] Derrida affirms that it is only in its aporetic nature that justice can become justice, and in the moment of undecidability often the possibility of belief. Reminding us of the Abraham of Kierkegaard's *Fear and Trembling*, Derrida speaks of the moment of decision in the face of the incalculable by which justice is sustained. He describes this also as the "desert in the desert,"[5] beyond rationality, but a moment – or place – where the claims and sacrality of the "other" are realized. It is a place – or moment – of destitution, beyond rule and order, that makes the impossible possible.

Another dense and difficult essay by Derrida, "Edmond Jabès and the Question of the Book," further sums up many of the themes of the present book. An intertext with Jabès' *Livre des questions* (1963), the essay begins with the close relationship between words and roots, and the capacity of the letter to take root in the no-place of the desert. Derrida speaks of the "adventure of the text as weed"[6] outlawed beyond the safety of cultivation into the Desert of the Promise, for the desert-book is made of sand, and the dwelling place of the poet "is a fragile tent of words erected in the desert where the nomadic Jew is struck with infinity and the letter."[7]

For Jabès, as we have seen, the white sheet of paper is like the desert, empty but full of traces of paths, and to write is to draw back and become absent, to embark on a journey. It is a journey towards a vision of the Land:

> What are you dreaming of? – The Land. – But you are on the land. – I am dreaming of the Land where I will be. – But we are right in front of each other. And we have our feet on land. – I know only the stones of the way which leads, as it is said, to the Land.[8]

Absence is the very heart of the question, the place always anticipated in the infinite detour that is the text that both separates us and draws us. For Jabès, the poem is at once the desert and the garden that is the end of all desert travels, and in order to speak the poet must know how to leave speech: everything and nothing.[9] In other words, the writer must become like God, the writer's Passion experienced in the distress of writing. This distress is in language's *rupture* with totality, for in order to be made whole again it is necessary first that it be broken. For it is in the ruptures, the cracks and fissures of the parched land, the *caesura* of the poem, that life is to be found and from here alone meaning emerges. But first the poet must have the courage to die and not to be.

The letter, like the seed in St. Paul, grows only in the absence and hiddenness of solitude: "it is solitude, articulates solitude, and lives on solitude."[10] Only in solitude may it grow into the tree that may be fashioned by craft into the mast that bears the weight of progress. Thus the city is kept in being by the empty fertile desert. Going out into the desert of the text, the poet becomes the traveler who seeks to retake possession of his language on the boundaries of the articulate and beyond. It is to dare to challenge articulacy, for only in an "original illegibility is . . . the very possibility of the book,"[11] for this illegibility, which is beyond all being, is the Godhead itself. Thus the book becomes a world from which every possible exit is only within the book itself. Retreating to its deepest interiority is to reside in an absolute that is no-place and therefore there is no other. Thus, for Jabès, the book is not in the world, but the world is in the book.[12]

This is why the desert and the word have always coexisted, as we have seen. We are here close to the recovery of a genuinely theological language that has actually never been lost, but is rarely heard, and almost never in the churches and institutions which have appropriated to themselves the theological discourses of Christendom. Only with the radical dissolution of Christendom and its aftermath in the West can the radical theology that has always been the theology of the desert begin to be articulated again in a language whose end is always silence. But before the theology, the poetics – and that is all we can claim to have begun to recover. A pre/theology, perhaps, or even an a/theology. This is why those mystics who celebrate wordlessness are the most writerly of people. For poet and desert traveler are on an endless journey of wandering and mirage, led by the forgotten dream, and just as the desert negates every preoccupation, "life negates itself in literature, only so that it may survive itself. So that it may *be* better."[13] Pure desert, the *desert absolu*, and pure literature are death itself, as Roland Barthes acknowledges, when he writes in *Writing Degree Zero* (1953): "Literature is like phosphorous: it shines with its maximum brilliance at the moment when it attempts to die."[14] We might say that what we have been studying in this book is nothing less than the writing of the book of life, lives enscriptured and texts lived. In spite of, perhaps because of, its mysticism, this is grounded in a reality, as we saw at the very beginning, of actual rocks and real sand experienced and fought with. It is thus the very opposite of what Graham Ward has identified as the possibility of theology within the postmodern condition; that is, theology within cyberspace.[15] In cyberspace, surfing the Net, we encounter absolutely the implications of the contemporary crisis of humanist subjectivity, while time and space, in a grotesque parody of their transfiguration in the desert, simply collapse into omnipresence and multilocality. Here in cyberspace is the ultimate achievement of anarchic eclecticism, the avoidance of responsibility and definition, and a solitariness that is the very opposite of the liturgical life of the wilderness. In Ward's words:

> You act anonymously, simply as the unnamed, unidentifiable viewpoint of so many interactive network games and where identity is needed, you can construct one.[16]

Here God, too, can be absolutely deconstructed, constructed, reconstructed at will, in irresponsible games which lack governing metaphors or any claims made upon us, yet at the same time, they absorb us entirely. We become transfixed, like children, before the endless unreality of the computer screen. When this becomes the case the theological project must be pursued in what Philippa Berry has called "a shadowy in-between realm – a no-man's-land of thought"[17] characterized by the ever-present image in the twentieth century of the wasteland, experienced only in the devastations of war and famine, in the decay of the city, in nuclear and ecological anxiety. It is what Bill Viola[18] saw in the stripped bareness and aloofness of deserted city streets. This is no desert from which springs of living water will ever flow, but a wasted land in which the mind and spirit dwell without purpose or direction. In the deadness of cyberspace can we survive at all?

In the previous chapter we briefly encountered the work of Maurice Blanchot as he wrote on Franz Kafka. This we now need to expand a little. In his series of meditations entitled *The Space of Literature* (1955), Blanchot takes up what will now be, to us, a very familiar theme: "the solitude of the work." He writes:

> In the solitude of the work – the work of art, the literary work – we discover a more essential solitude. It excludes the complacent isolation of individualism: it has nothing to do with the quest for singularity . . . The writer never knows whether the work is done. What he has finished in one book, he starts over or destroys in another.
>
> He whose life depends upon the work, either because he is a writer or because he is a reader, belongs to the solitude of that which expresses nothing except the word being: the word which language shelters by hiding it, or causes to appear when language itself disappears into the silent void of the work.[19]

And so we have moved from a wasteland void of theology to the space or abyss of the work of literature. Blanchot, in a remarkable echo of the experience of the Desert Fathers, suggests that writing can only originate in "true" despair. That despair is writing's sole determination, powerfully present in Kafka, who is one of the most deeply religious of writers, preoccupied with questions of salvation and its impossibility. And yet at the same time writing and despair have nothing in common – one can only write "by faith" – except their own indeterminacy. Kafka, then, writes determined by despair, and as his character "K." he hopelessly and endlessly pursues the possibility of salvation. Yet the key to his condemnation lies in the very first sentence of *The Trial*: "Someone must have been telling lies about Joseph K., for without ever having done anything wrong, he was arrested one fine morning."[20] But K.'s crime is to believe that there is a solution somewhere out in the "real" world of the judicial system beyond the desert of the text, while Kafka, like Jabès – both Jewish, whose ancestors wandered in the desert for forty years – knows that the world is in the book, and that K. never acknowledges. Joseph K., who only exists in the text of the novel, combats the text itself without realizing that in its space only is salvation. Literature is never merely a means to an end, as Kafka is well aware, and so K.'s case remains hopeless and he dies, in the end, like a dog, for as the priest in the cathedral says to him after recounting the great parable of the doorkeeper, "Before the Law": "it is not necessary to accept everything as true, one must only accept it as necessary." "A melancholy conclusion," K. replies. "It turns lying into a universal principle." Indeed, his only firm belief is that someone must have been telling lies.

And yet the words of the text remain, defiantly: someone *must* have been telling lies. Is it the case that somewhere in the maze of textuality there is truth? K. never finds it, if that is so, for in Kafka it is never that simple. Yet Blanchot realizes that the key – never easy in its demands – is the move Kafka is always making from literature to religion, within the text, demanding

> in a rather confusing way by passing from the desert of faith to faith in a world which is no longer the desert but another world, where liberty will be returned to him.[21]

In short, Kafka is to be read as another writer of utopia. In his writing his interior dissolves[22] and, in Blanchot's wonderful words, "there exists for him only the outside, the glistening flow of the eternal outside." There can hardly be a better description of Kafka's texts and what makes them so difficult and disturbing. Their crushing honesty – or the truth, in spite of itself – is that there is only outside and no hidden meaning, only the words themselves, and yet here alone is the impossible space of the text, determined by despair yet prompted by faith. That is all there is, and it is what Blanchot calls "the work's space and its demand." The crime is to fail to take that space seriously in and for itself – an empty space, its immanence absorbing every transcendence.

This is truly a desert space, without conclusion and yet always longing for closure. Literature is thus already a posthumous affair: as we read the writer is, in effect, always already dead, for the indeterminate space opened up by the text is lived *entirely* in the eternal present, without either past or future, for these, too, it has absorbed. There is nothing outside the text and it is, like God, Everything and Nothing. At its maximum brilliance, the work's space and its demands recreate the moment of death which is at the same time the only true moment of life fully lived, undisplaced by past or future and yet utterly real.

Yet modern literature in the West, perhaps uniquely, knows another place, one perhaps anticipated by T. E. Lawrence as he finally left the desert and sought oblivion and anonymity. This is the place of true despair where there is no journey, and the waiting is endless, for there is nowhere to go except to be trapped in an eternally recurring present that has no point of contact with anything that we can name as love. The classic instance of this literature of the wasteland is Beckett's *Waiting for Godot* and its conclusion:

> *Vladimir:* Well? Shall we go?
> *Estragon:* Yes, let's go.
> *They do not move.*[23]

As we draw near to the end of our travels, we return to the mad scullery maid of the *Lausiac History* with whom we began in chapter 1, and who has been with us throughout our journey.[24] She is precisely the opposite of Beckett's two tramps, for she has found what she is looking for, and has become nothing, a void – utterly avoided. The sponge who is nothing herself and therefore can absorb all the filth of the world, the one by whom it is therefore kept in being, she is what Michel de Certeau calls the "abject nothing" and the "unsymbolizable thing that resists meaning."[25] And so Palladius concludes her story:

> A few days later, unable to bear her sisters' esteem and admiration, overwhelmed by the demands for pardon, she left the convent. Where she went, where she hid herself, how she ended her days, no one has found out.

It is this woman's non-being which makes being and theology possible. She is a perfect example of the desert saint described by Edith Wyschogrod, who finds and loses herself through self-abandonment to the needs of the other. This, indeed, may be the truly postmodern turn, found in reality:

> Such saintliness is not a nostalgic return to a premodern hagiography but a postmodern expression of excessive desire, a desire on behalf of the Other that seeks the cessation of another's suffering and the birth of another's joy.[26]

Through her reading of Levinas, Wyschogrod characterizes the saintly life as the total loss of self, so that "the power to bring about new moral configurations is authorized by the prior renunciation of power."[27] The resultant vulnerability, however, is to be carefully distinguished from masochism, which finds satisfaction in pain, although in practice the two are often hard to separate – hence our references from time to time to the "asceticism" of de

Sade. Nothing, however, could be further from the deep interiority of the desert or from its *cleanness*, noted by travelers from Lawrence to Abbey and Thesiger.

Finally, Wyschogrod notes the ecstasy of the saint – for "the desire for the Other is excessive and wild."[28] Throughout this book, in novels, art, film, and travelers' tales, we have encountered a *fierce* mysticism, a single-minded purpose that defies the rational. It is a self-abandonment that is drawn to an ever-receding horizon, to a meeting point reached only in endless, restless journeying impelled by stillness.

Writing of the poetry of St. John of the Cross, Michel de Certeau takes us to the utopia of the Paradise Garden. But it is real, and therefore found to be no utopia – it is the utterly other, even to itself:

> The poem does what it says; it itself creates what it makes space for. But like the musician in Bosch's *Garden of Earthly Delights*, who is caught in his harp, his arms outstretched as though dead or passed out, played by the song that sends him into ecstasy, insane from being imprisoned in his instrument, that is, in the body of the voice of the other – the poet, too, is robbed by that excess which names but remains unnamable.[29]

We have one final journey to make. I have emphasized throughout this book the intense *reality* of the desert which is our subject. It has not been Wordsworth's poetic creation in *The Prelude*, but a harsh environment of extremes of heat and cold, rock and sand. Yet in chapter 6 I described this paradoxically as also a "virtual reality" and a "true cyberspace"[30] that is yet quite opposite to the cyberspace and computerized virtual reality that increasingly govern and administer our lives. It is a real place, yet it becomes the place of dream and vision, the Other that makes life itself possible. It is therefore a place supremely of the word and text, the end of a journey into the unnamable that can *be* nowhere but in the word. In the end, therefore, it matters little, perhaps, if John C. Van Dyke never entered the deserts of the American Southwest as he claimed, for that does not make them any the less real, and he realized them in a fiction that is parallel in some sense to the decentered fictional life of Lawrence, a mystery that nevertheless made things possible. It brought the Arab Revolt to the gates of Damascus. St. Augustine is possibly one of the greatest of desert saints precisely inasmuch as his own contemplated flight into the desert was countered by God himself (*Confessions* X.43.70),[31] his desert therefore a text. One of the greatest of desert texts, almost hidden and unmentioned so far in this book, is the last of the *Four Quartets* (1936–42) of T. S. Eliot – no rugged traveler he – which brings me, an Englishman, back to the desert that has been there all the time, a few miles from a town where I lived for years, that is "the place [I] would be likely to come from."[32] The journey from Cambridge to Little Gidding in the fens is not far, but it sums up a theme that is at the heart of Eliot's writing from *The Waste Land* (1922) onwards. In the final section of that poem, "What the Thunder said," Eliot turns to the Upanishads for the Sanskrit words:

> Datta. Dayadhvam. Damyata.
> Shantih shantih shanti

Shantih, or "The Peace which passeth understanding": as Andrew Louth has pointed out, the second part of the title of the Upanishad – Aranyaka – means forest,[33] and that this is the equivalent in North India to the desert as the place where ascetics and solitaries, like the Buddha, retired. The forest is the wild, lonely place. In "The Dry Salvages," the second of the *Quartets*, Eliot returns to the Hindu scriptures in a reference to the *Bhagavad-Gita* and to Krishna's articulation of the spirituality of the forest to Arjuna. Krishna's teaching, in turn, takes us back in Eliot's work to the Chorus at the end of *Murder in the Cathedral* (1935), where in a meditation on Archbishop Beckett's martyrdom there is a reference to "the death in the desert" from which "ground springs that which forever renews the earth."[34] This theme, indeed this very phrase, is returned to in a broadcast of 1941, in which Eliot speaks of the death of Charles de Foucauld, whose biography by René Bazin he had read, and affirms:

> There is no higher glory of a Christian empire than that which was brought into being by a death in the desert.[35]

This links once again with the teaching of Krishna, a meeting of East and West in the wisdom of the desert, in two lines at the end of part three of "Little Gidding" which look back also to the medieval mystic, Dame Julian of Norwich:

> By the purification of the motive
> In the ground of our beseeching.

Such purification, for her, is nothing other than an utter conformity to the life of Christ who is the ground of our beseeching: the *imitatio Christi*.

Throughout the plays, from *Murder in the Cathedral* to *The Cocktail Party* and *The Family Reunion*, there are constant references to the desert, but it is at the end of *The Four Quartets* that the theme reaches a new profundity and stillness, "a further union, a deeper communion / Through the dark cold and the empty desolation."[36] In part three of "East Coker" there is a long section translated from *The Ascent of Mount Carmel* of St. John of the Cross, concluding with the lines:

> You must go through the way in which you are not.
> And what you do not know is the only thing you know
> And what you own is what you do not own
> And where you are is where you are not.[37]

These words prepare us for the journey to Little Gidding, accompanied by Julian of Norwich, the author of *The Cloud of Unknowing*, and by all the desert travelers in the apophatic tradition of negation with whom we have been walking. I shall concentrate only on part one. That will be enough. For it is here that the desert is referred to, but to be here, in the fens of Eastern England, is finally enough. Here, too, is to be found the end of the world.

> There are other places
> Which are also at the world's end, some at the sea jaws,
> Or over a dark lake, in a desert or in city –
> But this is the nearest, in place and time,
> Now and in England.[38]

We find the themes we have been exploring coming together here: the specifics of place and the reality of its physical conditions; the blurring of categories of time and space; the utopic vision of the garden; the journey whose "purpose is altered in fulfillment."

Already in the first two lines of "Little Gidding" we are in a season that is suspended in time, like the Fathers and Mothers who dwelt on earth yet as true citizens of heaven. We are in a real moment in time, yet "sempiternal" – a moment which is never and always. It is a place and time of pure in-betweenness – in the dialectic of the tropic and the pole, between the light and the dark, at the depth of winter and yet the moment of growth. Here we cannot dwell, but only journey on. Here the light blinds, like the winter sun on the frozen pond, its rays almost horizontal, not vertical, and the cold burns more intensely than the blaze of branch. The soul is caught in that transitory moment between melting and freezing. What is extraordinary is that this is a moment that is all too familiar – an experience known on a winter's walk in England, but never acknowledged as anything but ordinary. Yet the wisdom of the desert, like all true poetry, takes the plain and everyday and makes it "unimaginable." For it is by this wisdom that we realize our true being.

We may begin our journey in the depths of winter or in the early summer of May, and it would be the same, and its end the same. In May the hedges are still white, though with blossom, not snow, a "voluptuary sweetness." Nor is the purpose of our journey the issue. It is the journey itself. As we have seen, men and women have gone out into the desert and made this journey for many different reasons, by no means all of them religious. Some have gone to war, some have gone simply to explore that which is unknown, some have gone seeking healing, and some have gone for no reason at all – yet there is a coherence in their journeying that binds them all together. The end of the journey is the same, though for some it is a judgment, as in McCarthy's terrifying novel *Blood Meridian*; for some, like Wilfred Thesiger, it brings nostalgia for lost cultures; for others it ends in a mystery like the fate of Sentain at the end of *Beau Travail*. For Charles de Foucauld, it was assassination. For the Jesus of Matthew 4 and Mark 1, it is the beginning of a ministry; for others, like the Jesus of *Quarantine*, it is, it seems, the end. The real meet the fictional – perhaps there is no difference. Perhaps these differences meet as in the great cry from the cross in John 19:30, the Greek verb in the perfect tense, *Tetelestai* – "It is finished," which is also a new beginning, for, as we are reminded in "Little Gidding,"

> What we call the beginning is often the end
> And to make an end is to make a beginning.

The end of the journey is the same – Little Gidding is always there with its pig-sty, its dull façade and the tombstone: always the tomb as a reminder. And every purpose becomes only a "husk of meaning," for the end is always other than our intentions, is always the unexpected "other" precisely because it is now and here, where we least expect it.

This is what Antony discovered in the interior mountain, and Teresa, in her way, in the *Interior Castle*: that this most real of all places is not a place, though there is no other. It is a space beyond the reach of enquiry or knowledge, and we are not come to it for instruction, to satisfy curiosity or report back. All these things have driven men and women into the desert, and yet there has always been something more than that. For a few, it is prayer – for others, it is a mystery that some choose to face and others finally do not. For all of them it is what Eliot calls "the intersection of the timeless moment," a reconciliation of opposites when time and space become one and singular in a landscape that is always more and other; a landscape that both kills and redeems and is absolutely indifferent and pure. It is never and always. As Thesiger found, "Round us was a silence in which only the winds played, and a cleanness that was infinitely remote from the world of men."[39]

Notes

1 Jacques Derrida, "Before the Law," in Derek Attridge (ed.), *Acts of Literature* (London: Routledge, 1992), pp. 203–5. I am grateful to Lori Branch for directing me to this passage.
2 Valentine Cunningham, *In the Reading Gaol: Postmodernity, Texts and History* (Oxford: Blackwell, 1994), p. 402. See also Jacques Derrida, "Post-Scriptum: Aporias, Ways and Voices," in Harold Coward and Toby Fashay (eds.), *Derrida and Negative Theology* (Albany: State University of New York Press, 1992), pp. 73–142.
3 Jacques Derrida, "Edmond Jabès and the Question of the Book," in *Writing and Difference*, translated by Alan Bass (London: Routledge and Kegan Paul, 1981), p. 72.
4 See Jacques Derrida, "Force of Law: The Mystical Foundation of Authority," in Druscilla Cornell, Michael Rosenfield, and David Gray (eds.), *Deconstruction and the Possibility of Justice* (London: Routledge, 1992), pp. 3–67.
5 Jacques Derrida, "Faith and Knowledge: The Two Sources of Religion at the Limits of Reason Alone," in Jacques Derrida and Gianno Vattimo (eds.), *Religion* (Stanford, CA: Stanford University Press, 1998), p. 21.
6 Derrida, "Edmond Jabès and the Question of the Book," p. 67.
7 Ibid, p. 69.
8 Edmond Jabès, *Le Livre des questions* (Paris: Gallimard, 1963), quoted in Derrida, "Edmond Jabès and the Question of the Book," p. 66.
9 Derrida, "Edmond Jabès and the Question of the Book," p. 70.
10 Ibid, p. 72.
11 Ibid, p. 77.
12 Ibid, p. 76.
13 Ibid, p. 78.
14 Susan Sontag, "Writing Itself: On Roland Barthes," in Susan Sontag (ed.), *Barthes: Selected Writings* (London: Fontana), p. viii.
15 Graham Ward (ed.), *The Postmodern God: A Theological Reader* (Oxford: Blackwell, 1997), p. xv.
16 Ibid.
17 P. Berry and A. Wernick (eds.), *Shadow of Spirit: Postmodernism and Religion* (London: Routledge, 1992), p. 1.
18 See chapter 8, p. 117.
19 Maurice Blanchot, *The Space of Literature*, translated by A. Smock (Lincoln: University of Nebraska Press, 1982), pp. 21–2.
20 Franz Kafka, *The Trial*, translated by W. Muir and E. Muir (Harmondsworth: Penguin Books, 1974), p. 1.
21 Blanchot, *The Space of Literature*, p. 83.
22 See chapter 10, p. 156.
23 Samuel Beckett, *Waiting for Godot* (London: Faber and Faber, 1956), p. 94.

24 See above, pp. 11–12.
25 Michel de Certeau, *The Mystic Fable, Vol. 1: The Sixteenth and Seventeenth Centuries*, translated by Michael B. Smith (Chicago: University of Chicago Press, 1992), pp. 33–4.
26 Edith Wyschogrod, *Saints and Postmodernism: Revisioning Moral Philosophy* (Chicago: University of Chicago Press, 1990), p. xxiv. See also Mark A. McIntosh, *Mystical Theology* (Oxford: Blackwell, 1998), p. 216.
27 Wyschogrod, *Saints and Postmodernism*, p. 58.
28 Ibid, p. 255.
29 Michel de Certeau, "Mystic Speech," in Graham Ward (ed.), *The Certeau Reader* (Oxford: Blackwell, 2000), p. 203.
30 See p. 74.
31 See also Andrew Louth, *The Wilderness of God* (Nashville, TN: Abingdon Press, 1991), p. 152.
32 T. S. Eliot, *The Four Quartets*, in *The Complete Poems and Plays, 1909–1950* (New York: Harcourt, Brace and World, 1952), pp. 117–48.
33 Louth, *The Wilderness of God*, p. 153. Louth points out that Eliot used the word Aranyaka in a draft of "East Coker," but later deleted it.
34 T. S. Eliot, *Murder in the Cathedral*, in *The Complete Poems and Plays, 1909–1950*, p. 221.
35 T. S. Eliot, "Towards a Christian Britain," *The Listener* 25 (January–June, 1941), pp. 524ff. See also Lyndall Gordon, *Eliot's New Life* (Oxford: Oxford University Press, 1988), p. 318.
36 The end of "East Coker."
37 Eliot, *The Complete Poems and Plays*, p. 127.
38 Ibid, p. 139.
39 Wilfred Thesiger, *Arabian Sands* (Harmondsworth: Penguin Books, 1991), p. 32. See also above, chapter 6, p. 77.

Postscript
The Desert and the Recent Wars in Iraq

In his novel *The English Patient*, Michael Ondaatje writes of how from the
Greek historian Herodotus in the fifth century BCE to the "sunburned,
exhausted" European explorers of the nineteenth century, the desert has burned
itself upon the Western imagination, its mythology rejuvenated by the discoveries of America and Australia. Ondaatje is speaking, of course, of the
deserts of Egypt and the Sahara, which in Arabic means, roughly, "the brown
void," but can also mean "nothingness," a forgetting of the world rather
akin to the Greek word *lethe*. But the European mind has been even more
profoundly moved by tales of travelers in deserts further east than Egypt –
the biblical wanderers who begin with Abram, followed by Moses and the
Israelites, Elijah, and finally the Jesus of the gospels. Abram, with his father
Terah, came from Ur of the Chaldees, linked by a later incident with the
theme which will run as a thread throughout this postscript. For Ur of the
Chaldees was one day to be buried by a ferocious dust-storm, prompting
the Assyrians to send an army of archers to fight the approaching sand-laden

wind. This odd, and presumably vain, military tactic was not unique in ancient history. For Herodotus, also, recounts how, two and a half thousand years ago, a Libyan army marched into the Sahara to subdue the terrible lord of the desert wind. The troops vanished for ever, "disappearing," says Herodotus, "in battle array, with drums and cymbals beating, into a red cloud of swirling sand."[1] If we find this naive and foolish, I wonder if we today have yet learned our lesson.

The theme of wind is a constant one in all desert literature. Where there is nothing else, there is always the wind blowing across the wilderness, described by all wanderers – a wind benign or angry. Spirit or *ruach*, once the cool evening breeze enjoyed by the Lord God in Genesis 3:8, is also found in the Sahara blowing as the *simoun* (the Arabic word for poison): the Moroccan *sirocco* or the Indian *loo*, described by Rudyard Kipling as a "red-hot wind from the westward, booming among the tinder-dry trees and pretending that the rain was on its heels." And remembering the storms that raged on Mount Sinai when Moses ascended to speak with God, or the winds on Mount Horeb when Elijah meets God there, it is not unreasonable to regard Yahweh as originally a Semitic storm god, like his later, demonized rival, Baal. It is probable, too, that the legend of Prester John, made famous in the *Travels* of John Mandeville, published in 1361, began in stories of an ancient desert storm god interpreted by European travelers on the Silk Route to the East to suit their own fancy and doctrine. The armies of ancient Libya and Assyria marched out to wage war on a terrible deity who was everywhere and nowhere and who was indifferently both god and devil, and there was no telling the difference. For, as Ernest Rénan once remarked, "Le Désert est monothéiste" – its god is one, and brooks no rivals and no opponents, which is why the theology of the Desert Fathers, like that of the New Testament, is full of demons, but fiercely and absolutely monotheistic, all being finally absorbed into the one being of God. But the desert wind does not only rage. It has other voices, and not least the still small voice of silence that finally speaks to Elijah on Horeb. The phrase is almost untranslatable from the Hebrew of 1 Kings 19. It denotes the stillness between silence and whisper that is felt and heard when the elements are in repose after a storm, as in Psalm 107:29: "He made the storm be *still* and the waves of the sea were hushed." It is a silence heard in the purest of winds that features in all writings of those who have traveled in the desert – T. E. Lawrence begins his great *Seven Pillars of Wisdom* with a reference to it: it is the best of all – it has no taste.

The wind is one and without age, blowing through the vast variety of the literature of the desert and binding it into a strange unity that our scholarship finds it hard to embrace and give any focus. It is ubiquitous and has powerful effects – indeed it defines the nature of existence in these desert places – and yet it is nowhere and is nothing. It lies at the heart of necessary fictions, from the accounts of the Exodus, to the gospels, to the fantastic lives of the Desert Fathers of Egypt, to the modern fiction of Rider Haggard, Michael Ondaatje, Jim Crace, and Cormac McCarthy.

What do we mean by "necessary fictions"? As a preface to his novel *Quarantine*, Jim Crace quotes a few words from a book entitled *The Limits of Mortality* (1993) by Ellis Winward and Michael Soule:

> An ordinary man of average weight and fitness embarking on a total fast – that is, a fast during which he refuses both his food and drink – could not expect to live for more than thirty days, not to be conscious for more than twenty-five. For him, the forty days of fasting described in religious texts would not be achievable – except with divine help, of course. History, however, does not record an intervention of that kind, and medicine opposes it.

By this account, then, the narrative of Jesus' forty days in the Judean wilderness is not true. He managed forty days – and the gospel tells us that he was hungry and certainly conscious enough to have a pretty good debate with the devil. In the end the angels intervene – divine help – and all is well. But this is not history and is medically off the scale of possibility. No doubt Winward and Soule would equally say that the accounts of the incredible fasting of the desert monks – one loaf a week for years on end – are just made up. But they make good and very persistent stories, and so Jim Crace, a modern novelist, jumps onto the bandwagon and tells the story of Jesus fasting in the desert again in *Quarantine*. But Crace admits that he is just a novelist – he makes things up. He is a writer of fiction and his primary tool is the imagination. In his novel he plays both sides of the court. Crace is not as naive as the evangelists – and his Jesus dies, having pushed the limits of mortality too far. But at the same time this does not seem to be an end. There is something more, mysteriously, something that can only be described as in that no-place and no-time of the desert wind. Crace is in his element as a novelist – he has to make this world up – it does not exist. Or perhaps it does exist very powerfully, but not in the categories of history or medicine. He makes it up because he has to, because his fictional world is something we take with absolute seriousness as the only "place" – an utterly deserted place without verification – and a vision from which all else flows. Here we may begin to suspect that the theologian should be contributing something, but he or she is rendered speechless and strangely skeptical, satiated by too many historical quests and burdened by a language that fails to take Jim Crace seriously (he just makes things up) and equally fails to take the Bible seriously (though in the opposite way, wrapping it up in cotton wool) when it does the same as Crace – makes it up. But in this place, in the desert, that is all you can do, and only then can it become a place of vision from which all else flows. That is the secret of the Desert Fathers and why we take them seriously, and yet we have systematically forgotten that it is so.

And so we move to the company of desert travelers who come after Abram, Moses, and Elijah. There is Jesus himself, of course, in Matthew 4 and elsewhere in the gospels where he goes out into the desert. Here also is just a sample from the writings of travelers who are not noted for their piety or religious concerns, yet who begin to speak a common language that is remarkably consistent across vast differences of culture, time, and place. Gertrude Bell (1868–1926) was a remarkable woman, an early graduate of Lady Margaret Hall, Oxford, who became a leading Arabic scholar and spent the last seven years of her life in Iraq as Oriental Secretary to the British Civil Administrator. In her book *The Desert and the Sown* (1907),[2] she is struck again by the profound importance of the biblical and early Christian desert traditions, still surviving in the monasteries of the Middle Eastern deserts, as she crosses the wilderness of Judea that has been, she writes, "nurse to the fiery spirit of man."

> Out of it strode grim prophets, menacing with doom a world of which they had neither part nor understanding; the valleys are full of the caves that held them, nay, some are peopled to this day by a race of gaunt and starved ascetics, clinging to a tradition of piety that common sense has found it hard to discredit.[3]

A very different writer, William Henry Hudson (1841–1922), contemporary with Gertrude Bell, was an Englishman who lived for 33 years in the deserts of Patagonia, in South America, where he discovered in solitude something of the spirit of the desert ascetics of Egypt. In his book *Idle Days in Patagonia* (1917), Hudson writes of the "gray, monotonous solitude" that became so important for him so that he sought it daily, "going to it in the morning as if to attend a festival." And yet, he continues, he had no object in going out into the desert in solitude. He went to respect the silence, and to *listen* to it. Furthermore, Hudson goes on, "during those solitary days it was a rare thing for any thought to cross my mind . . . In that novel state of mind I was in, thought had become impossible . . . my mind had suddenly transformed itself from a thinking machine into a machine for some other unknown purpose."[4] Hudson describes the change in his condition as if he had changed his very identity: himself as another – *soi-même comme un autre*; a phrase to which I shall return a little later. Hudson's narrative, as I have reported it, is pretty dry and prosaic, and yet his descriptions would be immediately familiar to anyone who has read Palladius, Rufinus, John Moschos, or the other reporters of the Christian desert monastics of the fourth and fifth centuries.

Very different is the bizarre French novelist who wrote under the name of Pierre Loti (1850–1923), who at various times was also a soldier, a painter, an acrobat, and a female impersonator. Crossing the Sinai Desert in 1894, Loti records his experiences in his book *Le Désert* (1895), in which the actual blends seamlessly with the fantastic – another trait of the stories of the Desert Fathers. Loti regards the desert from the Bible, and the Bible from the desert, interpolating descriptions of his own journey with biblical descriptions, largely from Exodus, of the wanderings of the Israelites in the same wilderness. What is remarkable (Loti having no particularly religious or theological concerns) is how accurately the biblical descriptions match his own experience; for example, the desert storm which precedes the theophany of Exodus 19 precisely describes Loti's experience of the same place with its echo like an unearthly voice:

> In the middle of the night, we are awakened by the racket of thunder made outsize and terrible here in this resonant echoing valley. A violent wind shakes our fragile canvas houses and threatens to blow us away. And our camels moan in the sudden and torrential downpour.[5]

Compare the description of the storm in Exodus 19:16.

Loti is a shameless romantic, and the desert has always given rise to a romanticism that found new life in the aestheticism of the nineteenth century, but is clearly discernible in the *Lives of the Desert Fathers* also. St. Antony of Egypt was one of the great romantics of world history. But, as always, there is another side to the picture. In *Roughing It* (1872), Mark Twain writes about his "vagabonding" through the deserts of the American West, and at one point recalls the country around Salt Lake City, Utah. Before the travelers set out, all is eager anticipation for their dramatic adventure. But, Twain admitted, "this enthusiasm, this stern thirst for adventure, wilted under the sultry August sun and did not last above one hour. One poor little hour – and then we were ashamed we had 'gushed' so. The poetry was all in the anticipation." By the end of the journey, Twain admits, the romance had faded away and "left the desert trip nothing but a harsh reality."[6] More than that, Twain the writer, never at a loss for words, admits that the desert experience defeated the power of words to describe it, and he is left speechless. He tells us all this quite beautifully, of course, but the point is an important one – and somehow reminiscent of the stories in the great collections of the *Sayings of the Desert Fathers*, of the Elders who warned off young aspiring monks who came to them with romantic notions of the desert life, using wise but few words so as not to disturb the silence to which their lives were attentive.

Then there is the strange and learned English traveler and explorer Charles M. Doughty (1843–1926), for whose book *Travels in Arabia Deserta* none other than T. E. Lawrence himself wrote a preface. Doughty, who was the first known Christian to enter Mecca, was a brilliant Arabic scholar, and his strange literary style is the result of seeking the inflections and rhythms of Arabic in English – a verbal example of the way in which the desert tends to elide differences of culture, religion, and even language, its truth, perhaps, universal, its storm god the willing guest of many traditions but finally fully appropriated by none. Doughty begins the account of his journey with these strange words: "The new dawn appearing we removed not yet. The day risen the tents were dismantled, the camels led in ready to their companies, and halted beside their loads. We waited to hear the cannon shot which should open that year's pilgrimage."[7]

And lastly, a few words from a journal I myself kept while I spent some time as a solitary in the wilderness of southern Texas, the last and least in this company of travelers.

> It hasn't been quite what I expected, but then things rarely are. I had a much more romantic image, absurdly constructed from myth, film, books. Of course, it is different. It has not been the grand desert of limitless sands and rocks and hills. But it has been something more than that – a place which is neither exterior nor interior, and remote. I should have expected as much, of course – to travel all this way and find a place which has been familiar all along but hitherto largely unfrequented by me. It is a place we all know, individually, but rarely if ever visit. I don't think I could live here for very long.

The enduring themes, then, are present, in the most hard-bitten and most inexperienced of travelers, and they are the themes which the Fathers and Mothers of the monastic rules of the West that followed Antony, Pachomius, and others, rooted at the heart of a theological tradition whose profound wisdom has been long almost unheard and is only now re-emerging in sometimes radical and startling ways. It is a tradition that finally "common sense has found it hard to discredit."

It has been long unheard in the Christian West because theology itself has been too attached to its parent institutions, too brash and often too dogmatic to attend to the voices of the poets who have continued to speak it. For poetry and the desert have had from the first a deep and intimate relationship. One need only read Deutero-Isaiah or the Psalms to be reminded of this. Or, less well known, there is the extraordinary desert rabbi and mystic of the seventh century CE, Eleazar ha-Kallir, whose beautiful "Invocation to the Prince of Rain" rehearses biblical history from the patriarchs as a celebration of water, the gold of the desert:

> remember the one they drew out
> > from a reed boat
> > > in the water
> they commanded
> > & didn't he water his flock
> > > with water
> the people you chose
> > when they thirsted
> > > for water
> he beat on the rock
> > it opened & gave out
> > > water
> because of him pour down your water
> remember the temple priest
> > who bathed 5 times
> > > in water.[8]

And so he goes on. In Chile, the poet Pablo Neruda (1904–73) found he could speak with the people of the deserts of Chile because his poetry provided a way of talking, and wherever he went, people asked to hear his poems. "I never knew," he said, "if my audience understood all or even some of my poems; it was hard to tell in that absolute silence, in the sort of awe with which they listened." Yet Neruda admits that he is a poet of the desert precisely because "the desert does not speak. I could not comprehend its tongue: its silence."[9] Perhaps the poet alone – regardless of culture – is content to speak from and of silence. The greatest mystics are poets – truly people of the desert, though often an interior one. And if, for us, the desert is a place to leave – to *desert* because it is deserted – Arabic poetry is not a "desertion" of the wilderness, but rather an entering into it, and into its secret and mysterious life that is often hidden in wells that are buried deep below the surface. In the same way, the ancient Hebrew poet enters into the vale of misery and finds there a well. The modern poetry of Edmond Jabès, an Egyptian Jew who spent most of his life in exile in France, combines the Arab-Islamic imagination with his deep study of Kabbalah and Jewish mysticism. The Sahara was central to his work; a place that was intensely a part of his upbringing and yet also a metaphor and symbol. In the interviews published as *From the Desert to the Book*, Jabès says:

As far as the word *desert* is concerned, what fascinates me is to see how far the metaphor of the void, from being used so much, has permeated the whole word. The word itself has become a metaphor. To give it back its strength, one has therefore to return to the real desert which is indeed exemplary emptiness – but an emptiness with its own, very real dust. Think also about the word *book*.[10]

Jabès' poetry moves endlessly between the actual sand of the desert and the word and book. But at its silent heart his poetry is deeply religious, and, it seems to me, deeply rabbinic. He writes: "Man does not exist. God does not exist. The world alone exists through God and man in the open book."[11] Jabès reminds us that one of the Hebrew names of God is *Hammakom*, which means *Place*. God is the place – as the book is. He continues: "Bringing these two together is something that has always excited me. God, through His Name, is the book. In one of my works I noted that one writes only in the effacement of the Divine Name – of the place."[12]

This place can only be the place which is, in all human terms, the place of negation: the nothing: the effacement of the human. Jabès moves easily through the Egypt of Western Orientalist construction, brilliantly and per-versely analyzed by Edward Said, although he is himself at the same time deeply romantic. But Jabès' romanticism is spare and paradoxical, flourish-ing in the utopia of no-time and no-place: never and always. This, for him, is the utterly real. For, he likes to say, time is merely an artificial concept, "something artificial laid over something real." And so he looks to the fatal-ism and indifference of the desert dweller, lost in time and space, for "his words are the wisdom of millennia, drawn from the desert – they are the words of the sand, as vast as NOTHINGNESS."[13] In the desert, the poet who listens knows the rhythm from beyond silence in the tiniest trace and mark in the sands that are words to be read by those who are attentive to them. Reading Bruce Chatwin's book of the Australian desert, *The Songlines* (1987), I was struck by the echoes of Jabès in the ancient Aboriginal notion of music and the melodic contour of song as a map which is one in its rise and fall with the nature of the land over which it passes.

What has our forgetfulness, our amnesia, of this cost us? Before I return in a little more detail to the Desert Fathers and Mothers, I want to take a slight detour, the purpose of which will, I hope, become clear. But, although intellectual, it is not so very far from the desert where, says John Steinbeck in *The Log from the Sea of Cortez*, "the great concept of oneness and of majestic order seems always to be born" and "in such a place lived the hermits of the early church piercing to infinity with uninhibited minds."[14]

First, Derrida's 1990 essay, "Force of Law: The 'Mystical Foundation of Authority.' "[15] From its undecidable moment of foundation, a legal system, says Derrida, cannot be described in terms of its origins as undergoing a continuous historical development, but rather as a rupture from the past that establishes the new system. The "force of law" is a performative and interpretive violence – performative in the declaration of the new law, and interpretive in its particular claims to be legitimate. A *logos*, Derrida suggests, is established and claims its right by interpretive force which negates interpretive undecidability. However, it is precisely at this negation that a limit and a silence are reached, and Derrida concludes, "It is what I here propose to call the mystical." But this is not a limit that is outside the law. Quite to the contrary, it is absolutely *of* the law, that which makes law law; in Derrida's words, "Walled up, walled in because silence is not exterior to language."[16] It is here, indeed, that one discovers the possibility of a recovery of the notion and practice of "justice." What is clear is that Derrida has made a move in the radical (dare one say, postmodern?) recovery of the aporetic and probably impossible necessity inherent in the very practice of law, that exactly tracks the movement of the early Desert Fathers in their radical critique of Roman law and society and their trek into the desert to find a silence that is not exterior to language but its very heart – a vital move for human "being" that has been whispered through the Christian centuries by a few mystics (who have more often than not found themselves standing outside the law) and by one or two poets or holy fools.

Second, and even more briefly: the philosopher Emmanuel Levinas in *Totality and Infinity* (1961) affirms: "Goodness consists in taking up a position in being such that the Other counts more than myself. Goodness thus involves the possibility for the I that is exposed to the alienation of its powers by death to not be for death."[17] It is thus in death that Levinas discovers the radical and *ethical* alterity of the Other. Such a radical and ethical shift or "reconditioning" is precisely enacted by St. Antony, as we have the account of his life in the work almost certainly written by St. Athanasius. For in the desert were the cities of the dead – the most ancient of all cities – where the dead were entombed beyond the boundaries of the human world, sent away for fear of contamination. Here Antony took up residence in a tomb, embracing death and the other in a total exchange of self for the Other – only to emerge, like Lazarus, in perfect health of mind and body. The desert is utter alterity, the nothing to life's demand for "being," and yet it is precisely here that life is to be found in the Other. But we must go just a little further with Levinas. If the ethical obligation to the Other and also to a future which never becomes, and never can become, present is a move against the synthesizing nature of the ego, such also is the structure of language and the significance of signification, as we find in Levinas' use of the terms "trace" and "expression." What he explores in his article of 1963, "The Trace of the Other," is an alterity in language that also, I suggest, lies at the heart of the poetic and literary traditions of the desert. Language as a shifting network of signs and deferrals cannot be other than familiar to those who live within the shifting landscape of sand, traces, and mirage.

Furthermore, in the work of Levinas, and in Paul Ricoeur's master-work *Soi-même comme un autre* (*Oneself as Another*) (1990), the absolute central-ity of the theological motivation is guarded against the dangers of hubris by a hiddenness that at the same time ensures its deepest presence. This is apparent even in Ricoeur's preface to his book, where he states "all my philo-sophical work, leads to a type of philosophy from which the actual mention of God is absent and in which the question of God, as a philosophical ques-tion, itself remains in a suspension that could be called 'agnostic.'"

In these briefest of excursions into contemporary thought we have glimpsed, I suggest, intellectual and ethical moves that offer us in our own time the gleams of light that the desert experiments of the early Christian church also offered. One could, I am sure, find similar examples in other religious traditions. Furthermore, they are moves that are crucial for theo-logy, although theologians then as now have too often been unwilling to follow the lead, for it is a hard road and demands much of us in mind, body, and spirit. In addition, those who lead have too frequently been outside the charmed circle of theological orthodoxy or expression – the poets or mystics, even the Fathers themselves, who have cared little or not at all whether their travels take them beyond the acceptable or the respectable. To the company of desert travelers, we must now add an unlikely crew – from St. Antony, to the Spanish mystic St. John of the Cross, to the English poet William Blake. There is in each the soul of the mystic – and we remember that term as it was used by Derrida in "Force of Law." In his *Ascent of Mount Carmel*, St. John of the Cross insists upon the necessity of passing through the dark night of sense into a true darkness that is either the heart of darkness, the hell discovered by Joseph Conrad at the soul of the modern empire, or the darkness of Antony's interior mountain, a darkness visible as the presence of the wholly other, and therefore necessarily absent, God. To enter this darkness demands a journey that few of us are prepared to make, for it is to enter into a vision that demands not less than everything, a total vision as in the prophetic texts of Blake, that cannot finally be taught, or even com-municated, for it can be made only in utter solitude, which is what the Fathers sought above all. For only in such solitude can be discovered the true nature of human being understood as Total Presence, an absolute realization of the chiasmic reversals of the gospels themselves: only in the utter indifference to life is life truly discovered. Thus – and this will be my final excursion into contemporary theology and thought – that true desert traveler of the spirit, the theologian Thomas Altizer, concludes his book *Total Presence* with these words:

> Genuine solitude is a voyage into the interior, but it is a voyage which cul-
> minates in a loss of our interior, a loss reversing every manifest or established
> center of our interior so as to make possible the advent of a wholly new but
> totally immediate world . . . But the real end or reversal of an individual interior
> makes possible the actual advent of a universal presence, a presence transcending
> all interior and individual identity, and presenting itself beyond our interior,
> and beyond every possible interior, as a total and immediate presence.[18]

This, it seems to me, describes perfectly the journeys and extraordinary asceti-
cism of the early desert monks of the fourth and fifth centuries, before their piercing to infinity with uninhibited minds began to be tamed and ordered in the monastic rules that started to emerge in the West through men like John Cassian and later St. Benedict. They enacted in their actual journeys into the interior a mystery which was subsequently largely forgotten and for which we have paid the price, both theologically and ethically. In the prologue to the *Lives of the Desert Fathers* they are described in biblical terms:

> They have slain wild beasts. They have performed cures, miracles and acts of
> power like those which the holy prophets and apostles worked. The Savior
> performs miracles through them in the same way. Indeed, it is clear to all who
> dwell there that through them the world is kept in being, and that through
> them too human life is preserved and honored by God.[19]

We see them in the desert, waiting on God, "waiting for Christ like loyal sons watching for their father, or like an army expecting its emperor, or like a sober household looking forward to the arrival of its master and liberator." Trained in indifference, they wait with perfect equanimity, perfect rest or *quies*. They understood exactly the word "liberate," and for this reason it can be affirmed that through them the world is indeed liberated and kept in being. Speaking little of Christ, and hating absolutely the heresy of the Arians, for whom Christ is part of the created world, they identified absolutely with the Christ who goes out into the wilderness to fight with the devil and who meets death in utter solitude on the cross: absolutely. Their sole preoccupation was a total unity with Christ, so that through the trans-
parent membrane of their fragile lives the passage between the divine and human, by which our most fundamental being, as made in the image and likeness of God, is preserved. Here the prologue to the *Lives* is quite precise:

"But while dwelling on earth in this manner they live as true citizens of heaven."[20] The language is almost Christological.

When the young Antony left the civilized world of his childhood and stepped out into the desert, sometime just after 270 CE, he was making a radical political statement in defiance of the principles and claims of the Roman Empire – a crazy enough gesture in the face of a power that effectively ruled the whole Western world. While the Fathers and Mothers followed a biblical tradition, it was neither the story of Israel's wanderings in Sinai (though that would be crucial in the later mystical traditions of the desert that flowered in the writing of the Pseudo-Dionysius), nor even the forty days of Jesus while he prepared for his ministry (though the theme of temptation is present in all the literature of these ascetics, and they, too, fought with their demons of lust and hunger). Rather, it was the story of Elijah that lay at the very heart of the enterprise. For, in 1 Kings 17, Elijah warns Ahab of a coming drought in the land, and is himself guided by God to the Wadi Cherith where he is sustained, even in the desert, by the ravens who feed him morning and evening. For the Egypt of Antony, the "present age" of the fertile Nile valley was but a fragile stay against the ever-present threat of famine, bounded by the clear ecological boundary of the limitless desert beyond. It was a world with no "outside," for the desert was to be shunned, the absolute "other" upon which one turned one's back. Indeed, the same could be said of the rim of the entire Roman Empire. Beyond it lay the endless and trackless wilderness. Of the terrible deserts beyond the river valley, Peter Brown has said "there was no outside viewing-point from which to take the measure of [their] faceless immensity, and no hope of disengagement from [their] clutches other than through drastic rituals."[21]

What Antony did was provide an outside viewing-point, both for the world and for Christian theology: a perspective from which both could be viewed and reassessed. He crossed the boundary into the "other" in a gesture that was actual, political, and (recalling Levinas) ethical. He made the impossible possible in a primal counter-cultural move that made the desert itself a "counter-world" and, in the famous image from the *Life of St. Antony*, the desert becomes a "city." Thus the first great monastery communities of Pachomius, who died in 346, were nothing short of Christian theology in the making – cities of the world where men and women lived as "true citizens of heaven." Not surprisingly, the image of the lost paradise and the true kingdom quickly followed in the literature that was written about these pioneers. At the same time, their asceticism, and above all their ability to survive and flourish on either next to nothing or even just the eucharistic elements themselves (that is, spiritual food), was both a living proof of the gospel reminder from Jesus' temptations, recalling Deuteronomy 8:3, that "one does not live by bread alone," and equally a powerful sign to those within the fertile, but fragile, zone of the Nile Valley that the threatening "other" can be embraced and even be a place of flourishing – what therefore have *we* to fear? God will provide, as he did for Elijah. In other words, Antony's move represented and effected a huge symbolic shift in how the world was to be perceived – by renouncing the world, the fears which bound the world are altered in a theological gesture taken to the extreme in the human body, and thus the world is kept in being and at the same time its whole power structure, politically built by the imperial rulers from within, is altered by an alterity that Levinas was to describe in *Time and the Other* as nothing short of a "transubstantiation." It was, so to speak, a sacramental move. Peter Brown expresses it more immediately in the example of Antony:

> It was his triumph in the struggle with hunger that released in the popular imagination the most majestic and the most haunting images of a new humanity. Nothing less than the hope of Paradise regained flickered, spasmodically but recognizably, around the figures who dared to create a human "city" in the landscape void of human food.[22]

I have deliberately brought together this far an assorted company of desert wanderers and poets, thinkers, and theologians who finally speak together with a strange and insistent harmony. Nor do I underestimate the growing chorus of ecological reminders telling us of the absolute necessity for the preservation of this fragile, indifferent, empty "other": in 1851 Henry David Thoreau, from his solitude by Walden Pond, asserted: "in Wilderness is the preservation of the World."[23] And so, what of our present world crisis? Here I can only speculate. But as our armies create havoc in the deserts of Iraq, their ghastly instruments of war etching no delicate traces wherein may be read the words of the open book in which alone exists, as Jabès reminds us, both God and man, but rather deep ruts and wounds, I recall the ancient image of the army sallying forth in battle array to subdue the lord of the desert wind, never to be seen again. In the first Gulf War of 1991, named Operation Desert Storm, the allied armies had already crossed the fatal boundary by arrogating to themselves the title of the Storm God who is Yahweh, Baal, the eternal "Other." They became themselves as gods – recalling Satan's fateful words to Eve before the Fall in Milton's *Paradise Lost*.

At the same time it has been necessary to invent a devil, the embodiment of all evil – Saddam Hussein, undoubtedly a conveniently wicked candidate. But, as we have seen, in the deep interior of the desert there is a place which is no-place, a utopia or a dystopia, either the lost paradise or the heart of darkness. In its latter guise, Conrad describes it brilliantly in his novella – a gray, insubstantial place of terrible indifference, caring neither if we live nor die – making us forgetful in our rage that it is precisely this indifference (spoken of also by T. S. Eliot in "Little Gidding") that the Fathers made the basis of their *quies*, or rest and peace in their being. Make of the God your opponent and he will become all the evil imaginable, and become the eternal opponent in a dualistic vision that forgets Rénan's words of wisdom, "Le Désert est monothéiste." If it is not Osama bin Laden it will be Saddam Hussein, and the face of evil can never cease there, because it is always necessary for the vision that has brought the "other" back into the fold that Antony broke from in a reversal of his ethical gesture, and now a gesture ensuring an eternal, demonic dualism. If Antony's journey was profoundly Christian, generously religious and a courageously, radically theological experiment – then the recent war against Iraq is, at its very heart, the antithesis of all these. (I am not speaking here at the level of either politics or economics – for these things, in my argument, merely flow from more primary sources in human being.)

As it was for the Roman Empire, so it was for the British Empire, and so will it be for all who follow. The Romans brought, they claimed, law and order to an unruly world, and there may be some truth in that. But there was an inevitable corruption at its heart, and they forgot what Derrida only now reminds us of – the mystical foundation of authority and the aporetic silence which makes the law law. The British, in their turn, brought the gospel to the heathen in their blindness, but it was the gospel of an alien culture too often imposed from within the structures of imperial power. And now – will the new Empire bring peace? No, because it has, quite simply, dared to break the fundamental sanctity and law of the desert itself. An earlier soldier who went into the deserts of Arabia, T. E. Lawrence, learned a very different truth. As we read in *The Seven Pillars of Wisdom*, from the beginning Lawrence's view of the Sinai Desert was religious and precise. He was successful precisely because he recognized that the war between Great Britain and Turkey could not be fought there with conventional modern armor and weapons. His genius was to use the desert itself against the technology that both threatened to destroy it and was itself finally destroyed by it. Against the Arab tribesmen of Prince Feisal, under the leadership of Lawrence, the Turkish army became another vain military operation that was lost in the desert – in Medina to be precise. Ultimately, Lawrence's tragedy was that he could never achieve the sanity and poise of the true desert ascetic: perhaps he was ultimately too much of a showman, without the necessary common sense. But in the final, understated words of the *Seven Pillars* (a fine example of British litotes), he himself acknowledges his tragedy – that he had to return to the "world," but only in the returning realized what he had lost: "In the end he [General Allenby] agreed [to let me go]; and then at once I knew how much I was sorry."[24]

The desert, as I have tried to demonstrate, provokes and demands a complex response. I have deliberately mixed journals and travel diaries with poetry, theology, and philosophical reflection – though at the heart there is, I believe, a profound and universal theological language whose images and rhythms govern all. Increasingly, as we erode the physical surface of our world, the voices of ecological anxiety are heard in defense of the fragile wilderness, and beneath their romanticism is a hard message. But I have left until almost the end the voice of fiction, although it has been present all the time. For the great biblical narratives and the gospels are best read as true fiction, while the narrators of the *Lives of the Desert Fathers* describe the extraordinary, larger-than-life men and women whom they encounter with the imaginative pen of the poet and novelist. It is too soon, even after the first Gulf War, for much of a literature to have emerged from it. Once the shrill and unreflective voices of politicians and military leaders have ceased and have moved on to other more immediate targets, the poets generally take time before they speak with the maturity of hindsight. One novel, however – Dominique Sigaud's *Somewhere in a Desert* (1998) – has emerged from Desert Storm, and with a remarkable revisiting of the ancient language of the wilderness. With a death that resembles life (to adapt the words of T. S. Eliot), the American soldier of the novel speaks from a desert place that has become nowhere, somewhere between Iraq and Saudi Arabia, the theater of war replaced by a meditation on its futility and consequences as the sands begin once more to cover its tracks and resume their ancient forms. As in the poetry of the Great War, especially the tragic verse of Wilfred Owen, the novel seeks to give no answers, but only to show, and to begin to dissolve the necessary, and necessarily short-lived, political myths and chimeras of the fighting, so that proper ethical and theological reflection might begin afresh. Sigaud revisits the haunting meeting of Owen's poem "Strange Meeting" with its words of the dead German soldier: "I am the enemy you killed, my friend." The ethical indifference of the people of war becomes the quiet indifference of the desert with, in the concluding words of Jim Crace's novel *Quarantine*, "the evening peace that's brokered not by a god but by the rocks and clays themselves, *shalom*, *salaam*, the one-time, all-time truces of the land."[25]

It was a long time before the true import of those words began gradually to dawn on me. They make possible the necessary death of God, the death in the desert on the cross, or the absolute kenosis, or self-emptying, that is absolutely and utterly necessary if the Storm God is to reconcile in himself, and by a total sacrifice, the warring dualism of God and Satan. The desert must be empty, empty of all our gods and demons, so that it might become again the garden where Allah can walk in peace or the Lord God walk at the time of the evening desert breeze before it all went wrong. Antony knew that the demons had to be fought before he discovered this truth in the emptiness and solitariness of the inner mountain. And when the emperor has gone and been forgotten and the demons whom he sent his army to defeat have moved on to occupy another place in the fertile human imagination, I imagine that there may be one or perhaps two gentle folk of common sense left, who matter so little that they have been forgotten by the world, to the point that they are entirely other than all its concerns, and for that very reason, as the prologue to the *Historia Monachorum* puts it, human life will be preserved and honored by God – for then he or she, too, will have a garden where he can walk in peace, and all opposites will be reconciled in Total Presence.

Notes

1 Quoted in Gregory McNamee, *The Desert Reader: A Literary Companion* (Albuquerque: University of New Mexico Press, 1995), p. xvii.
2 The original title of the book was *Syria*.
3 Gertrude Bell, *The Desert and the Sown* (New York: Cooper Square Press, 2001), p. 10.
4 W. H. Hudson, *Idle Days in Patagonia* (1917), quoted in McNamee, *The Desert Reader*, pp. 52–7.
5 Pierre Loti (Julien Viaud), *Le Désert* (1895), quoted in McNamee, *The Desert Reader*, pp. 158–64.
6 Mark Twain, *Roughing It* (1872), quoted in McNamee, *The Desert Reader*, pp. 34–7.
7 Charles M. Doughty, *Travels in Arabia Deserta* (London: Jonathan Cape, 1926), p. 6.
8 Eleazar ha-Kallir, "A Prayer & Invocation to the Prince of Rain," translated by Jerome Rothenberg and Harris Lenowitz. Quoted in McNamee, *The Desert Reader*, pp. 149–53.
9 Pablo Neruda, *Confieso que he vivido: Memorias* (*I Confess That I Have Lived*) (1974), quoted in McNamee, *The Desert Reader*, pp. 88–91.
10 Edmond Jabès, *From the Desert to the Book* (1980), quoted in McNamee, *The Desert Reader*, pp. 113–16.
11 Edmond Jabès, *Return to the Book* (1977), quoted in Rosmarie Waldrop, *Lavish Absence: Recalling and Rereading Edmond Jabès* (Middletown, CT: Wesleyan University Press, 2002), p. 133.
12 Jabès, *From the Desert to the Book*, quoted in McNamee, *The Desert Reader*, p. 114.

13 Ibid, pp. 114–15.
14 John Steinbeck, *The Log from the Sea of Cortez* (1962), quoted in McNamee, *The Desert Reader*, p. xxi.
15 Jacques Derrida, "Force of Law: The 'Mystical Foundation of Authority,'" *Cardozo Law Review* 11 (1990), pp. 919ff.
16 Ibid, p. 943.
17 Emmanuel Levinas, *Totality and Infinity*, translated by Alphonso Longis (The Hague: Nijhoff, 1969), p. 247.
18 Thomas J. J. Altizer, *Total Presence: The Language of Jesus and the Language of Today* (New York: Seabury Press, 1980), pp. 106–7.
19 *The Lives of the Desert Fathers (Historia Monachorum in Aegypto)*, translated by Norman Russell (Kalamazoo, MI: Cistercian Publications, 1981), p. 50.
20 Ibid.
21 Peter Brown, *The Body and Society: Men, Women and Sexual Renunciation in Early Christianity* (New York: Columbia University Press, 1988), p. 214.
22 Ibid, p. 216.
23 Henry David Thoreau, "Walking," in *Excursions: The Writings of Henry David Thoreau*, Riverside Edition, 11 vols. (Boston, MA: 1893), vol. 9, p. 275.
24 T. E. Lawrence, *The Seven Pillars of Wisdom: A Triumph* (London: World Books, 1939), vol. 2.
25 Jim Crace, *Quarantine* (Harmondsworth: Penguin, 1998), p. 243.

Bibliography

Abbey, Edward *Desert Solitaire: A Season in the Wilderness* (New York: McGraw-Hill, 1968).

Abbey, Edward *Fire on the Mountain* (New York: Avon Books, 1992).

Alloway, Lawrence *Barnett Newman: The Stations of the Cross*. Exhibition catalogue (New York: Guggenheim Museum, 1966).

Al'Quran Translated by Ahmed Ali (Princeton, NJ: Princeton University Press, 1994).

Altizer, Thomas J. J. *Oriental Mysticism and Biblical Eschatology* (Philadelphia, PA: Westminster Press, 1961).

Altizer, Thomas J. J. (ed.) *Toward a New Christianity* (New York: Harcourt, Brace and World, 1967).

Altizer, Thomas J. J. *The Descent into Hell: A Study of the Radical Reversal of Christian Consciousness* (Philadelphia, PA: J. B. Lippincott, 1970).

Altizer, Thomas J. J. *The Self-Embodiment of God* (San Francisco: Harper and Row, 1977).

Altizer, Thomas J. J. *Total Presence: The Language of Jesus and the Language of Today* (New York: Seabury Press, 1980).

Altizer, Thomas J. J. *Genesis and Apocalypse: A Theological Voyage Towards Authentic Christianity* (Louisville, KY: Westminster/John Knox Press, 1990).

Altizer, Thomas J. J. *The Genesis of God: A Theological Genealogy* (Louisville, KY: Westminster John Knox Press, 1993).

Altizer, Thomas J. J. *The Contemporary Jesus* (Albany: State University of New York Press, 1997).

Altizer, Thomas J. J. *The New Apocalypse: The Radical Christian Vision of William Blake* (Aurora: The Davies Group, 2000).

Altizer, Thomas J. J. "Van Gogh's Eyes." Unpublished manuscript.

Altizer, Thomas J. J. and Hamilton, William *Radical Theology and the Death of God* (Harmondsworth: Penguin Books, 1968).

Antier, Jean-Jacques *Charles de Foucauld (Charles of Jesus)*, translated by Julia Shirek Smith (San Francisco: Ignatius Press, 1999).

St. Antony, The Life of A Select Library of Nicene and Post-Nicene Fathers of the Christian Church. Second Series. Vol. 4, St. Athanasius: *Select Works* (Edinburgh: T. & T. Clark, 1991).

Auden, W. H. *The Enchafèd Flood, or the Romantic Iconography of the Sea* (London: Faber, 1951).

Bachelard, Gaston *The Poetics of Space* (Boston, MA: Beacon Press, 1994).

Baelz, Peter *The Forgotten Dream: Experience, Hope and God* (London: Mowbrays, 1975).

Ballard, J. G. *The Atrocity Exhibition*, annotated edition (London: Flamingo, 1993).

Barth, Karl *The Epistle to the Romans*, translated from the 6th edn. by Edwyn C. Hoskyns (Oxford: Oxford University Press, 1933).

Barth, Karl *Church Dogmatics*, translated by G. T. Thomson, T. F. Torrance, G. W. Broiley et al., 13 vols. (Edinburgh: T. & T. Clark, 1936–69).

Barthes, Roland *Selected Writings* (London: Fontana, 1983).

Barton, John and Muddiman, John (eds.) *The Oxford Bible Commentary* (Oxford: Oxford University Press, 2001).

Baudrillard, Jean *America*, translated by Chris Turner (London: Verso, 1988).

Bazin, René *Charles de Foucauld* (Paris: Librairie Plon, 1921).

Beckett, Samuel *Waiting for Godot* (London: Faber and Faber, 1956).

Begbie, Jeremy *Theology, Music and Time* (Cambridge: Cambridge University Press, 2000).

Bell, Gertrude *The Desert and the Sown* (London: Virago Press, 1985).

Benjamin, Walter *Illuminations*, translated by Harry Zohn (London: Fontana, 1973).

Berry, P. and Wernick, A. (eds.) *Shadow of Spirit: Postmodernism and Religion* (London: Routledge, 1992).

Blackstone, Bernard *English Blake* (Cambridge: Cambridge University Press, 1949).

Blackwell, Albert L. *The Sacred in Music* (Louisville, KY: Westminster/John Knox Press, 1999).

Blanchot, Maurice *The Space of Literature*, translated by Ann Smock (Lincoln: University of Nebraska Press, 1992).

Blanchot, Maurice *The Gaze of Orpheus and Other Literary Essays*, translated by Lydia Davis (Barrytown, NY: Station Hill Press, 1981).

Bonaventure, St. *The Journey of the Mind to God*, translated by Philotheus Boehner, OFM (Cambridge: Hackett Publishing, 1993).

Bonhoeffer, Dietrich *The Cost of Discipleship*, revd. edn. (New York: Macmillan, 1959).

Bonnefoy, Yves *Hier régnant* (Paris: Mercure de France, 1964).

Bonnefoy, Yves *In the Shadow's Light*, translated by John Naughton (Chicago: University of Chicago Press, 1991).

Bradshaw, P. F. "Celebration," in R. C. D. Jasper (ed.), *The Eucharist Today* (London: SPCK, 1974).

Branch, Lori "The Desert in the Desert: Faith and the Aporias of Law and Knowledge in Derrida and *The Sayings of the Desert Fathers*." *Journal of the American Academy of Religion* December 2003, Vol. 71, No. 4, pp. 811–34.

Britt, David (ed.) *Modern Art: Impressionism to Post-Modernism* (London: Thames and Hudson, 1989).

Brown, Peter *The Body and Society: Men, Women and Sexual Renunciation in Early Christianity* (New York: Columbia University Press, 1988).

Bruns, Gerald L. *Hermeneutics Ancient and Modern* (New Haven, CT: Yale University Press, 1992).

Burton, Sir Richard F. *A Personal Narrative of a Pilgrimage to Al-Madinah and Meccah* (1893), in Robyn Davidson (ed.), *Journeys: An Anthology* (London: Picador, 2002).

Cadava, Eduardo, Connor, Peter, and Nancy, Jean-Luc (eds.) *Who Comes After the Subject?* (London: Routledge, 1991).

Calvino, Italo *Invisible Cities*, translated by William Weaver (London: Vintage, 1997).

Caputo, John D. *The Mystical Element in Heidegger's Thought* (New York: Fordham University Press, 1986).

Caputo, John D. "Mysticism and Transgression: Derrida and Meister Eckhart," in Hugh J. Silverman (ed.), *Continental Philosophy III: Derrida and Deconstruction* (New York: Routledge, 1989).

Caputo, John D. *Demythologizing Heidegger* (Bloomington: Indiana University Press, 1993).

Carmen, A. E., Jr. "The Church Project: Pollock's Passion Themes," *Art in America* 70.6 (1982), pp. 110–12.

Cashen, Richard Anthony *Solitude in the Thought of Thomas Merton* (Kalamazoo, MI: Cistercian Publications, 1981).

Certeau, Michel de *The Practice of Everyday Life*, translated by Steven Randall (Berkeley: University of California Press, 1984).

Certeau, Michel de *The Mystic Fable, Vol. 1: The Sixteenth and Seventeenth Centuries*, translated by Michael B. Smith (Chicago: University of Chicago Press, 1992).

Certeau, Michel de "Mystic Speech," in Graham Ward (ed.), *The Certeau Reader* (Oxford: Blackwell, 2000).

Chadwick, Owen *John Cassian*, 2nd edn. (Cambridge: Cambridge University Press, 1968).

Chitty, Derwas *The Desert a City* (New York: St. Vladimir's Seminary Press, 1999).

Claeys, Gregory and Sargent, Lyman Tower (eds.), *The Utopia Reader* (New York: New York University Press, 1999).

Clark, Timothy *Martin Heidegger* (London: Routledge, 2002).

Climacus, John *The Ladder of Divine Ascent*, translated by C. Luibheid and N. Russell (New York: Paulist Press, 1982).

Cohen, J. M. (ed.) *The Penguin Book of Spanish Verse* (Harmondsworth: Penguin Books, 1956).

Corbin, Henry *Creative Imagination in the Sufism of Ibn Arabi* (Princeton, NJ: Bollingen Press, 1969).

Cornell, Druscilla, Rosenfield, Michael, and Carlson, David Gray (eds.) *Deconstruction and the Possibility of Justice* (London: Routledge, 1992).

Cowan, James *Journey to the Inner Mountain: In the Desert with St. Anthony* (London: Hodder and Stoughton, 2002).

Coward, Harold and Fashay, Toby (eds.) *Derrida and Negative Theology* (Albany: State University of New York Press, 1992).

Crace, Jim *Quarantine* (Harmondsworth: Penguin Books, 1998).

Cunningham, Valentine *In the Reading Gaol: Postmodernity, Texts and History* (Oxford: Blackwell, 1994).

Cupitt, Don *Taking Leave of God* (New York: Crossroad, 1981).

Cupitt, Don *Mysticism After Modernity* (Oxford: Blackwell, 1998).

Dalrymple, William *From the Holy Mountain* (London: Flamingo, 1998).

Davidson, Robyn (ed.) *Journeys: An Anthology* (London: Picador, 2002).

Defoe, Daniel *Robinson Crusoe*, ed. Michael Shinagel (New York: W. W. Norton, 1975).

Delooz, Pierre "Towards a Sociological Study of Canonized Sainthood in the Catholic Church," in Stephen Wilson (ed.), *Saints and Their Cults: Studies in Religious Sociology, Folklore and History* (Cambridge: Cambridge University Press, 1983).

Depardon, Raymond "Deserts," in *The Desert*. Fondation Cartier pour l'art contemporain (London: Thames and Hudson, 2000).

Derrida, Jacques "Edmond Jabès and the Question of the Book," in *Writing and Difference*, translated by Alan Bass (London: Routledge and Kegan Paul, 1981).

Derrida, Jacques *The Truth in Painting*, translated by Geoff Bennington and Ian McLeod (Chicago: University of Chicago Press, 1987).

Derrida, Jacques "Eating Well, Or, The Calculation of the Subject: An Interview with Jacques Derrida," in Eduardo Cadava, Peter Connor, and Jean-Luc Nancy (eds.), *Who Comes After the Subject?* (London: Routledge, 1991).

Derrida, Jacques "Force of Law: The Mystical Foundation of Authority," in Druscilla Cornell, Michael Rosenfield, and David Gray Carlson (eds.), *Deconstruction and the Possibility of Justice* (London: Routledge, 1992).

Derrida, Jacques "Before the Law," in *Acts of Literature*, ed. Derek Attridge (London: Routledge, 1992).

Derrida, Jacques "Post-Scriptum: Aporias, Ways and Voices," in Harold Coward and Toby Fashay (eds.), *Derrida and Negative Theology* (Albany: State University of New York Press, 1992).

Derrida, Jacques *Memoirs of the Blind: The Self-Portrait and Other Ruins*, translated by Pascale-Anne Brault and Michael Naas (Chicago: University of Chicago Press, 1993).

Derrida, Jacques "Faith and Knowledge: The Two Sources of Religion at the Limits of Reason Alone," in Jacques Derrida and Gianno Vattimo (eds.), *Religion* (Stanford, CA: Stanford University Press, 1998).

Derrida, Jacques and Vattimo, Gianno (eds.) *Religion* (Stanford, CA: Stanford University Press, 1998).

Dickinson, Emily *The Collected Poems*, ed. Thomas H. Johnson (London: Faber and Faber, 1970).

Dix, Dom Gregory *The Shape of the Liturgy* (London: Dacre Press, 1945).

Doughty, Charles M. *Travels in Arabia Deserta*, with an introduction by T. E. Lawrence (London: Jonathan Cape, 1921).

Duncan, Robert "The Delirium of Meaning." Afterword to *if there were anywhere but desert:The Selected Poems of Edmond Jabès*, translated by Keith Waldrop (Barrytown, NY: Station Hill Press, 1988).

Eckhart, Meister *The Essential Sermons, Commentaries, Treatises and Defense*, translated by Edmund Colledge and Bernard McGinn (New York: Paulist Press, 1981).

Eliot, T. S. "Towards a Christian Britain," *The Listener* 25 (January–June, 1941), pp. 524ff.

Eliot, T. S. *The Complete Poems and Plays, 1909–1950* (New York: Harcourt, Brace and World, 1952).

Everett, Anthony "Abstract Expressionism," in David Britt (ed.), *Modern Art: Impressionism to Post-Modernism* (London: 1989).

Farrer, Austin *A Celebration of Faith*, ed. Leslie Houlden (London: Hodder and Stoughton, 1970).

Finaldi, Gabrieli *The Image of Christ* (London: National Gallery, 2000).

Findlay, J. N. "Hegel's Study of the Religious Consciousness," in Thomas J. J. Altizer (ed.), *Toward a New Christianity* (New York: Harcourt, Brace and World, 1967).

Flaubert, Gustave *La Tentation de saint Antoine*, 3rd edn. (Paris: Charpentier, 1875).

Flaubert, Gustave *Flaubert in Egypt*, translated by Francis Steegmuller (Harmondsworth: Penguin Books, 1996).

Flaubert, Gustave *The Temptation of St. Anthony*, translated by Lafcadio Hearne (New York: Modern Library, 2001).

Gordon, Lyndall *Eliot's New Life* (Oxford: Oxford University Press, 1988).

Guillaumont, A. "La Conception du desert chez les moines d'Égypte," *Revue de l'Histoire des Religions* (1975) 188: 3–21.

Hadewijch, *The Complete Works*, translated by Mother Columba Hart, OSB (New York: Paulist Press, 1993).

Hampson, Daphne *After Christianity*, 2nd edn.(London: SCM, 2002).

Harold, Jim (ed.) *Desert* (Southampton: John Hansard Gallery, 1996).

Harpham, Geoffrey Galt *The Ascetic Imperative in Culture and Criticism* (Chicago: University of Chicago Press, 1987).

Harrigan, Peter "Art Rocks in Saudi Arabia," *Saudi Aramco World* vol. 53, no. 2 (March/April 2002).

Hart, Ray L. *Unfinished Man and the Imagination* (Atlanta, GA: Scholars Press, 1985).

Hazard, David *You Set My Spirit Free: A 40-Day Journey in the Company of St. John of the Cross* (Minneapolis, MN: Bethany House Publishers, 1994).

Hegel, G. W. F. *The Phenomenology of Spirit*, in Stephen Houlgate (ed.), *The Hegel Reader* (Oxford: Blackwell, 1998).

Hopkins, Gerard Manley *The Poems*, ed. W. H. Gardner and N. H. Mackenzie (Oxford: Oxford University Press, 1989).

Hopps, Walter "The Rothko Chapel," in *The Menil Collection*, new edn. (New York: Harry N. Adams, 1997).

Hounam, D. Review article on *Paris, Texas. In Dublin*, 214 (1984), pp. 10–11.

Jabès, Edmond *if there were anywhere but desert: The Selected Poems of Edmond Jabès*, translated by Keith Waldrop (Barrytown, NY: Station Hill Press, 1988).

Jabès, Edmond *From the Desert to the Book: Dialogues with Marcel Cohen*, translated by Pierre Joris (Barrytown, NY: Station Hill Press, 1990).

Jabès, Edmond *The Book of Resemblances 2. Intimations: The Desert*, translated by Rosmarie Waldrop (Middletown, CT: Wesleyan University Press, 1991).

Jabès, Edmond *From the Book to the Book: An Edmond Jabès Reader*, translated by Rosmarie Waldrop (Hanover, NH: Wesleyan University Press, 1991).

Jabès, Edmond *The Book of Margins*, translated by Rosmarie Waldrop (Chicago: University of Chicago Press, 1993).

Jasper, R. C. D. (ed.) *The Eucharist Today* (London: SPCK, 1974).

Jenkins, David "Literature and the Theologian," in John Coulson (ed.), *Theology and the University: An Ecumenical Investigation* (London: Darton, Longman and Todd, 1964), pp. 219–20.

Jerome, St. *Letters*, translated by T. C. Lawler (London: ACW, 1963).

John of the Cross, St. *Selected Writings*, ed. Kieran Kavanagh, OCD (New York: Paulist Press, 1987).

Johnson, Phyllis and Cazelles, Brigitte *La Vain Siècle Guerpier: A Literary Approach to Sainthood through Old French Hagiography of the Twelfth Century* (Chapel Hill: North Carolina Studies in the Romance Languages and Literature, 1979).

Johnston, William *The Inner Eye of Love: Mysticism and Religion* (London: Collins, 1978).

Kafka, Franz, *The Trial*, translated by W. Muir and E. Muir (Harmondsworth: Penguin Books, 1974).

Kandinsky, Wassily *Concerning the Spiritual in Art*, translated by M. T. H. Sadler (New York: Dover Publications, 1977).

Kearney, Richard *The Wake of Imagination* (London: Routledge, 1988).

Keble, John *The Christian Year* (1827).

Khemir, Mounira "The Infinite Image of the Desert and its Representations," in *The Desert*. Fondation Cartier pour l'art contemporain (London: Thames and Hudson, 2000).

Kierkegaard, Søren *The Concept of Irony: Schelling Lecture Notes*, translated by Howard V. Hong and Edna H. Hong (Princeton, NJ: Princeton University Press, 1989).

Lançon, David *Jabès l'Egyptien* (Paris: Jean Michel Place, 1998).

Lane, Belden C. *The Solace of Fierce Landscapes: Exploring Desert and Mountain Spirituality* (New York: Oxford University Press, 1998).

Lawrence, T. E. Introduction to C. M. Doughty, *Travels in Arabia Deserta* (London: Jonathan Cape and the Medici Society, 1921).

Lawrence, T. E. *The Seven Pillars of Wisdom: A Triumph* (London: World Books, 1939).

Lawrence T. E. *Letters*, ed. M. Brown (London: J. M. Dent, 1988).

Lévi-Strauss, Claude *The Savage Mind* (Chicago: University of Chicago Press, 1966).

Lindqvist, Sven *Desert Divers*, translated by Joan Tate (London: Granta Books, 2002).

Lives of the Desert Fathers, The, translated by Norman Russell; introduction by Benedicta Ward, SLG (Oxford: A. R. Mowbray, 1981).

Louth, Andrew *The Wilderness of God* (Nashville, TN: Abingdon Press, 1991).

Lucie-Smith, Edward *American Realism* (London: Thames and Hudson, 1994).

Lyotard, Jean-François *The Differend: Phrases in Dispute*, translated by George Van Den Abbeele (Manchester: Manchester University Press, 1988).

McCarthy, Cormac *Blood Meridian, or The Evening Redness in the West* (London: Picador, 1989).

McElrath, D. (ed.) *Franciscan Christology* (New York: Franciscan Institute, 1980).

McGinn, Bernard *The Presence of God: A History of Western Christian Mysticism, Vol. 1: The Foundations of Mysticism* (London: SCM, 1991).

McIntosh, Mark A. *Mystical Theology* (Oxford: Blackwell, 1998).

McNamee, Gregory *The Desert Reader: A Literary Companion* (Albuquerque: University of New Mexico Press, 1995).

Marin, Louis *Utopiques: jeux d'espaces* (Paris: Minuit, 1973).

Marion, Jean-Luc *God Without Being*, translated by Thomas A. Carlson (Chicago: University of Chicago Press, 1991).

Melville, Herman *Billy Budd, Sailor* (Harmondsworth: Penguin Books, 1970).

Merton, Thomas *The Wisdom of the Desert: Sayings from the Desert Fathers of the Fourth Century* (London: Sheldon Press, 1961).

Merton, Thomas *Zen and the Birds of Appetite* (New York: New Directions, 1968).

Merton, Thomas *The Asian Journals of Thomas Merton* (New York: New Directions, 1975).

Merton, Thomas *Thomas Merton: Spiritual Master*, ed. Lawrence S. Cunningham (New York: Paulist Press, 1992).

Messinger, Lisa Mintz *Georgia O'Keeffe* (New York: Thames and Hudson, 1988).

Migne, Père *Patrologiae* (1844–66).

Moschos, John *The Spiritual Meadow*, translated by John Wortley (Kalamazoo, MI: Cistercian Publications, 1992).

Nash, Roderick *Wilderness and the American Mind*, 3rd edn. (New Haven, CT: Yale University Press, 1982).

Newhall, Beaumont *The History of Photography*, revd. edn. (London: Secker and Warburg, 1964).

Newman, Barnett "The Sublime is Now," *The Tiger's Eye*, no. 6 (December, 1948).

Norris, Kathleen *The Cloister Walk* (New York: Riverhead Books, 1997).

Ondaatje, Michael *The English Patient* (London: Picador, 1993).

Otto, Rudolf *The Idea of the Holy*, translated by John W. Harvey (Oxford: Oxford University Press, 1923).

Paglia, Camille *Sexual Personae: Art and Decadence from Nefertiti to Emily Dickinson* (New Haven, CT: Yale University Press, 1990).

Palin, Michael *Sahara* (London: Weidenfeld and Nicolson, 2002).

Palladius *The Lausiac History*, translated by Robert T. Meyer (New York: Newman Press, 1964).

Pasolini, Pier Paolo *Oedipus Rex*, translated by John Mathews (London: Lorrimer Publishing, 1971).

Pasolini, Pier Paolo *Poems*, selected and translated by Norman MacAfee, with Luciano Martinengo (New York: Random House, 1982).

Prickett, Stephen "Towards a Rediscovery of the Bible: The Problem of the Still Small Voice," in Michael Wadsworth (ed.), *Ways of Reading the Bible* (Brighton: Harvester Press, 1981).

Pseudo-Dionysius *The Complete Works*, translated by Colm Luibheid, with Paul Rorem (New York: Paulist Press, 1987).

Rice, Gene *Nations Under God: A Commentary on the Book of I Kings* (Grand Rapids, MI: Eerdmans, 1990).

Ricoeur, Paul *The Symbolism of Evil*, translated by Emerson Buchanan (Boston, MA: Beacon Press, 1969).

Ricoeur, Paul *Oneself as Another*, translated by Kathleen Blamey (Chicago, Chicago University Press, 1992).

Ringer, Alexander L. *Arnold Schoenberg: The Composer as Jew* (Oxford: Clarendon Press, 1990).

Robinson, John *Honest to God* (London: SCM Press, 1963).

Robinson, Roxana *Georgia O'Keeffe: A Life* (London: Bloomsbury Publishing, 1990).

Rohdie, Sam *The Passion of Pier Paolo Pasolini* (Bloomington: Indiana University Press, 1995).

Rosenblum, Robert "The Abstract Sublime," *Art News*, vol. 59, no. 10 (February 1961); reprinted in Henry Geldzahler, *New York Painting and Sculpture: 1940–1970* (New York: E. P. Dutton, 1969).

Rossellius, Cosmas *Thesaurus artificiosae memoriae* (1579).

Roszak, Theodore *Where the Wasteland Ends: Politics and Transcendence in Post-industrial Society* (London: Faber, 1974).

Rousseau, Jean-Jacques *A Treatise on Natural Education* (1762).

Rubens, Bernice *Our Father* (London: Abacus, 1988).

Rubenson, Samuel "St. Antony, The First Real Coptic Author?" in *Actes du IVe congres copte* (Louvain, 1992).

Rubenson, Samuel "Christian Asceticism and the Emergence of the Monastic Tradition," in Vincent L. Wimbush and Richard Valantasis (eds.), *Asceticism* (Oxford: Oxford University Press, 1998), pp. 53–5.

Said, Edward W. *Reflections on Exile and Other Literary and Cultural Essays* (London: Granta Books, 2001).

Saint-Exupéry, Antoine de *Wind, Sand and Stars*, translated by Lewis Galantière (New York: Harcourt Brace, 1940).

Saint-Exupéry, Antoine de *The Little Prince*, translated by Katherine Woods (New York: Harcourt Brace, 1943).

Saint-Exupéry, Antoine de *The Wisdom of the Sands*, translated by Stuart Gilbert (New York: Harcourt Brace, 1950).

Sandler, Irving *The Triumph of American Painting: A History of Abstract Expressionism* (New York: Harper and Row, 1970).

Scarry, Elaine *The Body in Pain: The Making and Unmaking of the World* (New York: Oxford University Press, 1985).

Schama, Simon *Landscape and Memory* (London: HarperCollins, 1995).

Scharlemann, Robert P. *Inscriptions and Reflections: Essays in Philosophical Theology* (Charlottesville: University of Virginia Press, 1989).

Schiff, Stacy *Saint-Exupéry: A Biography* (New York: Alfred A. Knopf, 1994).

Schoenberg, Arnold *Moses und Aron* (1930–). The English text used is by Allen Forte, published with the 1984 recording by Sir Georg Solti and the Chicago Symphony Orchestra (London: Decca Record Company, 1985).

Sheldrake, Philip *Spaces for the Sacred* (London: SCM, 2001).

Siciliano, Enzo Foreword to Pier Paolo Pasolini, *Poems*, translated by Jonathan Galassi (New York: Random House, 1982).

Sigaud, Dominique *Somewhere in a Desert*, translated by Frank Wynne (London: Phoenix House, 1998).

Silesius, Angelus *Le Pelerin cherubique*, translated by Eugene Susini (Paris: PUF, 1964).

Silko, Leslie Marmon *Ceremony* (Harmondsworth: Penguin Books, 1986).

Simic, Charles *Unending Blues* (New York: Harcourt, 1986).

Simeon Stylites, The Lives of, translated by Robert Duran (Kalamazoo, MI: Cistercian Publications, 1992).

Steiner, George *Heidegger* (London: Fontana, 1978).

Steiner, George *Real Presences* (London: Faber and Faber, 1989).

Symeon Stylites, Life of, translated by F. Lent. *Journal of the American Oriental Society* (1915), pp. 103–18.

Tall, Deborah *From Where We Stand: Recovering a Sense of Place* (New York: Alfred A. Knopf, 1993).

Taubes, Jacob "On the Nature of Theological Method: Some Reflections on the Methodological Principles of Tillich's Theology," *Journal of Religion* (January, 1954).

Taylor, Mark C. *Disfiguring: Art, Architecture, Religion* (Chicago: University of Chicago Press, 1992).

Templeton, Douglas A. *The New Testament as True Fiction: Literature, Literary Criticism, Aesthetics* (Sheffield: Sheffield Academic Press, 1999).

Thesiger, Wilfred *Arabian Sands* (Harmondsworth: Penguin Books, 1991).

Thomas, R. S. *Mass for Hard Times* (Newcastle-upon-Tyne: Bloodaxe Books, 1992).

Thoreau, Henry David "Walking," in vol. 9 of *Excursions: The Writings of Henry David Thoreau,* Riverside Edition, 11 vols. (Boston, MA, 1893).

Torp, H. "Le Monastère copte de Baouit: Quelques notes d'introduction," *Miscellanea Coptica, Acta Instituti Norvegiae Romani* (1981) 9: 1–8.

Turner, Denys *The Darkness of God: Negativity in Christian Mysticism* (Cambridge: Cambridge University Press, 1995).

Ujica, Andrei "2 Pasolini, June 2000," in *The Desert.* Fondation Cartier pour l'art contemporain (London: Thames and Hudson, 2000), pp. 207–8.

Van Dyke, John C. *The Desert: Further Studies in Natural Appearances* (Baltimore, MD: Johns Hopkins University Press, 1999).

Van Dyke, John C. *The Grand Canyon of the Colorado: Recurrent Studies in Impressions and Appearances* (New York: Scribner's, 1920).

Van Gogh, Vincent *The Letters,* ed. Mark Roskill (London: Fontana, 1983).

Viola, Bill *Reasons for Knocking at an Empty House: Writings 1973–1994* (London: Thames and Hudson, 1995).

Virilio, Paul "The Twilight of the Grounds," in *The Desert.* Fondation Cartier pour l'art contemporain (London: Thames and Hudson, 2000).

Waaijman, Wees "Towards a Phenomenological Definition of Spirituality," *Studies in Spirituality* 3/1993: 5–57.

Waddell, Helen *The Desert Fathers.* Translations from the Latin (London: Constable, 1936).

Waldrop, Rosmarie *Lavish Absence: Recalling and Rereading Edmond Jabès* (Middletown, NY: Wesleyan University Press, 2002).

Ward, Benedicta (trans.) *The Wisdom of the Desert Fathers: Systematic Sayings from the Apophthegmata Patrum*, new edn. (Oxford: SLG Press, 1986).

Ward, Graham (ed.) *The Postmodern God: A Theological Reader* (Oxford: Blackwell, 1997).

Ward, Graham *Cities of God* (London: Routledge, 2000).

Ward, Graham *True Religion* (Oxford: Blackwell, 2003).

Wenders, Wim *Paris, Texas* (script) (Berlin: Road Movies, 1984).

Wenders, Wim *The Act of Seeing: Essays and Conversations*, translated by Michael Hofman (London: Faber and Faber, 1997).

White, Patrick *Voss* (Harmondsworth: Penguin Books, 1983).

Wilson, Jeremy *Lawrence of Arabia* (New York: Atheneum, 1990).

Wyschogrod, Edith *Saints and Postmodernism: Revisioning Moral Philosophy* (Chicago: University of Chicago Press, 1990).

Yates, Frances *The Art of Memory* (Chicago: University of Chicago Press, 1966).

Index